Mastering SAP XI—Administration

Marcus Banner, Heinzpeter Klein

Contents

Introduction 3

1 The Architecture of SAP Exchange Infrastructure 5

1.1 System Landscape Architecture 5
SAP NetWeaver 5
Process Integration Using SAP XI 5
The Architecture of SAP XI 6
XI Landscape Topology 7

2 Basic Configuration of the XI Interface System 9

2.1 System Data and Sizing 9
System Data of the Example 9
Sizing SAP Exchange Infrastructure 3.0 9
2.2 Implementing the Architecture 10
Configuring the System Parameters 10
2.3 Configuration within the Repository and Directory 12
Initial Scenario 12
Configuring the Sending System for the Distribution 13
Configuring the IDoc Adapter 16
XI Tools 16
Importing a Software Component Version 19
Importing SAP Objects 19
Creating a Namespace in the Repository 20
Creating Message Mapping Objects 20
Example 22
Registering a Mapping Program 23
Creating an Interface Mapping Object 23
Defining Outbound and Inbound Interfaces 23
Configuration in the Integration Directory 24
Configuring the Receiving System 27

3 Configuring the System Landscape 29

3.1 Basic Administration of the SLD 29
Starting and Stopping the SLD Service 30
Server Log 30
Displaying System Information 30
Setting Up Data Persistence 30
Configuration of the SLD Profiles 31
Setting Up the SLD Bridge 32
System Message 34
Administration of the SLD Namespace 34
3.2 Customizing the System Landscape Directory 35
Main Menu of the SLD 35
Software Catalog 36
Technical System 37
Business System 39
Transport Groups 40
3.3 Change Management Service 41
CMS Architecture 42
Setting Up the Change Management Service System 43
Landscape Configurator 45
Transport Studio 48

3.4 Minimum Configuration of the Transport System (without CMS) 49

4 **Authorizations** 51
4.1 Single Sign-On 51
4.2 XI Role Concept 52
4.3 Web Administrator 55

5 **Performance Optimization Measures** 57
5.1 Adapting Web AS 6.40 for XI 3.0 57
RFC Quota on the R/3 Side 57
JCo Service Provider on the J2EE Side 58
5.2 Parameter Settings on the R/3 Side 60
Web AS 6.40—Gateway Parameters 60
Web AS 6.40—Communication Parameters 60
XI 3.0 Parameter Settings—Tuning Category 61
XI 3.0 Parameter Settings—Runtime Category 64
5.3 Archiving and Deletion Procedures in XI 3.0 66
Archiving 66
Deletion Procedure 67
5.4 Parameter Settings on the J2EE Side 69
J2EE ApplicationThreadManager 69
Tuning the Java VM 69
5.5 Application Tuning 70

6 **Central Monitoring in the XI Runtime Workbench** 71
6.1 Types of XI Monitoring 71
6.2 Monitoring Requirements and Options 72
6.3 Component Monitoring 74
6.4 Message Monitoring 75
6.5 End-to-end Monitoring 76
6.6 Performance Monitoring 79
6.7 Alert Monitoring 80
Configuring Java Monitoring (GRMG) 84
6.8 Cache Monitoring 86

Appendix 89
1 Overview of Relevant XI System Parameters 89
2 Checklist—Interface Configuration 93

Index 94

Introduction

This book is the synthesis of our experiences with SAP Exchange Infrastructure 3.0. As a component of the SAP NetWeaver '04 platform, SAP Exchange Infrastructure (SAP XI) has become increasingly important since the fall of 2004. The advantages of the current Release 3.0 over Release 2.0 are apparent in many respects. Several well-known companies have since decided to use SAP XI to establish a stronger integration of the individual systems in their system landscapes and to begin the necessary consolidation procedures using this integration tool.

Thanks to our daily work with SAP XI 3.0, we highly recommend the SAP XI platform as a valuable technical component for optimization and consolidation activities, as well as the flexible coupling of individual systems. Whereas in 2004, Enterprise Application Integration (EAI) experts in the US could do their work without being affected in any way by SAP products, today the new stable SAP XI release seems to have put an end to that isolation. In the future, companies and corporations with a highly sophisticated SAP landscape will most likely use the integration tool supplied by SAP for the integration of their legacy systems. EAI providers who have been specializing in those integration processes will notice this change both in Europe and in the US, where SAP is becoming a continuously growing presence.

Since the introduction of Service Pack (SP) level 11, SAP XI impresses the user with its robust and stable runtime, which raises the expectations for future releases. What makes the tool even more attractive is that a substantial number of various adapters is available to SAP partners to connect their legacy systems with SAP XI. Furthermore, according to various benchmark tests, it was thought that the internal conversion to XML had a negative effect on system performance, but we now know that is not the case. The integration with POS (point of sales) and SAP Business Warehouse (SAP BW) systems (with their large data volumes) provides excellent proof of this tool's potential.

This SAP Press Essentials book is intended for readers who are responsible for and experienced in the administration or monitoring of SAP systems.

In this book, we'll use a sample project taken from our daily work to describe the necessary steps that you must perform when setting up the SAP Exchange Infrastructure in your system landscape.

In **Chapter 1**, we'll describe the architecture, while in **Chapter 2**, we'll use an interface example to introduce you to the basic configuration in the repository and in the directory. Then, we'll describe the individual configuration steps required for the System Landscape Directory (SLD) in **Chapter 3**. **Chapter 4** focuses on authorization management. In **Chapter 5** and **Chapter 6**, we round off the SAP XI topic by providing you with useful tips for optimizing the system performance and for monitoring the system.

Acknowledgments

Marcus Banner: I would like to thank my family for their understanding and support throughout the project. Many hours that could have been spent with them were sacrificed for this book. This book is dedicated to my wife Tanja and my daughter Cassandra, the two most important people in my life, who I love more deeply than anything else in this world.

Heinzpeter Klein: I'd like to thank my colleagues of the retail basis team, Frank Ihnen, Vladislav Skala, and Bernard Klingen, for their great support. While I worked on the manuscript of this book, they assumed many basic and coordination tasks that would otherwise have absorbed much of my time.

Both authors would like to thank our editor, Florian Zimniak, and Christine Gustav of SAP for their support in reviecing this book.

1 The Architecture of SAP Exchange Infrastructure

1.1 System Landscape Architecture

This chapter provides you with an overview of the technical concepts and tasks that you have to perform when working with SAP Exchange Infrastructure (SAP XI) projects.

SAP NetWeaver

Figure 1.1 illustrates the four core areas of the overall SAP NetWeaver structure: people integration, information integration, process integration, and application platform. Each of these four areas represents an aspect of integration:

- SAP uses the people integration concept to describe a collaboration platform for teams, the technical integration of mobile employees (mobile infrastructure), and a role-based provision of applications and information required by individual employees in a standardized user interface (portal).
- Information integration refers to technologies used to enable a fast retrieval and a sophisticated aggregation and analysis of corporate information in an unstructured (Knowledge Management) and structured (Business Intelligence) storage. This concept also includes the component for harmonizing master data (Master Data Management).
- The third core area illustrated in Figure 1.1 is the concept of process integration, which is carried out by the technical component, SAP XI. This level involves the integration of process components across different technical components provided by different vendors.
- Due to its support of Java and ABAP developments and the database and operating system abtraction layer, the application platform supports a wide range of platforms and standards. Life Cycle Management is responsible for keeping the core areas current and in a valid, viable, and usable state. By using a system landscape directory (SLD), implementation tools, change management, software logistics, ugrade options, and installation wizards, the entire software life cycle is supported.

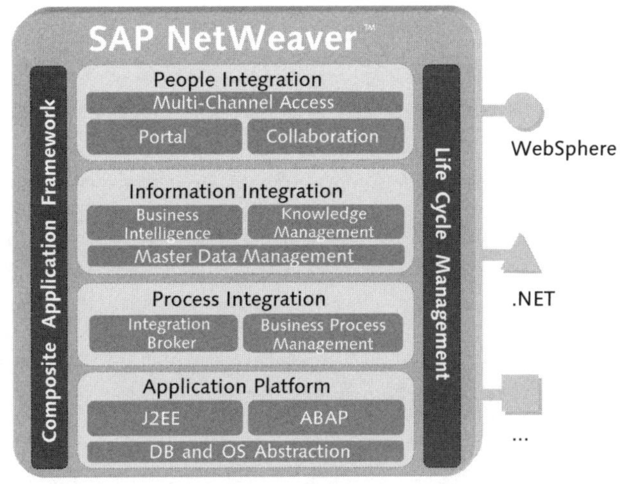

Figure 1.1 Overview of SAP NetWeaver

In this book, we'll focus on the process integration area and describe many aspects and solutions that are relevant for your daily work.

Process Integration Using SAP XI

SAP Exchange Infrastructure (SAP XI) and Business Process Management (BPM) form the basis for an optimized process management. Using the right interface management applications (ABAP + J2EE) enables you to integrate and control the different flows of information. In this context, it's not important whether the target-oriented communication is supposed to take place between several SAP applications or between SAP products and third-party products. Therefore, all process chains are technically feasible across products and vendors without any restriction, and can be checked at any time.

Figure 1.2 shows that there are no technical limits to a comprehensive integration, that is, if you use XI, you can link virtually everything.

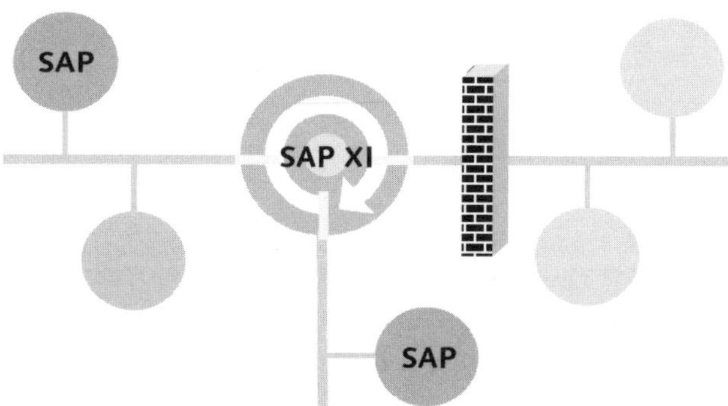

Figure 1.2 Process Integration—Exchange Infrastructure

The Architecture of SAP XI

Figure 1.3 illustrates the structure of SAP Exchange Infrastructure (SAP XI). We will now briefly describe the terminology used to help you link the specific terms to certain topics.

The figure contains the following elements:

Item	Description
1	Integration Builder (IB): The Integration Builder is a graphical Java environment that enables you to access the Integration Repository (IR) and the Integration Directory (ID) from your workstation to configure your interfaces.
2	Central Monitoring: Functions for monitoring the relevant SAP XI components, message processing by one or more components, and also, the message processing performance.
3	Integration Repository (IR): In the Integration Repository (that you can access using the Java front end, Integration Builder), you can define business scenarios, message interfaces, and interface data assignment mappings, as well as other metadata that is required at design time.
4	Integration Directory (ID): In the Integration Directory, you can model your individual interfaces by compiling individual modules from the repository into a functioning interface within the directory. Therefore, the Integration Directory is a configuration database that enables the management of routing relations, routing conditions, and executable mappings at configuration time.

Table 1.1 Legend for Figure 1.3

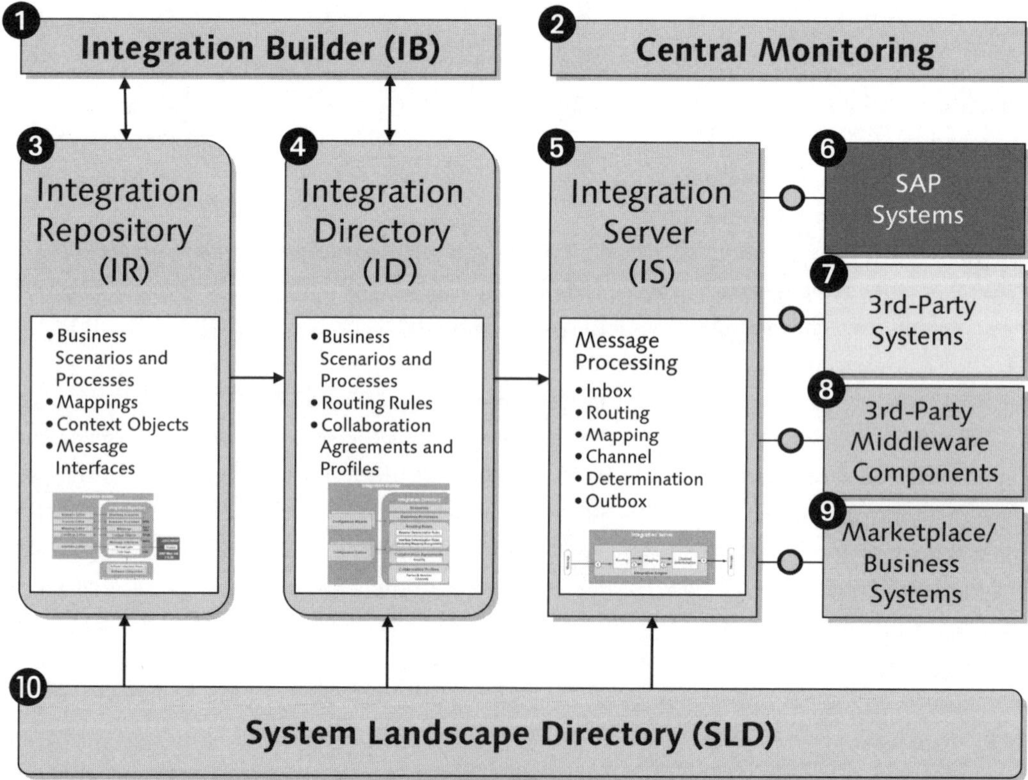

Figure 1.3 Architecture of the Exchange Infrastructure

Item	Description
5	Integration Server (IS): Represents the central integration component of the message processing flow. All sent messages related to SAP XI are processed by the Integration server. It is configured across the entire landscape that the Integration Server determines the recipient of a message, and that it performs the mapping and routing of all messages.
6	SAP Systems: For example, mySAP ERP, SAP BW, SAP APO, etc.
7	Third-Party Systems: For example, SeeBeyond, Baan, Broadvision, IDE World Software, Oracle Application, PeopleSoft, Siebel, etc.
8	Third-Party Middleware Components: For example, WebMethods Integration Server and Seeburger BIS
9	Marketplace/Business Systems: For example, Business Warehouse Java components: BI UDI 3.5 (Business Interface Universal Data Integration)
10	System Landscape Directory (SLD): In the System Landscape Directory, you record all information on the system landscape and provide that information centrally. The technical systems of the landscape are recorded with their technical attributes such as the computer name, system ID, and the like (technical system). In order to be able to map business processes, the technical systems are assigned business system names that represent logical business systems (business landscape). As shown in Figure 1.3, this data is made available to the individual SAP XI components.

Table 1.1 Legend for Figure 1.3 (cont.)

XI Landscape Topology

In our project, which we'll use as a basis for our descriptions in this book, we followed the recommendations made by SAP and created a central system landscape directory (central information provider) for XI. For Web Dynpro and other J2EE developments, we'll use two local SLDs (T and Q systems) together with the central SLD. The two local SLDs are synchronized using the data supplier bridge. During the implementation and testing of J2EE applications (e.g., Web Dynpro), the two local SLDs are supposed to reduce the workload carried by the central SLD so that the latter can primarily be made available to the productive J2EE and XI applications.

In our example, the central SLD is the XI production system P47. The data of all existing and new reporting systems (both SAP and third-party systems) is stored centrally in this system and is automatically synchronized with the local SLDs by using the data supplier bridge (SLD data bridge). In that way, it is ensured that the system information is available for interface configuration and development purposes across the entire system landscape (T/Q/P). The setup of the SLD data bridge is described in Section 3.1 in the subsection *Setting Up the SLD Bridge* based on an example. Note that a data synchronization can be performed only by using the data that has been automatically reported by the connected systems (in R/3, this is done using Transaction RZ70). Manual changes to the SLD are not transported via the data supplier bridge into the local SLDs.

A process-oriented separation of SLD instances can be useful if the systems must be separated for reasons of security due to highly sensitive data (e.g., personal information, commissions, and sales data). Such a separation can be mandatory due to legal regulations or a company's security policy. Organizational reasons can also be the cause, for example, it may make sense to separate independent company areas from each other, or because different XI releases are being used. As expected, those measures increase the administration costs.

The synchronization of settings and developments from the integration repositories and directories of the testing and quality systems into a production repository or directory can be carried out via an internal transport system (import/export) or the Change Management Service (CMS). Section 3.3, *Change Management Service*, describes the installation of these two transport options in great detail.

Figure 1.4 illustrates system P47 (central SLD). The retail systems, T31, Q31, and P31, have been automatically entered into the central SLD via Transaction RZ70 and are automatically updated when modifications are made. The same applies to the vendor master data systems, T20, Q20, and P20. This means that the central SLD knows the system data. By using the aforementioned supplier bridge, this information can also be transferred to the local SLDs.

SAP Note 764393—*Configuring the SAP System Landscape Directory*—describes the problems and specific issues inherent in an SLD infrastructure that is created from scratch. In addition, this SAP note provides useful solutions. Please read the SAP note because it also provides many useful concepts and tips that we implemented in our own projects. The SAP note contains the following items:

- Communication between systems
- Increasing the administration effort by using several SLD instances
- Uniqueness of network-related addressees
- Defining and designing a security concept for separating the development, testing, and XI production system environments
- Configuring a central or separated transport landscape
- Specific items to be considered when upgrading or updating
- Recommendations on implementing the SLD configuration (e.g., host, port, logon data, and synchronization)

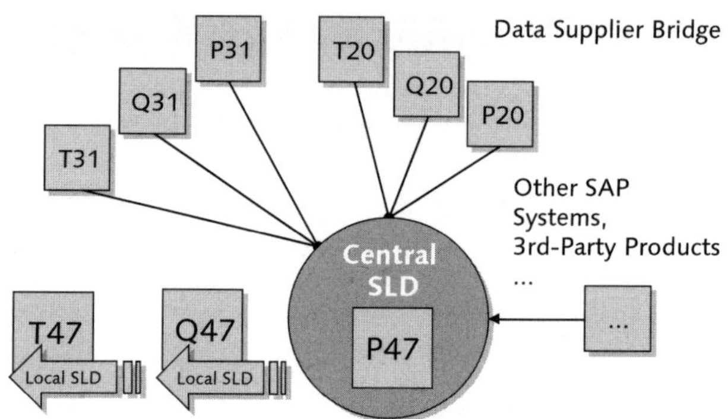

Figure 1.4 System Integration—Data Supplier Bridge

Chapter 3, *Configuring the System Landscape*, also contains additional information on these topics.

In the next chapter, you'll learn how to create an interface configuration in just a few steps.

2 Basic Configuration of the XI Interface System

2.1 System Data and Sizing

At the time this book was printed, we used the support package status 10/11. For this reason, all our descriptions and examples refer only to functions of that software component status. The Java environment was brought to the corresponding level.

When the manuscript was finished, we reached the following support package status in our production system, P47:

Software component	Release	Level	Highest support package	Short description of software component
SAP_BASIS	640	0011	SAPKB64011	SAP Basis component
SAP_ABA	640	0009	SAPKA64005	Cross-application component
ST-PI	003C_640	0001	SAPKITLPS1	SAP Solution Tools Plug-in (ST-PI 003C_6...)
PI_BASIS	2004_1_640	0005	SAPKIPYI65	Basis Plug-In (PI_BASIS) 2004_1_640
SAP_BW	350	0005		Business Information Warehouse
ST-A/PI	01E_BCO640	0000		SAP service tools (e.g., for GoingLive check, SAP support, EarlyWatch, etc.)

Table 2.1 Support Package Status of the Sample System

System Data of the Example

Our retail project example is based on an XI installation on an HP Integrity Superdome 64 server (Intel Itanium 2). We decided to use this platform to be able to quickly and efficiently customize the system with regard to changing requirements. The operating system we'll use is HP-UX (Version B.11.23 U ia64), and the database is an Oracle database (Version 9.2.0.4.0).

The following hardware resources were provided for the XI system:

Systems	SAPS	DB (GB)	RAM (GB)
T47, Testing and development	2000	100	6
Q47, quality assurance	4000	100	6
P47, Production	4000	100	8

When selecting your hardware and software platform, you should note that you must be able to significantly scale your platform to a higher level due to changing customer requirements, with regard to interfaces from existing projects or production systems. Moreover, we recommend that you distribute your production system to two cell boards to reduce downtimes in case of hardware problems.

Sizing SAP Exchange Infrastructure 3.0

From the SAP SDN portal (*http://sdn.sap.com*), you can download the document, *Sizing Guide—SAP XI 3.0.pdf*, which describes how you can size your XI system. You can easily find and download the document by using the search help and the **How-To-Guides** category.

The tables contained in the *Sizing Guide* provide important information on the necessary hardware equipment. To make an exact estimate, you should determine the precise quantity of messages per interface that you will have to cope with in the future. Based on that information, you can determine how much RAM you need, what the size of the hard disk should be, and what CPU performance is required.

2.2 Implementing the Architecture

Configuring the System Parameters

We'll now use the architecture example to describe the individual system parameters and their meaning. As described above, we want to equip our XI landscape with a central SLD. The central SLD runs on the P47 system. The development platform T47 and the quality platform Q47 are supposed to use the SLD. The individual repositories and directories will be used per system, that is, they'll be used for the T system, the Q system, and the P system individually, while changes will be transported via CMS from the T platform to the Q and P platforms. We'll describe the settings by using the sample configuration of the development platform.

Later on, you can transfer the necessary settings and descriptions to the QA system or the production system respectively.

You can access the settings by calling the menu item **Administration** from the XI start page, *http://[hostname]:[port]/rep*. When you're in the **Administration** menu, go to **Administration of Properties** and click on **Exchange Profile**. Figure 2.1 shows the corresponding navigation.

Once you have called the **Exchange Profile** link, a maintenance dialog opens in which you can view and change the existing parameters. Note that some changes won't take effect until you restart the J2EE stack. However, before you start maintaining the parameters, you should determine whether you're working on the right system. To do that, navigate to the **Connection** submenu. As shown in Figure 2.2, you can enter the technical connection to the system to be maintained in that submenu.

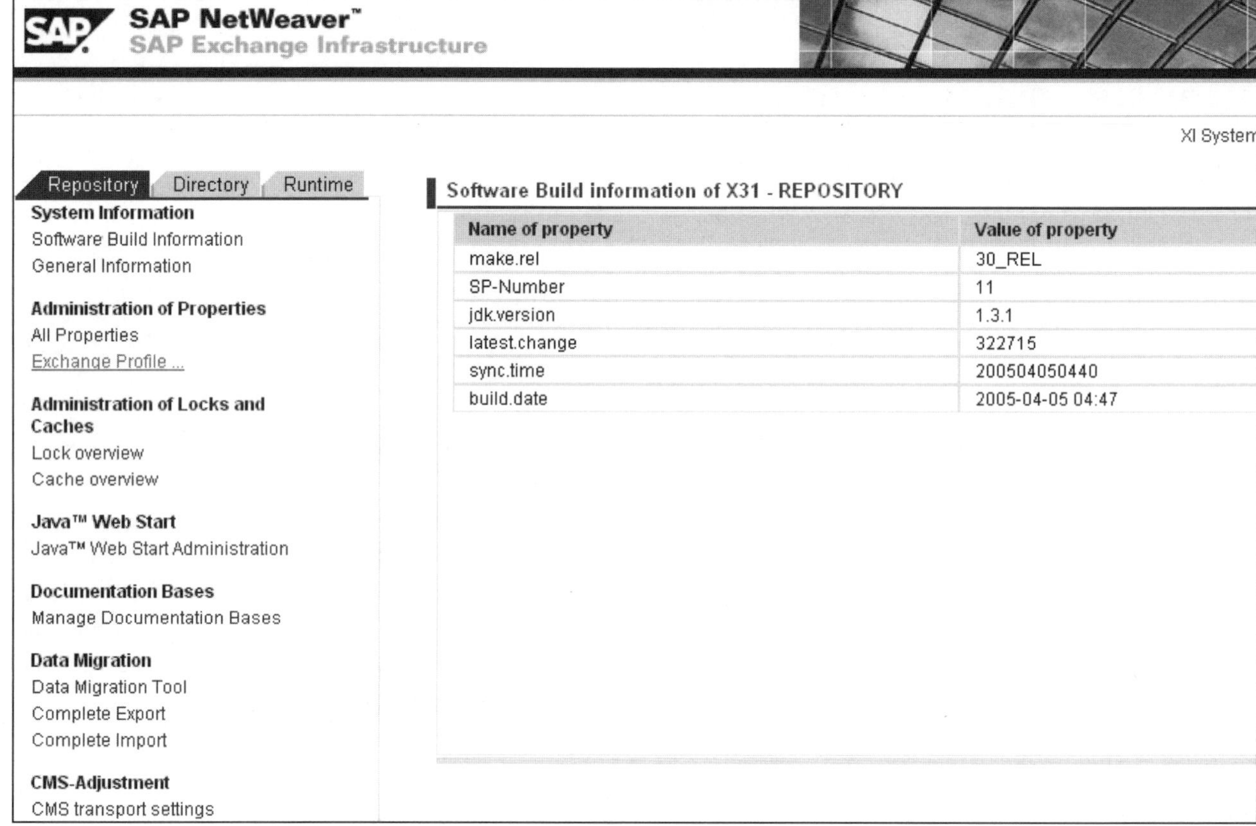

Figure 2.1 Overview of SLD Administration (Exchange Profile)

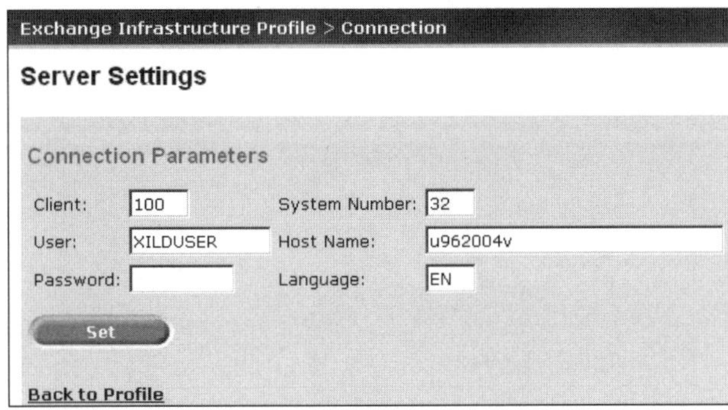

Figure 2.2 Setting Up the Server Settings Connection

In the **Client** field, you can enter the R/3 client and in the **System Number** field, you must specify the system number of your R/3 instance. Moreover, you have to specify a technical user, a password, and a logon language. Once you have verified that you're working on the correct system, we recommend that you back up your profile parameters locally on your machine. To do that, you can use the menu item **Export**. In the event that you encounter a problem, you'll be able to recover the parameters by using the menu item **Import**. The profile information will be provided for download to your workstation as an XML file within a ZIP archive. An upload is carried out by taking steps in the opposite direction.

In our sample architecture, the server names in the development system are *u962004v* and *sapt47*, and we'll use port *53200*. The central SLD is on system *sapp47* on port *56900*. Let's recall: We want to configure the development system with a local repository and a local directory, whereas the SLD is to reference the P47 system, which means that we'll use the central SLD on the production system.

We'll now describe the most important parameters that you need to configure your architecture. The relevant SAP documentation contains information on all the parameters available. As you can see in Figure 2.3, the maintenance menu is divided into the following subtrees:

- Adapter Framework
- Application System
- Connections
- Default
- Integration Builder
- Integration Server

The individual subtrees reflect the individual settings of the XI components. The **Connections** and **Default** subtrees are superordinate categories in which you can define the default values for documentation, SQL log levels, and the connection information for the other subtrees.

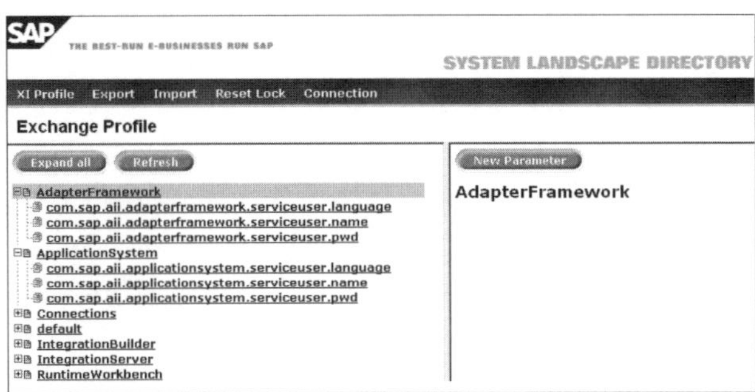

Figure 2.3 Configuring Parameters in the Exchange Profile

If you want to add a new parameter, you must highlight the corresponding subtree and then click on the **New Parameter** button in the right-hand pane. You can view the individual parameters by expanding the subtree. By highlighting the parameters, you can call them to change, delete, and save them in the right-hand pane of the dialog.

Let's begin with the **Connections** subtree and expand it as shown in Figure 2.4.

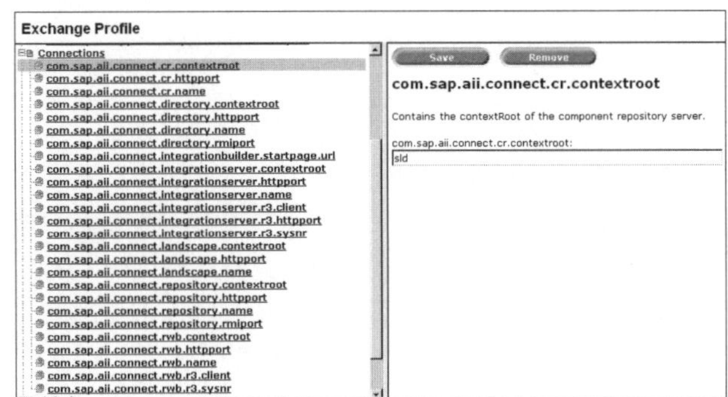

Figure 2.4 Connections Subtree in the Exchange Profile

The first parameter we'll work with is the parameter; *com.sap.aii.connect.cr.contextroot.* To simplify the notation, we'll abbreviate the name in our descriptions. This parameter defines the context root of the SLD. In our example we'll keep using the default name, *SLD*. The *cr.httpport* parameter is much more interesting. As we want to use our SLD on the P47 system, we must specify the port of the P47 system here. The parameter expects the http port; in our example, that's *56900*. As you may have already guessed, the *cr.name* parameter expects the name of the corresponding server; in our example, this is *sapp47*.

The structure and meanings of the parameters *directory.contextroot*, *directory.httpport*, and *directory.name* are similar to the parameters just described. Here you can define which directory is to be used at which port and on which server. Since we want to use a local directory, we'll store the server and the port of our development system here. Thus, for our example, we'll store the value *53200* for the *directory.httpport* parameter, and the value *sapt47* for the *directory.name* parameter. We won't change the default value *dir* for the context root for parameter *directory.contextroot*.

The parameters that contain the prefix *IntegrationServer* define the server and port of your runtime. Here, you must specify the local server and the corresponding ports.

The next parameters we want to look at are the SLD settings. You can use the parameters *landscape.contextroot*, *landscape.httpport*, and *landscape.name* to define the SLD that is to be used by the XI system that you want to administrate. As in our example, we decided to use a central SLD on the P47 system, we'll enter the value *sapp47* for the *landscape.name* parameter, and the value *56900* for the *landscape.httpport* parameter. We'll keep the value *sld* for the context root.

Since we have now set up the central SLD for our development system, we must set the parameters for our repository in the next step. As described above, we want the repository to run locally on the development platform. The relevant parameters are *repository.contextroot*, *repository.httpport*, and *repository.name*. For the *repository.contextroot* parameter, we'll use the default value *rep*. The *repository.httpport* parameter should be set to *53200*, and the value for the *repository.name* parameter is the server *sapt47*. The runtime parameters *rwb* are also set up using the values of the local system, that is, *sapt47*.

Figure 2.5 illustrates the architecture that we have just described. You must now connect the individual SAP systems to the central SLD via a data supplier bridge. Section 3.1 contains detailed information on how you should do this configuration. The appendix contains an overview of the individual parameters, including sample values and a short description.

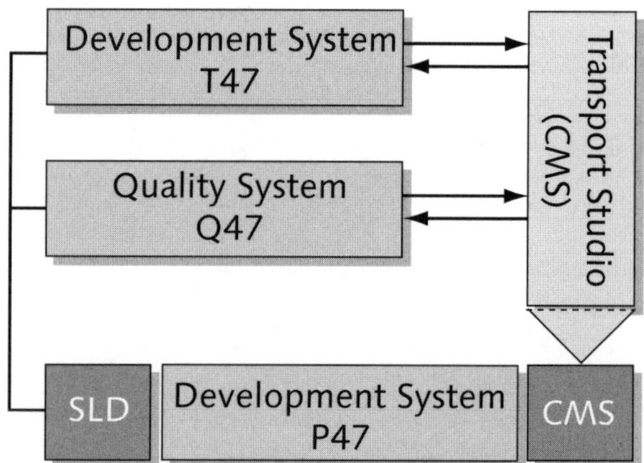

Figure 2.5 Sample Architecture—Overview

2.3 Configuration within the Repository and Directory

This section describes the configuration of an interface for distributing SAP vendor master data among two SAP R/3 systems by using SAP Exchange Infrastructure 3.0. You can use the procedure described here as a configuration example for your own XI connections.

To illustrate the example, we chose the processes of sending and receiving Financial Accounting (FI) supplier master data in an intermediate document (IDoc) message format. Figure 2.6 provides an overview of the complete scenario.

Initial Scenario

This section provides a detailed description of the individual concepts and process steps we used in our example so that you can gain profound insight into the SAP XI world. Once you have read this chapter, you should be able to solve many things that may still seem unclear. Moreover, the appendix contains a concise list of activities that describes all steps in brief. To simplify the descriptions in the following sections and chapters, we'll use a "two-way XI landscape" from now on. For this reason, we'll reduce the T47 and Q47 systems to the X31 system shown in Figure 2.6. Therefore, the example primarily refers to a connection using the "T and Q X31 system."

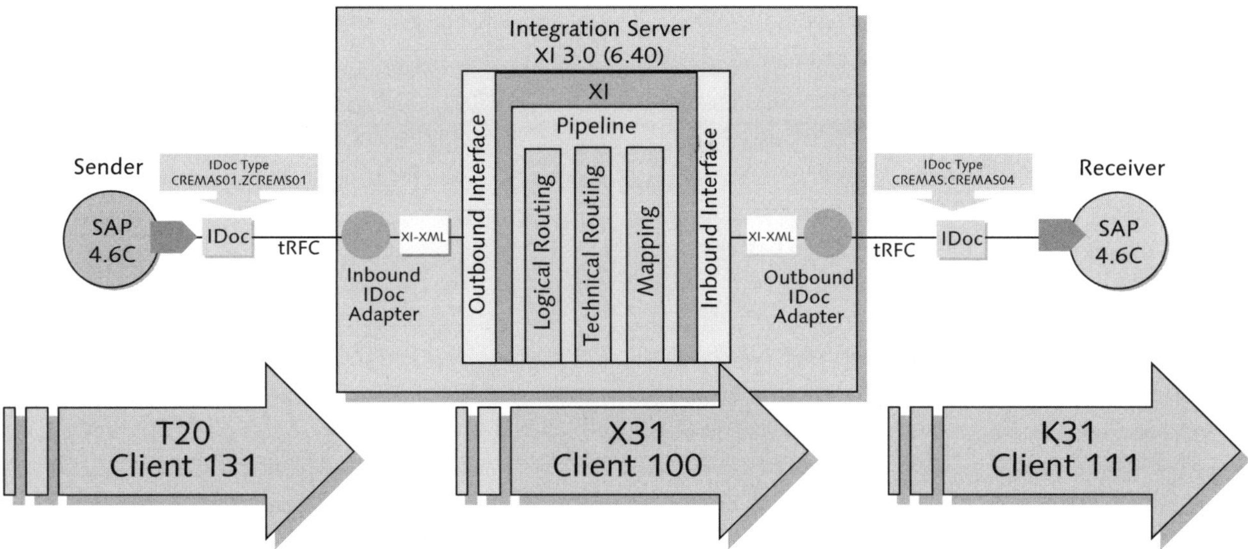

Figure 2.6 Interface Processing of the Integration Server

The SAP vendor master data is sent from client 131 in the sending system T20 through the ALE IDoc interface in accordance with the configuration in the outbound partner profile via tRFC to client 100 in integration server X31. The message type ZCREMS of the sent IDoc, which consists of the basic IDoc type CREMAS01 and the customer extension to ZCREMS01, represents the outbound interface of the sending T20 system.

As soon as the integration server receives an IDoc from the sending T20 system, the IDoc is automatically transferred to the inbound IDoc adapter. The inbound IDoc adapter is installed on the XI integration server and translates the IDoc format into the specific XI-XML message format of the integration server. Then, the data is transferred to the pipeline for processing.

The integration server receives the data in XI-XML message format and identifies the receiving business system and its inbound interface (logical routing). Then, it determines how the receiving system can be technically reached (technical routing). All information required for logical and technical routing is stored in the Service Level Directory (SLD) and in the integration repository of the XI component during the configuration of the XI interface. Moreover, mappings of the outbound interface of the sending system and of the inbound interface of the receiving system are also stored in the integration repository.

Since the outbound interface of the sending SAP system T20 in our example is different from the inbound interface (IDoc type CREMAS.CREMAS04) of the receiving SAP system K31, we implemented a message mapping in the integration repository of the XI component and registered that mapping for the two interfaces. In a mapping program, we defined the way in which the two interfaces are to be mapped.

An outbound IDoc adapter that is installed on the integration server translates the mapping data from the XI message format back into the IDoc message format of the inbound IDoc interface of the receiving SAP system. The data is sent via tRFC to the IDoc interface of the project target system K31, client 111.

The receiving system K31, client 111, receives the IDoc and transfers the message—according to the inbound partner profile configured in the receiving system—to the IDoc interface of the responsible software component, where it is forwarded to the relevant function module or workflow.

Configuring the Sending System for the Distribution

The following three requirements must be met so that IDocs can be sent from a sending SAP system to the integration server:

1. In the distribution model, you must define which message type should be distributed to the integration server.
2. You must configure an outbound partner profile that controls when and through which port or RFC destination an IDoc is sent.
3. The distribution of the model view must have been completed upfront.

In the following sections, we'll describe how you can make these configurations.

First, you must create an RFC user in both the sending and receiving systems. For our example, we have created the user ZSC_USER via Transaction SU01 with the user type *Communication* in client 131 of system T20 and in client 100 of XI system X31. For interface processing, the system user must have extensive ALE and RFC authorizations. In our go-live test, we assigned the authorization profiles SAP_ALL and SAP_NEW to the specific RFC user who is not dialog-enabled.

Secondly, you must create a logical system in both the sending and receiving systems, which you can do via using Transaction BD54. In the table, you must maintain the entry of the receiving system X31, client 100, as a logical system (in our example, *REFAX31100* and *REFAT20131*). Note that you should always use all caps to write the logical system name.

A logical system is stored in each client via Transaction SCC4. Typically, this happens after a system installation or after a client copy has been created, which should be carried out by the system adminstrators. You can use Transaction SCC4 to verify whether this has occurred in your sending and XI systems. If not, create the two logical systems in the sending system and the receiving XI system. The table that's used for Transaction BD54 is a cross-client table.

Then you must create an RFC destination, because an outbound partner profile in the sending system can only be used if an RFC destination for the integration server has been defined in the sending T20 system. The RFC destination defines the target system for RFC calls and controls the remote function calls. You can define and view RFC destinations via SAP Transaction SM59, *Display and Maintain RFC Destinations* (see Figure 2.7).

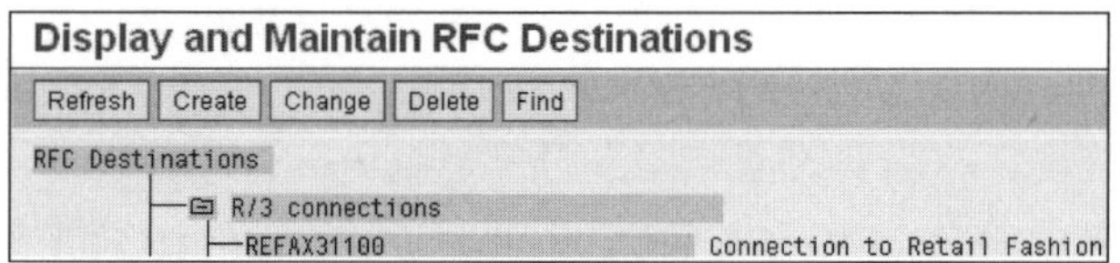

Figure 2.7 Transaction SM59—Displaying and Maintaining RFC Destinations

In our example, we created an RFC connection to a connection type 3 target system (R/3 connections). The name of the newly created RFC destination should be the same as the name of the logical target system. Therefore, in our example, the name of both the RFC destination and the logical target system is *REFAX31100*. During the creation of the RFC destination, we specified the server computer of the integration server, including its system number and client as the target computer. In addition, a valid user name and password must be specified (see Figures 2.8 and 2.9).

Figure 2.8 Creating an RFC Connection—Technical Settings

> **Note** Please check the connection and authorizations via the following menu path: **Test · Authorizations**. If the system doesn't return any RFC errors, you can continue with the next step.

In the following configuration step you will set up a distribution model. The ALE distribution model controls the message flow between SAP systems. It consists of individual model views in which all cross-system message flows that belong together are defined.

Start Transaction BD64, *Distribution Model*. Go to the **Change** mode and use the **Create model view** button to create the technical names for the model view. For our example, we have created the model view KKMT20 in client 131 so that IDocs of the message type *ZCREMR* can be sent to integration server X31, client 100 (see Figure 2.10).

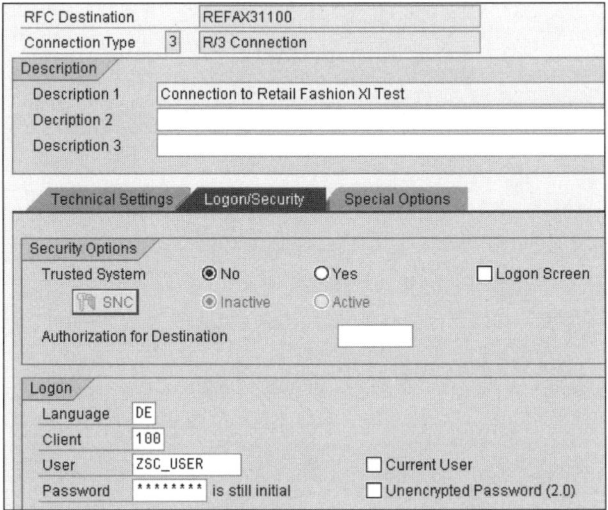

Figure 2.9 Creating an RFC Connection—Logon/Security

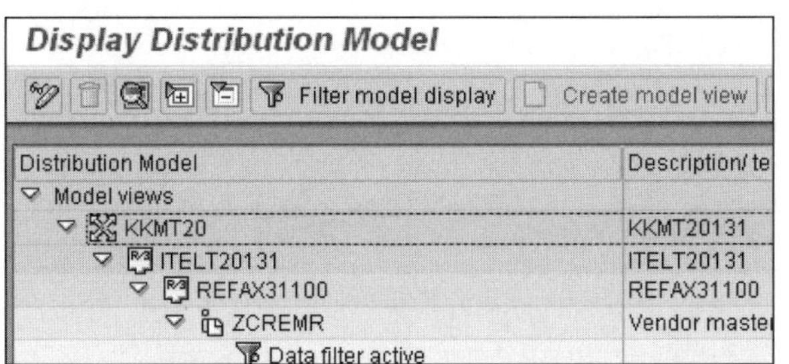

Figure 2.10 Transaction BD64—Displaying the Distribution Model

You can easily insert the modified message type *ZCREMR* via the Change command. Go to the **Change distribution model** mode and click on the **Add message type** button. Specify the model view, sender, receiver, and the message type. In our example, those are as follows: model view *KKMT20131*, sender *ITELT20131*, receiver *REFAX31100*, and message type *ZCREMR*.

Now you can use Transaction BD64 to generate the partner profile. You can easily do that via the following menu path: **Environment • Generate Partner Profiles**. Select the model view first. Then start the partner generation program via the menu path. You must specify the XI target system in the **Partner system** field. Click on **Execute**. The resulting log file should contain information confirming that the partners, the port, and the relevant outbound parameters were generated by the system.

You can verify the result by using Transactions WE21, *Ports in IDoc processing*, and WE20, *Partner Profiles*.

For our test purposes, we had to make the entries shown in Figures 2.11 and 2.12.

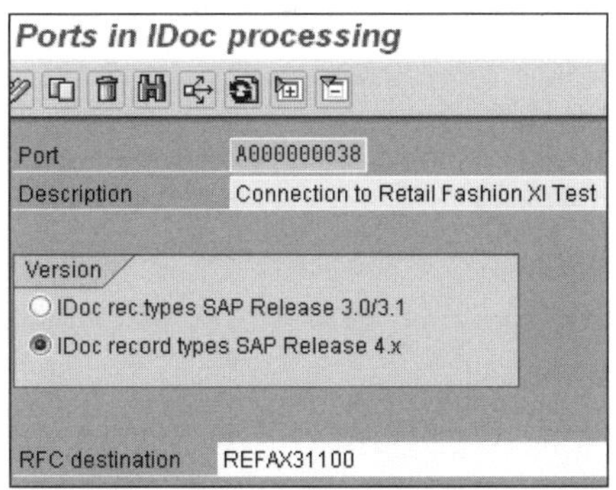

Figure 2.11 Transaction WE21—Ports in IDoc Processing

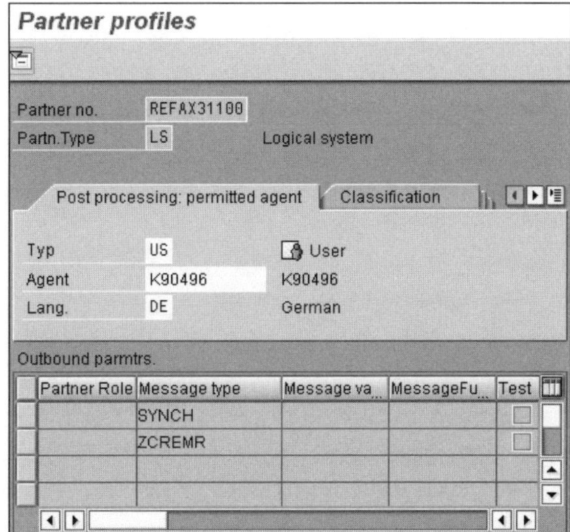

Figure 2.12 Transaction WE21—Partner Profiles

If, during the profile generation, the entries are missing due to an error, you can simply create them, Next, you must perform the distribution of the model view for the XI system via the menu path, **Edit • Model View • Distribute**. To do that, select the corresponding entry in your XI system. In our example, that's the logical system *REFAX31100*. Then, you can trigger the distribution of the model view for the XI system. The resulting log file indicates whether the distribution was successful, however, to ensure that it was, you should log on to the XI system and call Transaction BD64. If there's no error or problem, you can see the transferring model view KKM T20 immediately.

This means that the configuration of the sending system via ALE through the RFC port is completed.

Configuring the IDoc Adapter

The IDoc adapter on the integration server should contain up-to-date IDoc metadata of the IDoc types to be processed.

To load the metadata of the IDoc type from the sending system T20 into the integration server, the IDoc adapter must know the port of the sending system. If you have configured a port, you can establish a connection to the system from which the metadata of the IDoc type is loaded. The port and the corresponding RFC destination must be created upfront on the integration server. To do that, you can use Transaction SM59, *Display and Maintain RFC Destinations*.

To publish a port, you can use Transaction IDX1, *Port Maintenance in IDoc Adapter*. Use the menu item **Create** to include a new port into the list of ports that are available to the IDoc adapter. When you create a port in the IDoc adapter, you must select the relevant port, the RFC destination, and the source client (sender).

In our example, we created the port SAPT20 in client 100 on the integration server X31. Through this port, the necessary IDoc type metadata *CREMAS01/ZCREMS01* (basic type and extension) was loaded from client 131 in the sending system into the IDoc adapter. In the example, the created adapter port references port SAPT20 and uses the RFC destination *ITELT20131*.

You have already created the user and logical systems in both systems so that a correct connection can be established. Now you have to repeat two steps that have already been described earlier.

Use Transaction SM59 to create the RFC connection for the sending system in the XI system. In our example, this is RFC connection type 3, *ITELT20131*. Enter the relevant system data of the sending system and check whether a connection is actually being established and whether the communication user can log on to the target system.

Start Transaction IDX1 and click on the **Create** icon to create a port. Use the sample data shown in Figure 2.13 to create your port.

You can configure the IDoc adapter via Transaction IDX2. To do that, call the transaction and click on the **Create** icon. Enter the IDoc type, the extension, and the port that you have previously created. For our example, we entered the IDoc type *CREMAS01*, the extension *ZCREMAS01*, and the port *SAPT20*. The result is displayed in Figure 2.14.

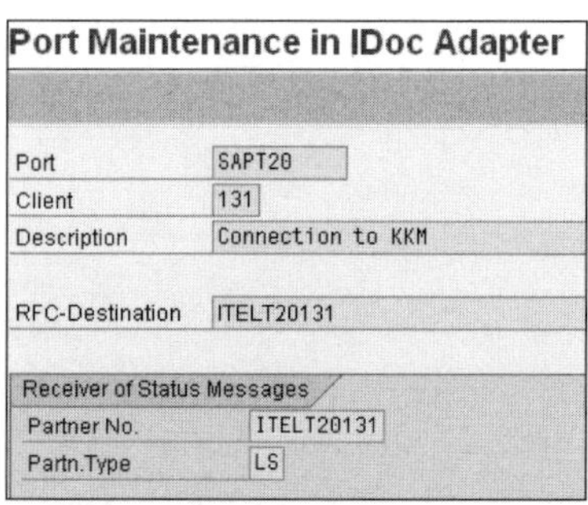

Figure 2.13 Transaction IDX1—Port Maintenance in the IDoc Adapter

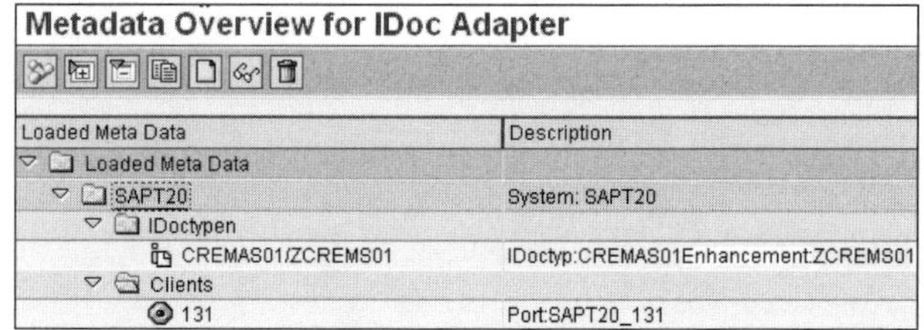

Figure 2.14 Transaction IDX1—Metadata for IDoc Adapters

You can use Transaction IDX2—*Metadata Overview for IDoc Adapter*—to load the IDoc type metadata from the sending system. The transaction provides an overview of the metadata that has already been loaded from each source system. By double-clicking on the icon of the respective IDoc type in the tree row, you can get more detailed information. Alternatively, you can select the entire row and click on the **Display** icon. The structural IDoc overview provides you with a lot of relevant information. Here too, you can view this information by either double-clicking on the relevant tree node for the IDoc structure, or by selecting the node and clicking on the **Display** icon.

XI Tools

You can access the Exchange Infrastructure via Transaction SXMB_IFR or Internet Explorer. If you enter the URL *http://[hostname]:[port]/rep/start/index.jsp* in your web browser, the SAP Exchange Infrastructure home page will be displayed, as shown in Figure 2.15.

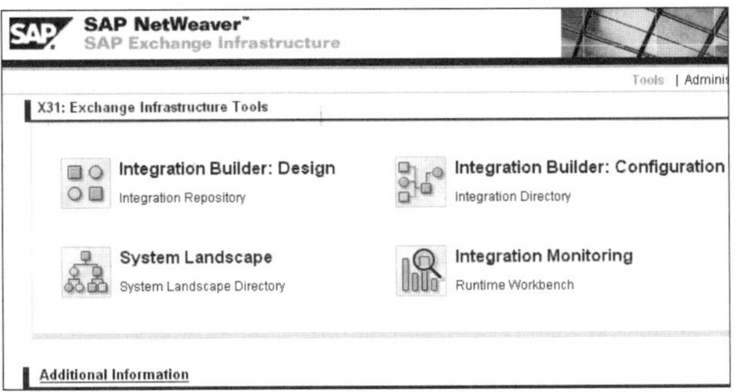

Figure 2.15 SAP Exchange Infrastructure Home Page—Transaction SXMB_IFR

To make the settings in the individual Exchange Infrastructure tools, you must first create a user with the necessary authorizations and a password for the XI system. Section 4.2 contains useful information on the necessary authorizations.

> **Note** In SAP systems, a business system is a real client. In this context, the business system describes the semantics of the corresponding technical system.
> It is mandatory that you record the technical systems and business systems in the SLD so that they can be used for all further configurations in the integration repository. The necessary information on the system landscape is made available to other XI tools such as the integration repository via a separate interface.

If you click on the **System Landscape Directory** link on the home page, you can call the SLD configuration. The **Technical Landscape** and **Business Landscape** links enable you to enter the configuration menus for the technical and business systems respectively.
All systems involved in the business process or the interface must be integrated as technical systems into the technical landscape. This means that in our example the sending system T20, the integration server X31, and the receiving system K31 must be created.

Technical systems are categorized and grouped according to their *system type*. Which attributes you can record is dependent on the system type. In our example, all systems involved in the interface are of the *Web AS ABAP* system type.

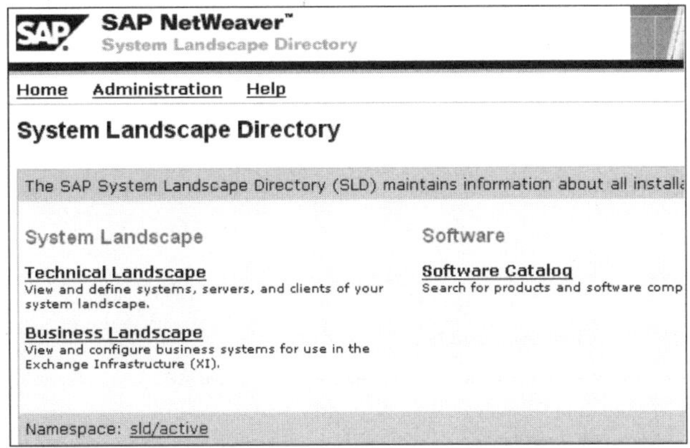

Figure 2.16 System Landscape Directory Link—SLD Configuration

Depending on the release and support package status, you can use Transaction RZ70 to enter the data automatically into the SLD of the systems involved (see Chapter 3 for detailed information). It also describes how you can manually create a technical system.

> **Note** Installed products and software components are entered at the level of the technical system since development objects are cross-client objects in SAP systems.

Figure 2.17 shows the details we entered for the sending system T20. Once you have created the technical system, you must continue creating the business system.

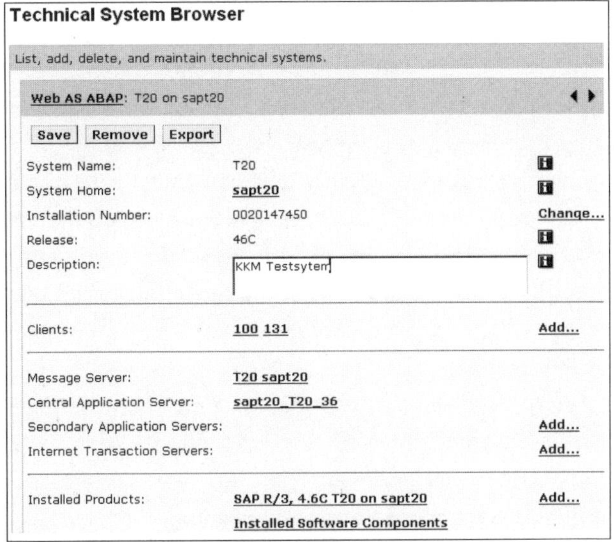

Figure 2.17 Technical System—Creating System Data

Each technical system must be assigned a business system name so that you can map your business processes in a distributed system landscape. A business system describes the semantics of a system, and in this way it acts like an SAP client. The configuration of the business systems is carried out within the business landscape (see Figure 2.18).

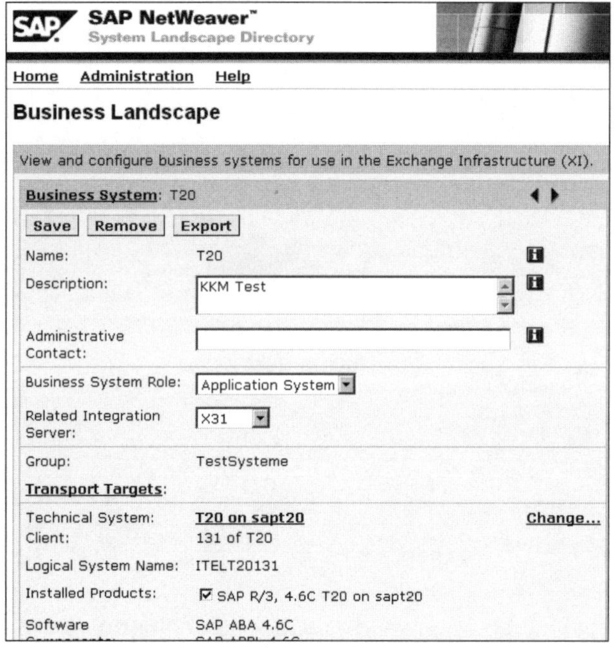

Figure 2.18 Business System T20

As you can see in Figure 2.18 of our example, the business system called T20 is assigned client 131 of the technical system T20 and the role of an *application system* because that is its function when sending master data to the related integration server X31 or to the application system K31. It is mandatory that you assign a technical system to each business system, and you must do that no later than at the time of configuration. Finally, you must enter the software products of the technical system that are relevant for the business system (or the client respectively).

As is the case with technical systems, you can create business systems by using a specific wizard. Section 3.2 contains detailed information on how you can create a technical system and a business system.

Once we have created the required business system, we will briefly describe the software catalog and the necessary settings for our example in the next step.

In addition to the information on the technical and business systems, you maintain information on the software components involved in an interface or a business process in the SLD. Therefore, a software component is regarded as a modular unit that can be used in various products of a software producer. A product is a combination of software components and can be available in different versions.

The connection between product versions and component versions is mapped in the SLD by using *software feature* type objects.

At design time, all components involved in a logical integration scenario are represented in the integration repository. Basically, these include the following components:

- software components used
- inbound and outbound interfaces
- mapping programs

At the time of configuration, the components that are represented in the integration repository are referenced to an existing system landscape in the integration directory during the distribution of an abstract integration scenario.

In the following section, we'll describe the use of components from the SLD. The creation and configuration of the SLD is described in great detail in Chapter 3.

As you can see in Figure 2.19, for our scenario we created a separate software component in the SLD. And, as mentioned above, you can find instructions on how to create such a software component in Section 3.2.

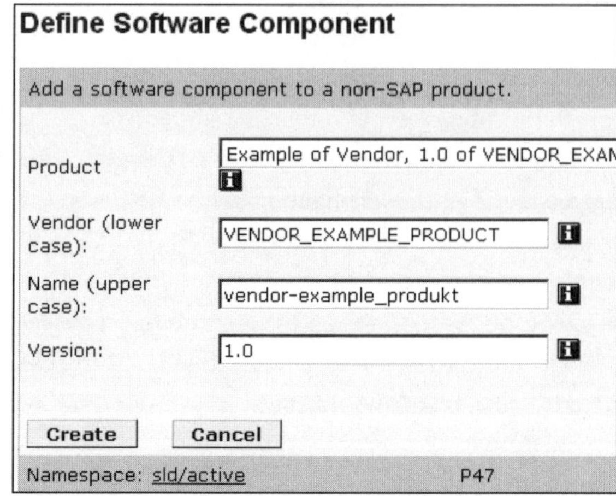

Figure 2.19 Defining a Software Component

In the following step, we'll import the software component version from the SLD into the XI repository.

Importing a Software Component Version

Software component versions are required for the creation of namespaces and are therefore a prerequisite for the creation of all dependent objects in the integration repository, such as interface structures, integration scenarios, and the like.

Call the Integration Builder from the XI home page. A Java application starts up, which can take several seconds.

Go to the menu **Tools • Transfer from System Landscape Directory • Import Software Component Versions** to call the dialog in which you can import a software component version from the SLD into the integration directory (see Figure 2.20).

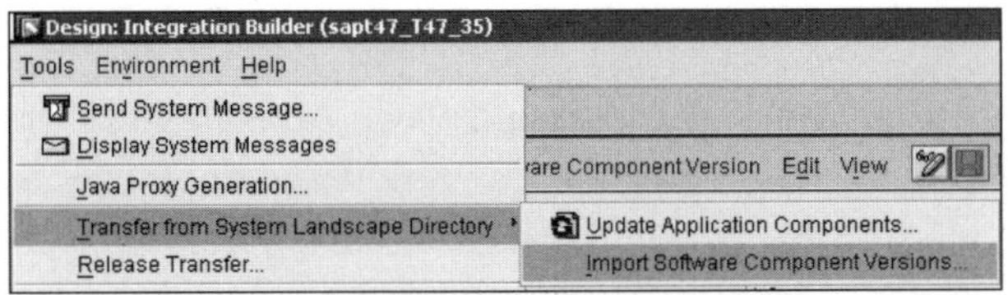

Figure 2.20 Importing Software Components

In the **Import Software Component Versions** dialog, you can select the required software component versions and use the **Import** button to load them into the integration repository.

For the IDoc interface prototype described earlier, the newly created software component version **Example of Vendor...** must be imported into the integration repository. Depending on the size of the existing catalog, this function can take several seconds.

After the software component has been imported, you must activate the software component version via the **Change Lists** tab in the left-hand pane of the screen.

Importing SAP Objects

In the properties section of the software component version, select the option **Import of RFC and IDoc Interfaces from SAP Systems Permitted** in the **Definition** tab (right-hand pane of the screen). Moreover, you must check the entries for the connection properties of an SAP system to ensure that the import of the corresponding objects is feasible.

The inbound and outbound interfaces are stored in the integration repository as XML schemas that map the form of the XML messages to be expected for the interfaces.

The import wizard is used to import IDoc interfaces into the integration repository. If you want to launch the import wizard, you must first expand the subnodes of the software component version from which you want to import an interface. Then you can call the menu item **Import of SAP Objects** via the context menu of the **Imported Objects** subnode. The system displays the import wizard, as shown in Figure 2.21.

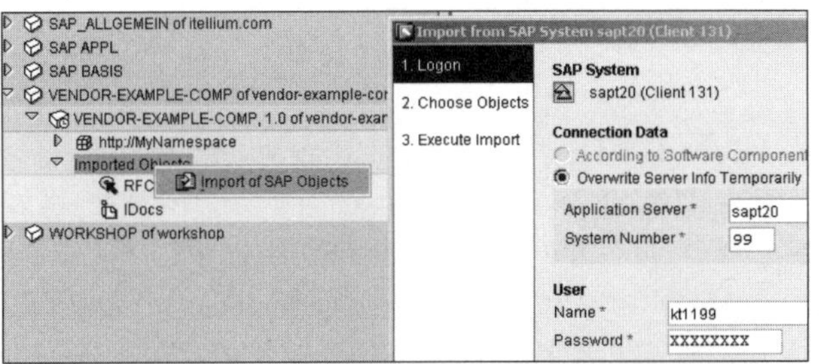

Figure 2.21 Integration Repository—Wizard for Importing SAP Objects

If the logon data is incorrect, you can re-enter it in the first step of the wizard. Next, you must select the IDoc you want to import. In our example, that's the IDoc object *ZCREMS.CREMAS01.ZCREMS01*. Then click on the **Next** button to start the automatic import. Now you must activate the objects again through the **Change Lists** tab in the left-hand pane. After you do that, the imported IDoc interfaces are available under the menu item **Imported Objects • IDocs**. All IDocs and RFCs that have been imported in this software component version are stored in the **Imported Objects** subfolder. The result of the import is illustrated in Figure 2.22.

As in our example, the outbound interface of the sending system is identical to the structure of the inbound interface of the receiving system, you must import the same IDoc interface twice into the integration repository. Therefore, the outbound interface and the inbound interface of the sending and receiving systems, T20, client 131, and K31, client 111, are assigned the same IDoc interface: *ZCREMR.CREAMS01.ZREMS01*.

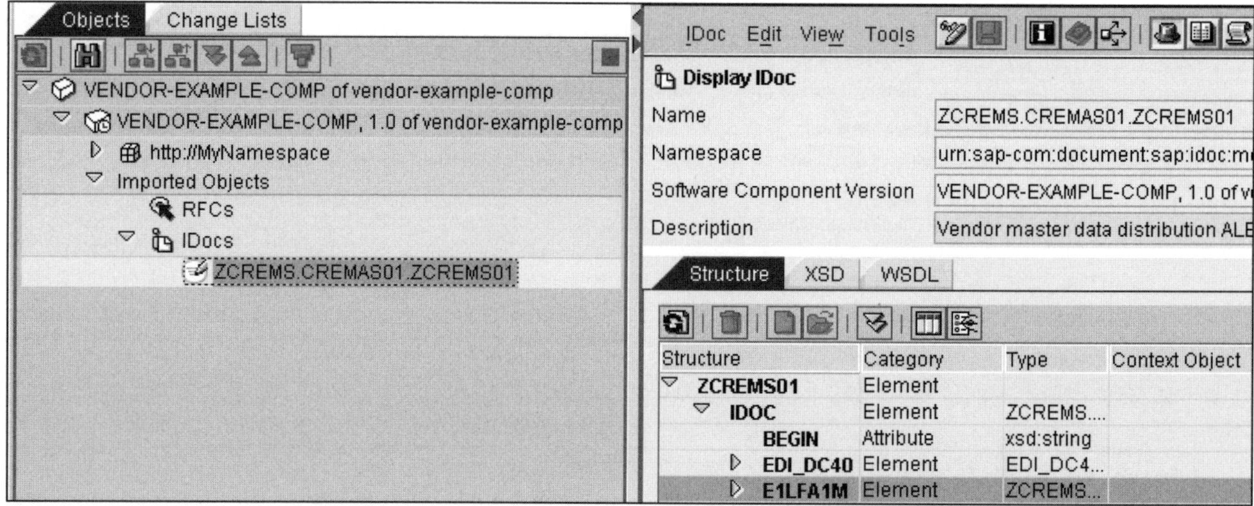

Figure 2.22 Result of the Import of SAP Objects (IDoc Interface)

If the outbound interface of the sender and the inbound interface of the receiver are not identical, that is to say if two different IDoc structures have been imported, it is necessary to define mapping rules to specify how the structure and values of the outbound interface can be mapped onto the inbound interface. You must store such mapping rules at design time by using a mapping object in the integration repository. There are several steps involved in creating a message mapping, which we'll briefly describe in the following sections.

Creating a Namespace in the Repository

To create the individual components, you must first create a separate namespace within the previously imported software component. Again, you can use the context menu to do that. Figure 2.23 illustrates this procedure.

Figure 2.23 Creating a Namespace in the Repository

Once you have saved the namespace, it is included in the tree structure below the software component node. After that, you can create the integration scenario, interface, mapping, and adapter objects.

For our example, we have to define the mapping objects in the next step.

Creating Message Mapping Objects

To create a new message mapping, go to the following menu: **Software Component · Namespace · Mapping Objects · Message Mapping**, open the context menu and click on **New...** The message mapping object can then be created in a new dialog where you can specify the object name and a description (see Figure 2.24). Then, you must activate the object via the **Change Lists** tab in the left-hand pane of the screen.

Once you have done that, you must create the actual mapping rules or mapping program by using a graphical mapping editor. The editor enables you to design a structure mapping and to establish a link with a value mapping.

To perform a mapping, you must first load the schemas of the source and target data structures from the integration repository into the structure overview of the mapping editor (in our example: *ZCREMS.CREAMS01.ZCREMS01*). In the editor, you must do that in both the left- and right-hand panes. After loading the schemas, they are displayed in the structure overview of the mapping editor. Then you must execute the function **Map Selected Fields and Substructures if Names Are Identical** (Figure 2.25, top right). In that way, you have established a direct connection.

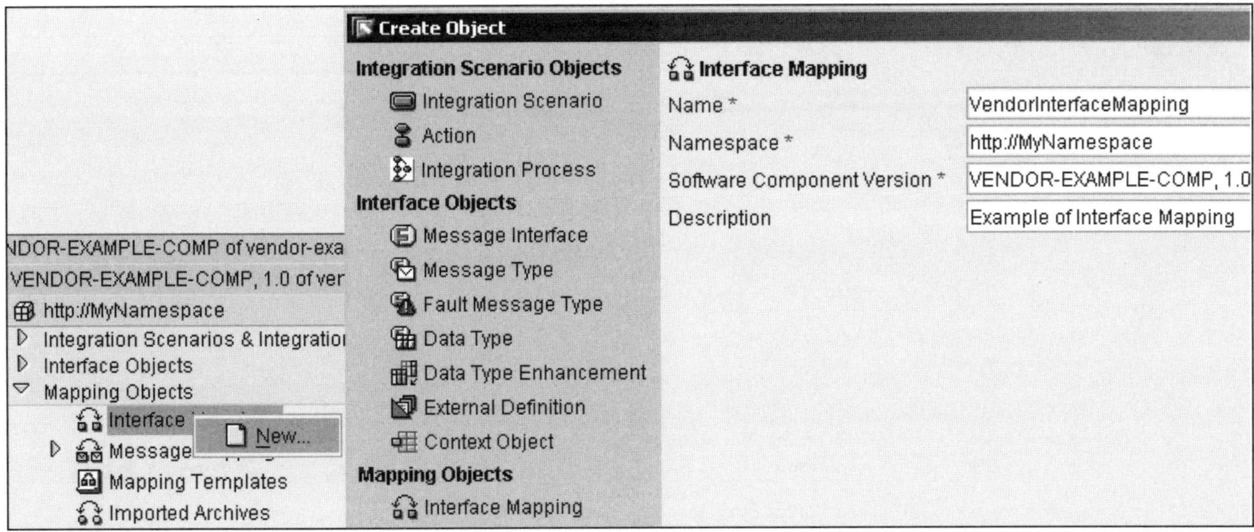

Figure 2.24 Integration Repository: Creating a Message Mapping Object

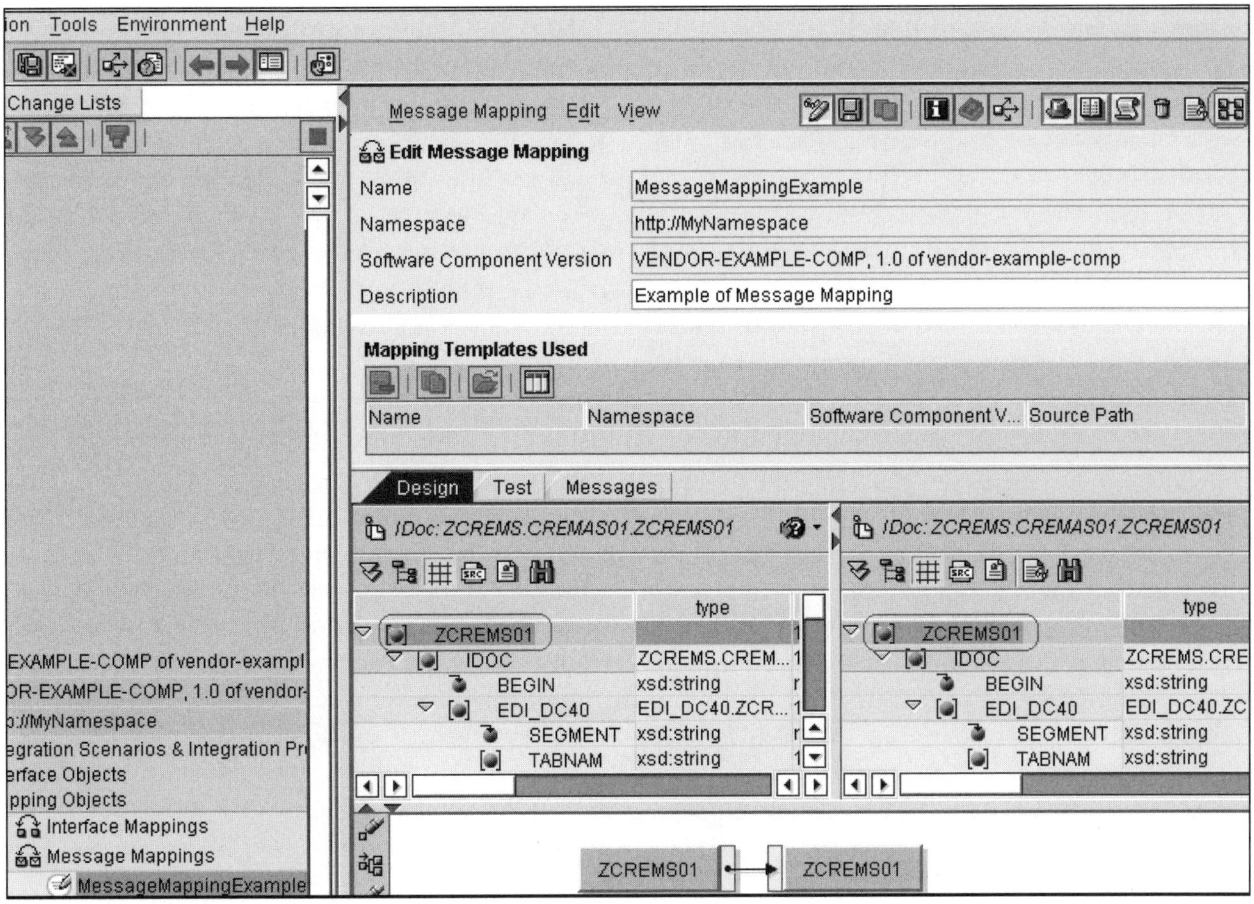

Figure 2.25 Mapping Editor: Structure Overview

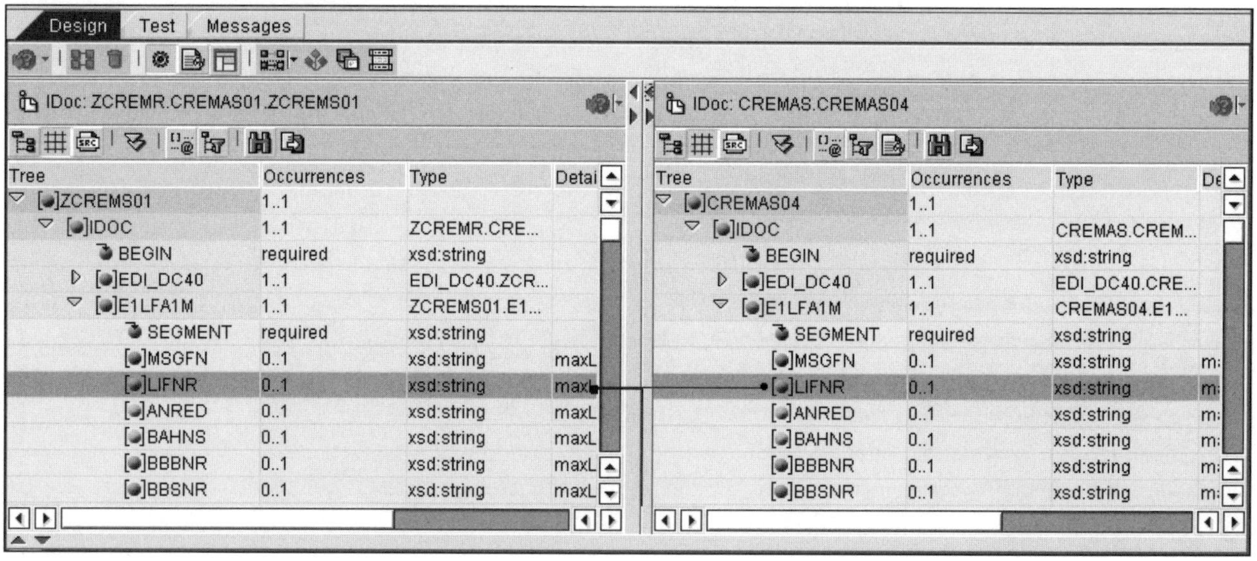

Figure 2.26 Mapping Editor: Assigning Fields

Save the results and perform an activation via the **Change Lists** tab.

In our example, we have performed a 1-1 mapping. If, however, you want to modify individual fields or fill a different source structure, the editor provides a smart configuration option.

By dragging a field from the source data structure and dropping it onto a specific field in the target data structure, you can manually establish a corresponding connection. The mapping editor then displays this manual assignment in the dataflow editor for further editing. The defined dependencies are displayed as a red line connecting the interdependent fields (see Figure 2.26).

In the simplest scenario, the field value is not changed. This means that the field value of the source data structure is transferred 'as is' into the assigned field of the source data structure. For complex mappings, however, it may be necessary to modify the contents or structure of the field values in the source data structure before transferring them into the assigned fields of the source data structure. Such modifications include the following:

- Changing the format of date fields
- Concatenating the contents of several fields in the source data structure (e.g., concatenating character strings) to transfer them into a single field of the target data structure
- Performing mathematical operations using several field values of the source data structure The result is transferred into a field of the target data structure.

You can define mapping rules by using the dataflow editor (i.e., the editor window below the structure overview). The dataflow editor provides standard functions for processing the field values of the source data structure (e.g., text: `substring( )`, `concat( )`, or arithmetic: `add( )`, `subtract( )`, and the like).

Example

Figure 2.27 shows a diagram of the dataflow editor. The diagram illustrates the concatenation of the field values of two fields in the source data structure (*firstName* and *lastName*) by using the standard text function, `concat( )`. The return value of the `concat( )` function (= *firstName* + *lastName*) is transferred into the *name* field of the target data structure.

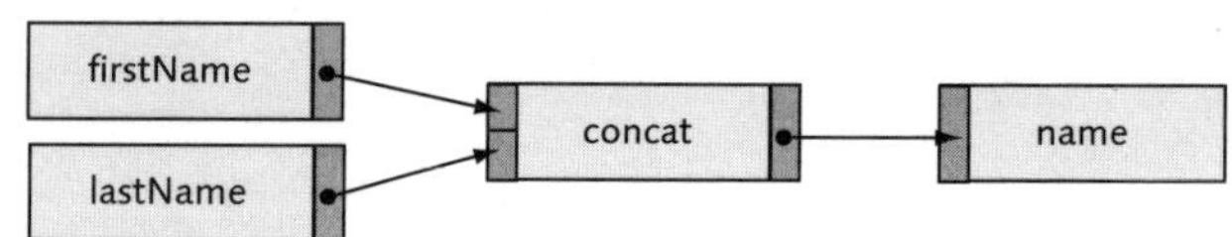

Figure 2.27 Dataflow Editor: Target Field Mapping Using the Standard String Concatenation Function

Of course, you can also develop your own Java mapping routines and combine and use them with the standard functions described above. There are other options available for mapping Java and ABAP. You can even directly connect a chain of customized Java modules to your adapters, for example, to force a global conversion. Those topics, however, are not addressed in this Essentials book.

Registering a Mapping Program

Interface mappings register mapping programs or message mappings for a specific pair of interfaces. An interface mapping can only reference a mapping program that belongs to the same software component version as the interface mapping itself. The integration server can identify mapping programs that are referenced by the interface mapping.

It is generally possible to create several different interface mappings for one pair of interfaces. The interface mapping that should be used in a logical solution scenario is defined along with the definition of the interface identification at the time of configuration.

Creating an Interface Mapping Object

To create a new interface mapping, go to the following menu: **Software Component · Namespace · Mapping Objects · Interface Mapping**, open the context menu, and click on **New...** (see Figure 2.28).

When you create a new interface mapping object, you must specify the name of the object and a description.

Defining Outbound and Inbound Interfaces

After creating the interface mapping object, you must specify the outbound and inbound interfaces for which you want to register the mapping program. You can do that by entering the respective interfaces into the tables with the same names in the central panes of the object editor. Then, you must import the properties of the individual interfaces by clicking on the **Read Interfaces** button. Once the properties have been imported, the table in the lower part of the object editor displays tabs for the source and target messages.

In that lower part of the object editor, you can select a mapping program that you want to register for the interface pair you specified in the central part of the editor. You can use the input help to select an existing message mapping from the integration repository (context menu or F4 key in the **Mapping Program** section of the object editor). The input help displays all message mappings that are stored in the integration repository. You can also create a message mapping in the object editor or select several mapping programs simultaneously.

Figure 2.29 shows the interface mapping we created for our example. The interface mapping (i.e., the mapping program) for the interface pair consists of the outbound interface *ZCREMR.CREMAS01.ZCREMS01* of the sending system T20 and the target interface *ZCREMR.CREMAS01.ZCREMS01* of the receiving system K31.

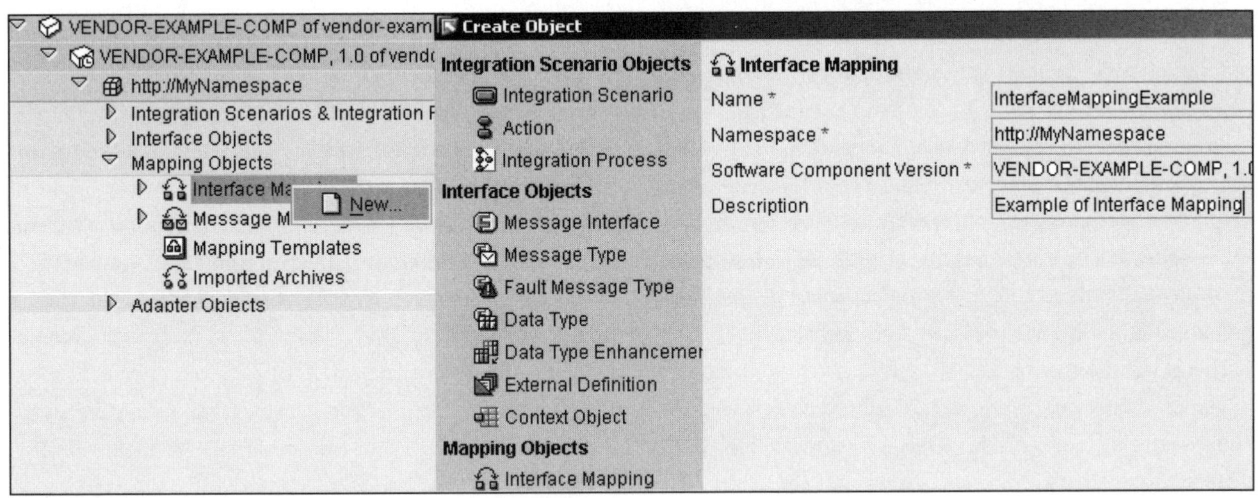

Figure 2.28 Integration Repository: Creating an Interface Mapping Object

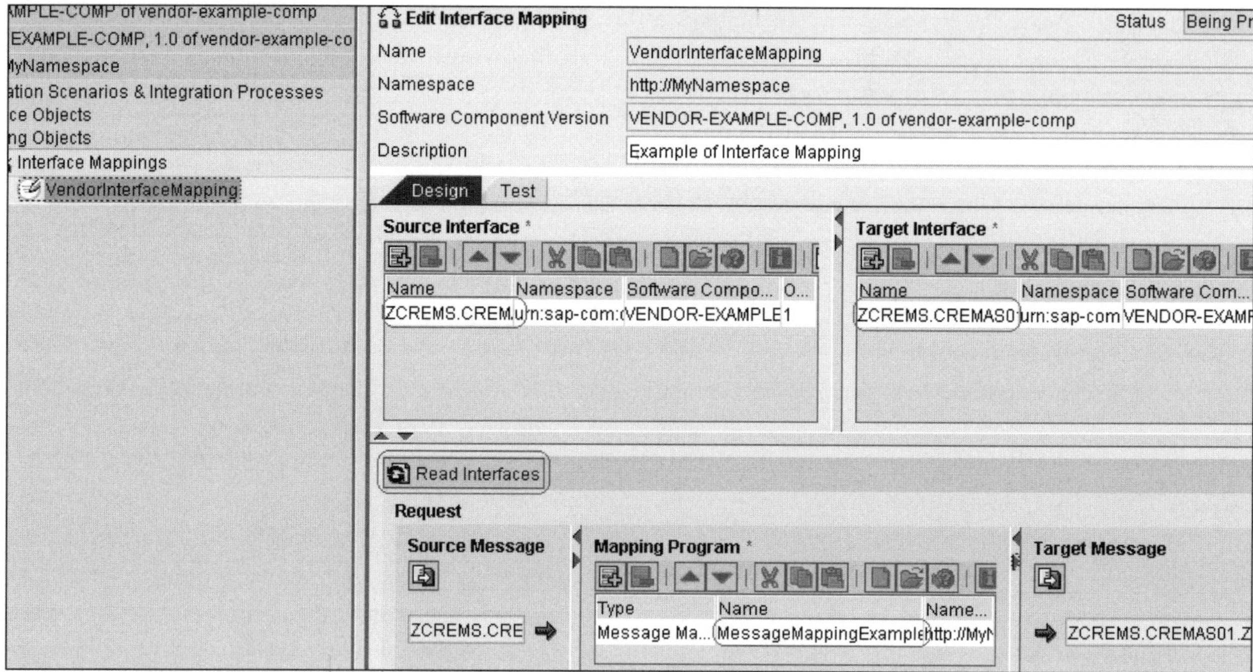

Figure 2.29 Integration Repository: Interface Mapping

Configuration in the Integration Directory

At configuration time, the logical components of a logical integration scenario that are represented in the integration repository are mapped to a specific system landscape within the integration directory. During that process, you specify from which system with which outbound interface messages are to be sent to which specific system with which specific inbound interface. The sender and the receiver are specified as business systems to which specific technical systems are assigned in the SLD.

Thus, all technical and logical routing, as well as all mapping configurations, are carried out in the integration directory.

You can access the integration directory via the link *http://[hostname]:[port]/rep/start/index.jsp*, which is used to call the Java application, *Integration Builder*.

To address a business system from the SLD as a sender or receiver of messages in the logical routing, you must ensure that the business systems are defined as services in the integration system.

To do that, you can use the Configuration Wizard, which can be called via the **Create** button (Figure 2.30, top left).

You can select only those business systems that you have previously created in the SLD.

In our example, you can only exchange messages within your own system landscape. For this reason, you must select the **Internal Communication** option to enable internal communication.

For each sending and receiving business system service, a communication channel must be created or assigned respectively. Communication channels define the actual rules according to which messages are handled during inbound or outbound processing. In particular, it is the type and configuration of the adapter to be used during inbound and outbound processing that are defined in the communication channel. Depending on whether a service is addressed as a sender or receiver of messages, the assigned communication channel assumes the role of a sending or receiving channel respectively.

In our example, we assigned an IDoc adapter as a communication channel in the role of a sending channel to business system service T20, and in the role of a receiving channel to K31. The assigned communication channel determines that messages sent from the integration server to the target system K31 are converted by an SAP IDoc adapter from the XI-XML format into the IDoc

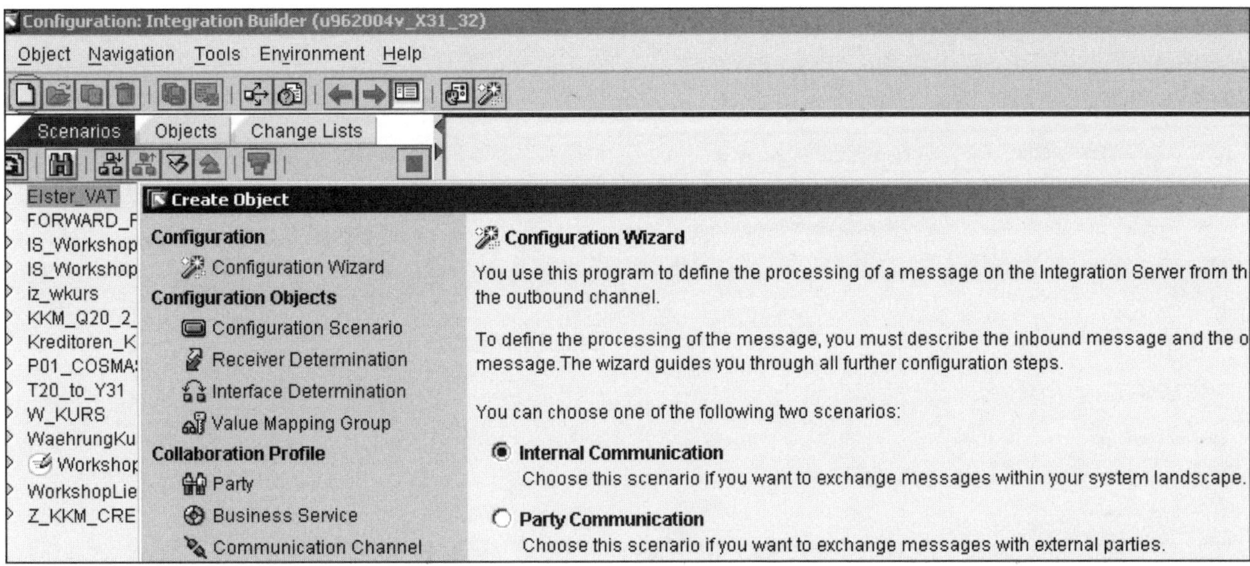

Figure 2.30 Configuration Wizard

format of the receiving system. To achieve this, you must carry out the configuration steps shown in Figures 2.31 and 2.32.

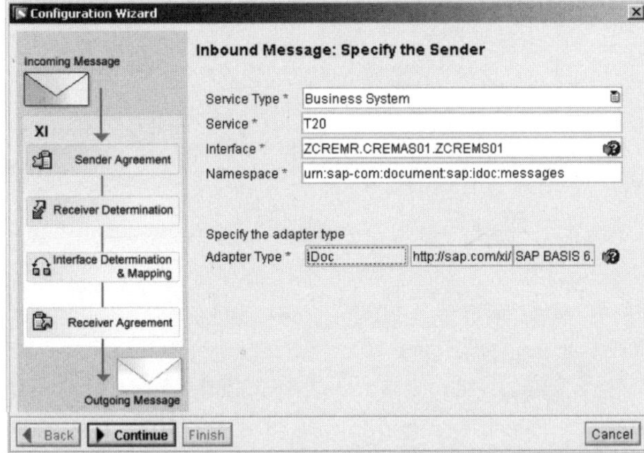

Figure 2.31 Inbound Message: Specifying the Sender (Sending Channel)

For the inbound message, you must specify the following data:

- Service
- Interface
- Namespace
- Adapter Type

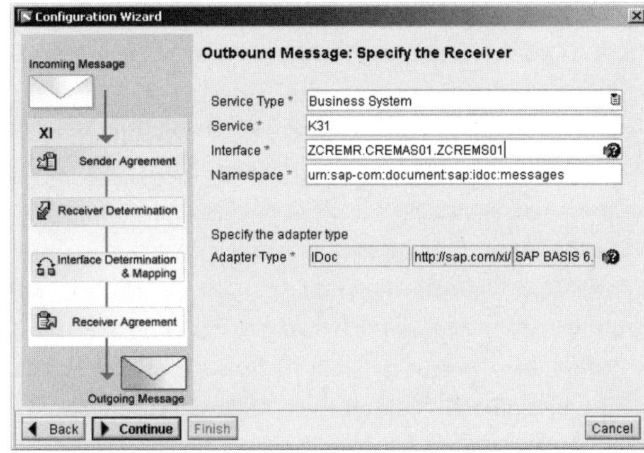

Figure 2.32 Outbound Message: Specifying the Receiver (Receiving Channel)

For the outbound message, you must specify the following data:

- Service
- Interface
- Namespace
- Adapter Type

Due to our choice of interfaces and communication in the previous configuration steps, we don't need to make any further specifications, as you can see in Figure 2.33.

In the next step, you must specify the receiving system(s) to which incoming messages from a sending business system service should be forwarded. You can do this via a receiver determination that must be created in the integration directory.

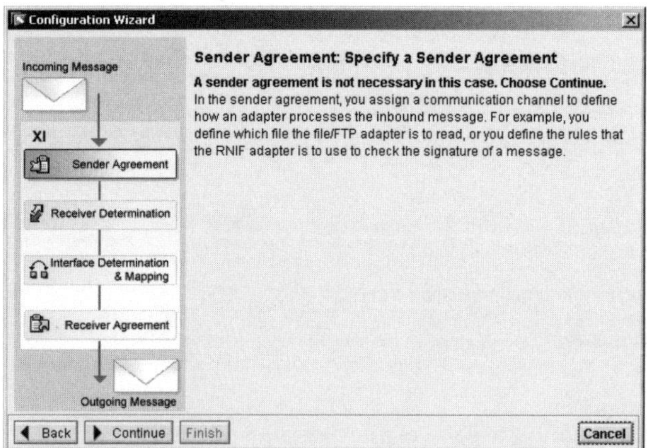

Figure 2.33 Sender Agreement

In a receiver determination, a sender and the corresponding outbound interface are assigned one or more receivers and optionally, message forwarding rules. Services are addressed as message receivers. To address a business system as the recipient of messages, a business system service must be assigned to it as a receiver. To address a business process as the recipient of messages, a business process service must be assigned to it.

In a communication agreement, you can specify the communication channel to be used for sending messages. A distinction is made between receiver agreements and sender agreements. In a receiver agreement, you specify a communication channel and the inbound interface of the target system for a specific sender/receiver pair.

In our example, we determined in the receiver determination *|T20|ZCRMR.CREMAS01.ZCREMS01* that all messages of the interface type *ZCREMR.CREMAS01.ZCREMS01* that are coming in through business system service T20 are to be sent to business system service K31. You can use the **Change** icon to manually change the automatically entered values (see Figure 2.34).

An interface determination specifies the inbound interface to be used for incoming messages for a specific sender/receiver pair. In the course of an interface determination, you assign the inbound interface of the receiving system to the outbound interface of the sending system, as well as the interface mapping to be used for a specific interface pair. A prerequisite for creating an interface determination is the implementation (message mapping) and registration (interface mapping) of a mapping program in the integration repository at design time.

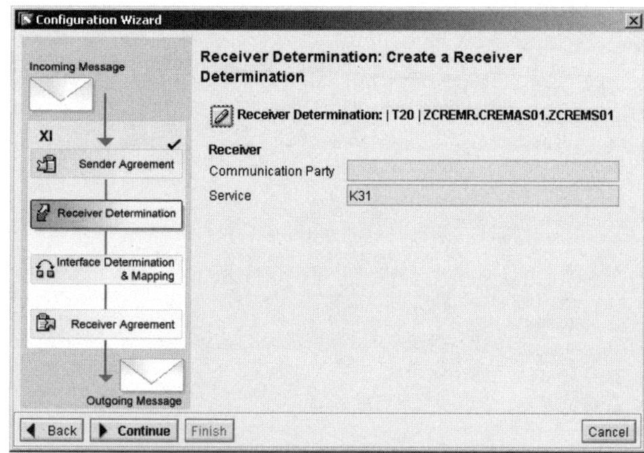

Figure 2.34 Receiver Determination

You can use the **Change** icon to manually change the automatically entered values. Figure 2.35 displays the required entries.

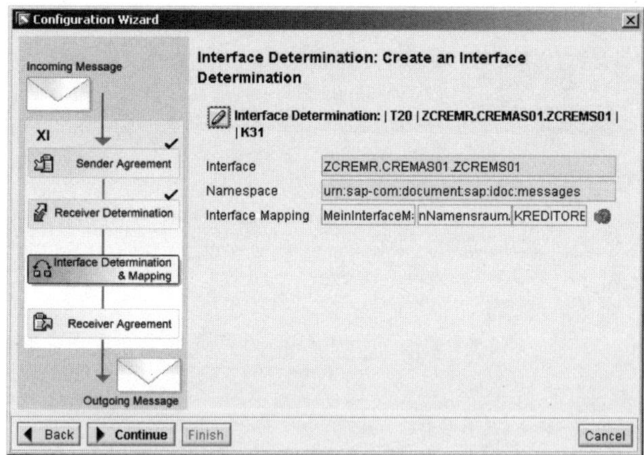

Figure 2.35 Interface Determination

In the next step you must specify the name of the communication channel.

You can use the **Change** icon to manually change the automatically entered values. Figure 2.36 displays the required entries.

In the penultimate step, you must specify the name of the scenario. You can either assign the new configuration to an existing scenario or create a new scenario by choosing a name that doesn't exist yet (Figure 2.37).

After clicking on the **Finish** button (see Figure 2.37), the objects are created, and the result is output in a small log file (Figure 2.38). At that point in time, you can still change warnings and errors in the configuration scenario via the nodes you have created.

In the last step, you must activate the objects via the **Change Lists** tab in the left-hand pane of the screen. Once the objects are activated, the scenario is *active*.

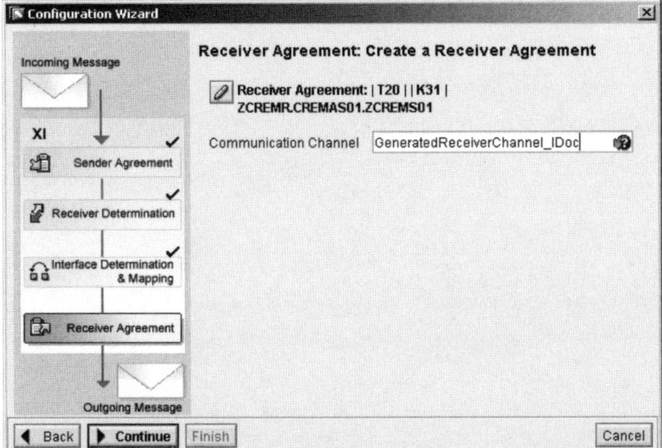

Figure 2.36 Receiver Agreement—Specifying the Communication Channel

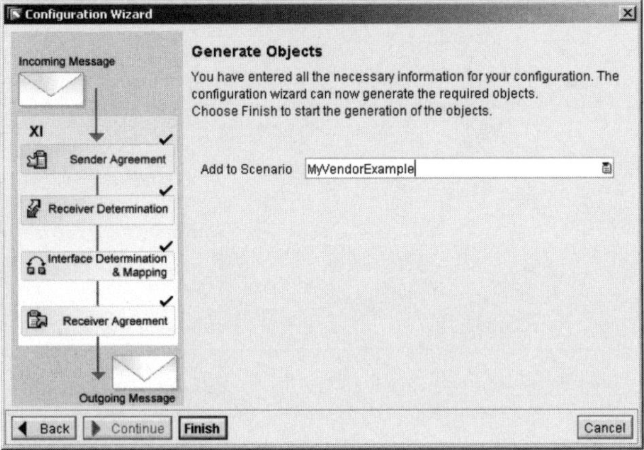

Figure 2.37 Generating Objects (Scenario)

Please note that we don't address the Business Process Management (BPM) subject in this book. Neither do we mention the option of using a specific wizard to import an integration scenario that has been created in the repository in the directory. For information on the configuration of such an integration scenario, as well as on using the import wizard, please refer to the appropriate SAP documentation.

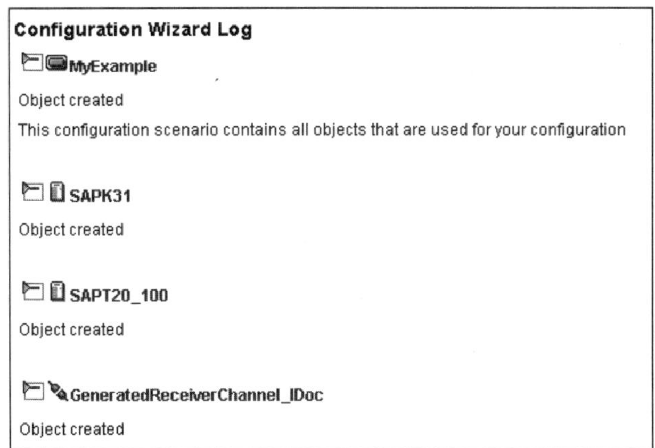

Figure 2.38 Configuration Wizard Log

Configuring the Receiving System

To process the IDoc sent from the integration server in client 111 of the receiving system K31, you must maintain the logical system, the IDoc port number, and the inbound partner profile for the message type transferred in the control record of the IDoc in the target system. At the beginning of this chapter, we described the configuration steps. For the XI system, you must create the following elements in the receiving system:

- The logical system via Transaction BD54
- The IDoc port number via Transaction WE21
- The partner profile via Transaction WE20

The sending system must be created in the list of logical systems (partner type LS). In our example, the sending system is the system with the logical system name *REFAX31100*. The message type of the IDoc sent must be included in the list of inbound parameters of the sending system. In our example, these are the message types *CREMAS* and *ZCREMR*.

In the detail view for the message type, the process code enables you to control through which function module or workflow task you want to process the IDoc. In our example, this is process code *CRE1*.

Note that the appendix of this book contains a checklist of the individual configuration steps.

3 Configuring the System Landscape

On the basis of several examples, this chapter will provide you with an understanding of the minimum configuration required for the first interface we'll use. For this purpose, we'll divide the subject into three sections:

- Configuring the System Landscape Directory (SLD)
- Setting up the Change Management Service (CMS)
- Using the SAP Exchange Infrastructure (SAP XI) transport system without CMS

The sections referring to the SLD will explain the basic set-up steps, the creation of technical and business systems, as well as required parameter settings and the associated XI tools. Section 3.3, *Change Management Service*, describes the required parameters and concisely explains the basic service setup. In an addendum to this second section, we'll address the tools that are provided by SAP for the sole purpose of carrying out transports without the CMS.

3.1 Basic Administration of the SLD

To navigate to the required settings, call the following URL: *http://[Hostname]:Port/sld/*.

Then, click on the **Administration** menu item. This brings you to the basic administration of the SLD. The corresponding submenu is shown in Figure 3.1.

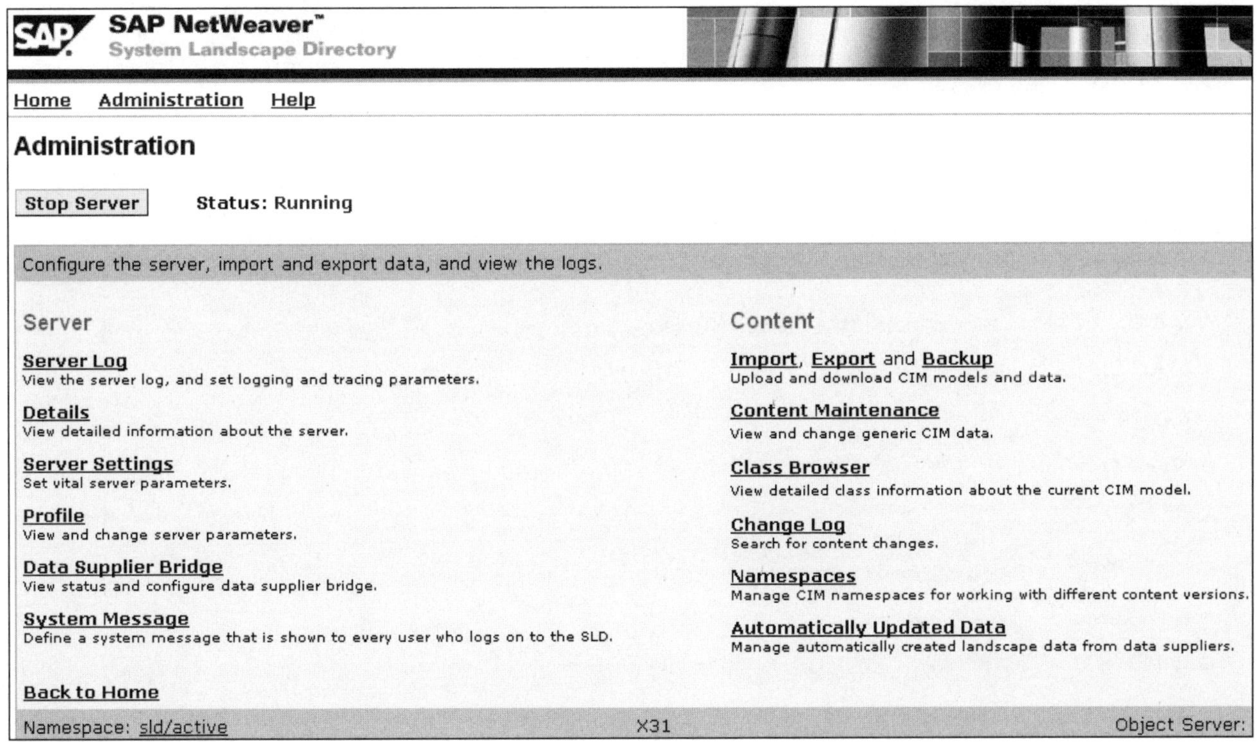

Figure 3.1 SLD Administration Overview

Within this menu, you can perform several activities. In the following, the available options are each described in a separate section.

Starting and Stopping the SLD Service

The upper area of the overview shows the server status: *Running* (Server active) or *Stop* (Server not active). Using the **Stop Server** or **Start Server** pushbuttons, you can easily start or stop the server to make or enable potential changes. The server is shut down within a few seconds and usually available again just as quickly. If you chose the architecture of a central SLD, you should consider that the server may not be stopped in active interfaces. The customizing of the R/3 stack permits you to temporarily close the system using a parameter in the runtime. For a description of the ENTRY_LOCK parameter, see Section 5.2 under *XI 3.0 Parameter Settings—Runtime Category*.

Server Log

The **Server Log** menu item provides a logging option for events taking place on the server. You can set the level of detail individually. More configuration options will be described below under *SLD Profile Configuration*.

Displaying System Information

The **Details** menu item provides detailed information about your J2EE server:

- Server (e.g., SLD version/patch level/VM version)
- Data (e.g., CIM model version/required version/last update)
- Persistence (location of the SLD settings/JCo version)
- Object manager (e.g., object manager version/CIMOM servlet version)
- Browser (e.g., session ID/browser settings)
- Supplier bridge (e.g., last data receive/supported types)

Figure 3.2 shows a corresponding example of this presentation of information.

Setting Up Data Persistence

The **Server Settings** menu item is for configuring the data persistence of the SLD. Selecting this menu item displays the menu shown in Figure 3.3.

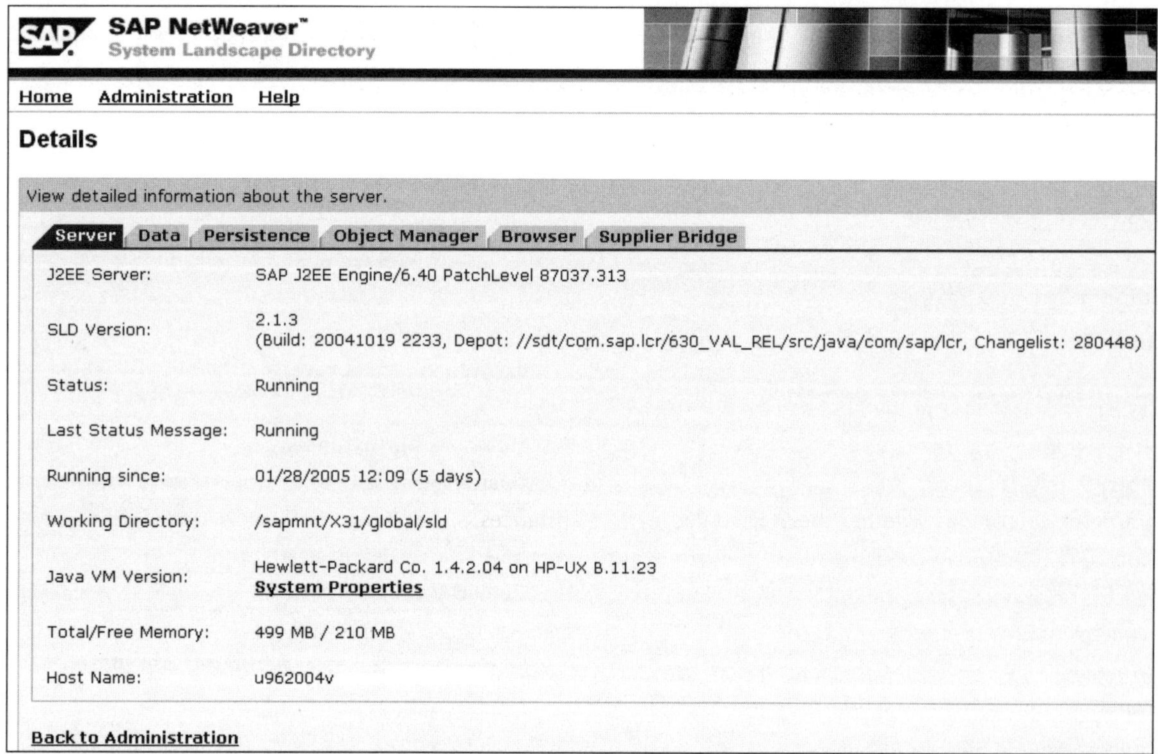

Figure 3.2 System Landscape Directory—Details

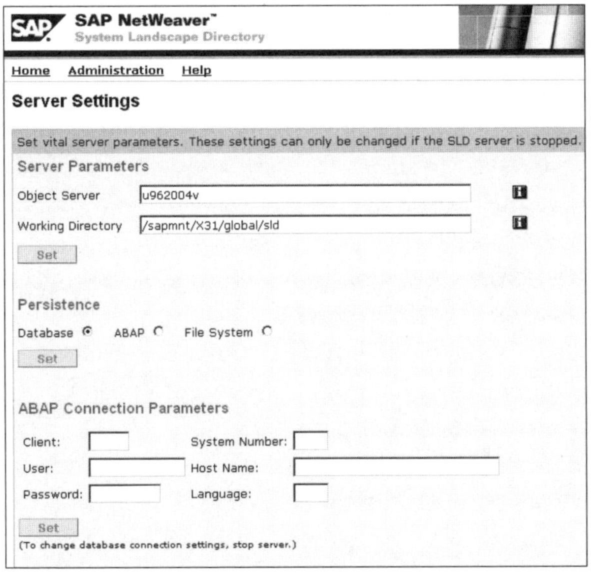

SAP NetWeaver
System Landscape Directory

Home Administration Help

Server Settings

Set vital server parameters. These settings can only be changed if the SLD server is stopped.

Server Parameters

Object Server u962004v

Working Directory /sapmnt/X31/global/sld

Set

Persistence

Database ABAP File System

Set

ABAP Connection Parameters

Client: System Number:

User: Host Name:

Password: Language:

Set

(To change database connection settings, stop server.)

Figure 3.3 System Landscape Directory—Server Settings

Please note that you should specify this setting only after you have stopped the SLD. The corresponding procedure was already described in the respective section. **Server Parameters** refer to the server name (in this example *u962004v*, as in the previous ones) and the definition of a working directory on this server. We recommend that you use the default installation path. Under **Persistence**, you can now specify whether the SLD data should be saved in the database, per RFC in an R/3 system to be defined under **ABAP Connection Parameters**, or on the file system in the working directory. We recommend that you use the **Database** setting.

Configuration of the SLD Profiles

The **Profile** menu enables you to change the individual profiles for the SLD per dialog. We only briefly describe a selection of the relevant parameters that can be changed online in the dialog.

- **Parameter: StartWithServer**
  This parameter determines whether the SLD server should be started automatically when the J2EE server is started. If this value is *true*, the SLD is started automatically. If this value is *false*, the SLD must be started manually after restarting the J2EE server. The corresponding procedure is described above under *Starting and Stopping the SLD Service.*
  Default value: true
- **Parameter: TraceLevel**
  This parameter defines the level of detail of the SLD log. You can specify the following settings:

Levels of Detail	Effect on Log Details
0	Errors (Error Messages Cannot Be Suppressed)
1	Plus Warnings
2	Plus Information
3	Plus Debug
4	Plus Fine Debug
5	Plus Finer Debug
6	Plus Finest Debug

  We recommend that you set the trace level to a higher value at the beginning and that you lower it to the default value at a later stage to avoid unnecessary log information.
  Default value: 2
- **Parameter: UserCacheLifetime**
  This value describes the maximum lifetime of the internal user cache for HTTP requests. If you set this value to 0, caching will be turned off. We don't recommend that you do this; instead, you should leave the default value as is to avoid performance problems.
  Default value: 300
- **Parameter: AutomaticModelImportOnStartup**
  If you want to prevent the data of the SAP CIM model from being applied automatically during SLD server startup, you can do so by setting this parameter to *false*. By setting the value to *true*, the data is usually loaded in the default namespace of the SLD. We recommend that you leave the default value *true*.
  Default value: true
- **Parameter: BufferInstances**
  If the parameter is stored as *true*, a cache for the CIM instances is used for the object manager in the main memory. This results in performance improvements. However, this option is not yet available for cluster systems, therefore, we recommend that you set this parameter to *false* in such an environment. Otherwise, we recommend the default value of *true*.
  Default value: true

- **Parameter: CIMOMSessionTimeout**
  This value controls the timeout value for an HTTP session of two executing WBEM requests to the object manager. In this case, too, you should leave the default value of 300.
  Default value: 300
- **Parameter: SchedulerWaitTime**
  This specifies how long the OM scheduler process will wait. If you find problems in the log, you can increase this value to avoid problems or set its value to 0 to remove the limit altogether. However, typically, this should normally not be necessary and, in theory, the default value could be reduced.
  Default value: 60000
- **Parameter: WriteChangeLog**
  If you set this parameter to *false*, changes reported by the object manager are no longer written to the change log. We recommend that you set this parameter to *true*.
  Default value: true
- **Parameter: JCOPoolSize**
  This parameter defines the size or number of the Java Connector (JCo) client pool, which is used if you selected the ABAP option when specifying the SLD persistence setting. A value of 0 disables the pool. We think that a value of 5 is sufficient at the beginning. This is discussed in detail in Chapter 5.
  Default value: 10
- **Parameter: SaveCompressedXml**
  You should leave the value of *true* to ensure that your XML documents are saved as compressed files. Note, however, that you need to pay attention to the dependency on the *PersistenceIndexXml* parameter.
  Default value: true
- **Parameter: UpdateQueryDB**
  If this parameter is set to *true*, query update information is written directly to the database.
  Default value: false
- **Parameter: DateFormat**
  Describes the format used for presenting and entering date fields.
  Default value: mm/dd/yyyy
- **Parameter: SessionTimeout**
  The number of seconds until the browser reports a timeout error and throws you out of the system.
  Default value: 1800

Setting Up the SLD Bridge

To avoid having to maintain each technical system in your SLD, along with its corresponding software components, SAP devised the SLD bridge. This tool allows you to register your SAP systems, with all their relevant information, automatically in the SLD. Therefore, the advantage of using the SLD bridge is that all changes of components and versions are automatically updated in the SLD, because a corresponding job handles a regular update of SLD data in the SAP systems after setup. Beside ABAP-based systems, you can also have J2EE-based SAP systems registered automatically. If you want to connect non-SAP systems to the SLD, you can do so individually in Java via an SAP interface. This interface allows for both the registering and querying of data and it can be implemented quickly (see Figure 3.4).

In this section, we describe the connection of ABAP-based systems. To configure the SLD bridge, changes are necessary both to the ABAP-based systems and to XI. We begin with the XI settings by calling the **Data Supplier Bridge** link in the main menu (see Figure 3.1 above).

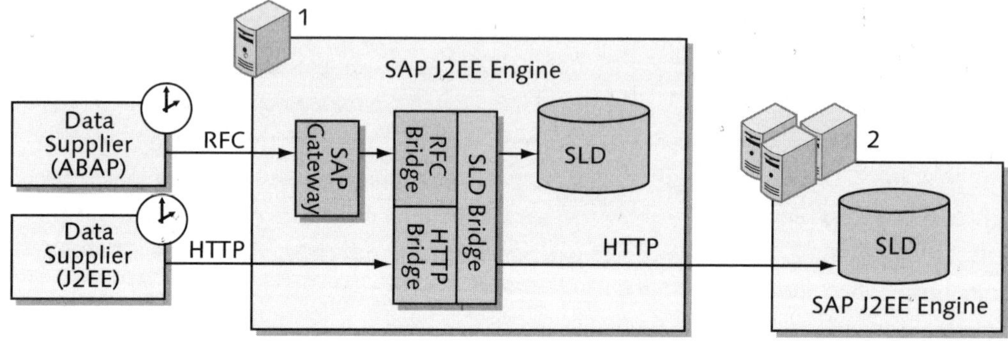

Figure 3.4 System Landscape Directory—SAP J2EE Engine

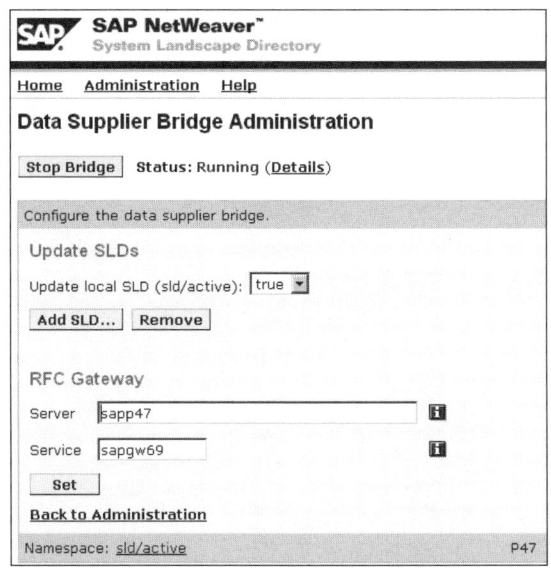

Figure 3.5 System Landscape Directory—Data Supplier Bridge Administration

In this menu, you can stop the data supplier bridge by selecting the **Stop Bridge** pushbutton. We recommend that you stop the bridge before making any changes to the configuration and restart it immediately afterwards.

In the **Server** and **Service** fields, enter the server name of your system and the gateway service name, which you should know from R/3.

Depending on the architecture, the **Update SLDs** function enables you to update other SLDs automatically when the central SLD is changed. The **Update local SLD** dropdown box allows you to protect the SLD that you're currently configuring from being updated by the data supplier bridge, if you set the parameter to *false*. To update external SLDs with changes, click on the **Add SLD...** pushbutton to open the configuration dialog shown in Figure 3.6.

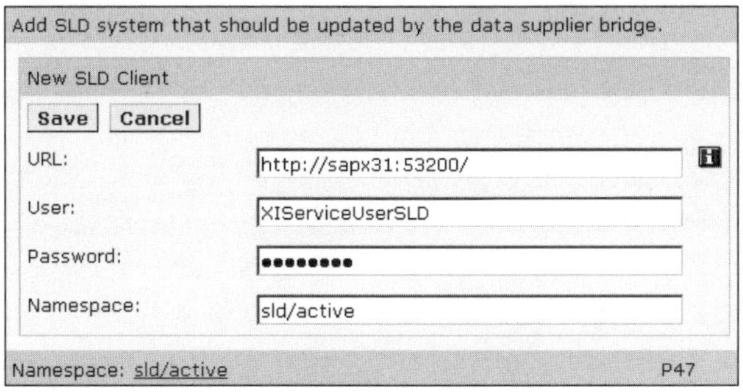

Add SLD system that should be updated by the data supplier bridge.
New SLD Client
Save Cancel
URL: http://sapx31:53200/
User: XIServiceUserSLD
Password: ••••••••
Namespace: sld/active
Namespace: sld/active P47

Figure 3.6 Setting Up the Update of Local SLDs

In the **URL** field, you store the SLDs of another NetWeaver system to be provided with data. In the **User** field, you store an existing system user of the target system. Remember to first assign the relevant roles to this user (see Chapter 4, *Authorizations*). Store the corresponding password of the selected system user and the namespace of the target SLD to be updated in the **Password** and **Namespace** fields.

For the meaning and creation of namespaces in the SLD, please refer to the *Administration of the SLD Namespaces* section.

After we specified all required settings on the exchange infrastructure page, we now switch to the data-sending side of our R/3 systems to be integrated. Using the SAP GUI, log on to the system to be integrated. Start Transaction RZ70. If the transaction is not known, install the current service packs on your R/3 system. You will see the dynpro shown in Figure 3.7.

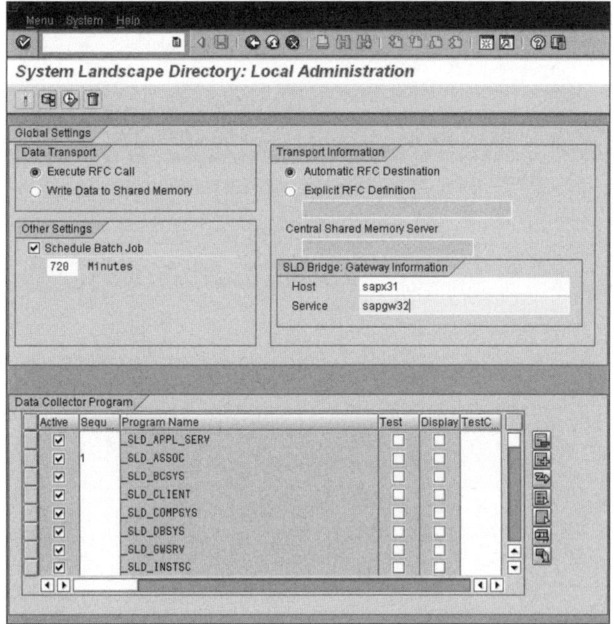

Figure 3.7 Local Administration (System Connection Via Transaction RZ70)

Using this transaction, you can enable the relevant data collection programs and enter your SLD as the target system for these data streams. In our example, we'll send the system information of the R/3 system T15 to the SLD of the *sapx31* development system. You can automatically allow for the following data collection programs:

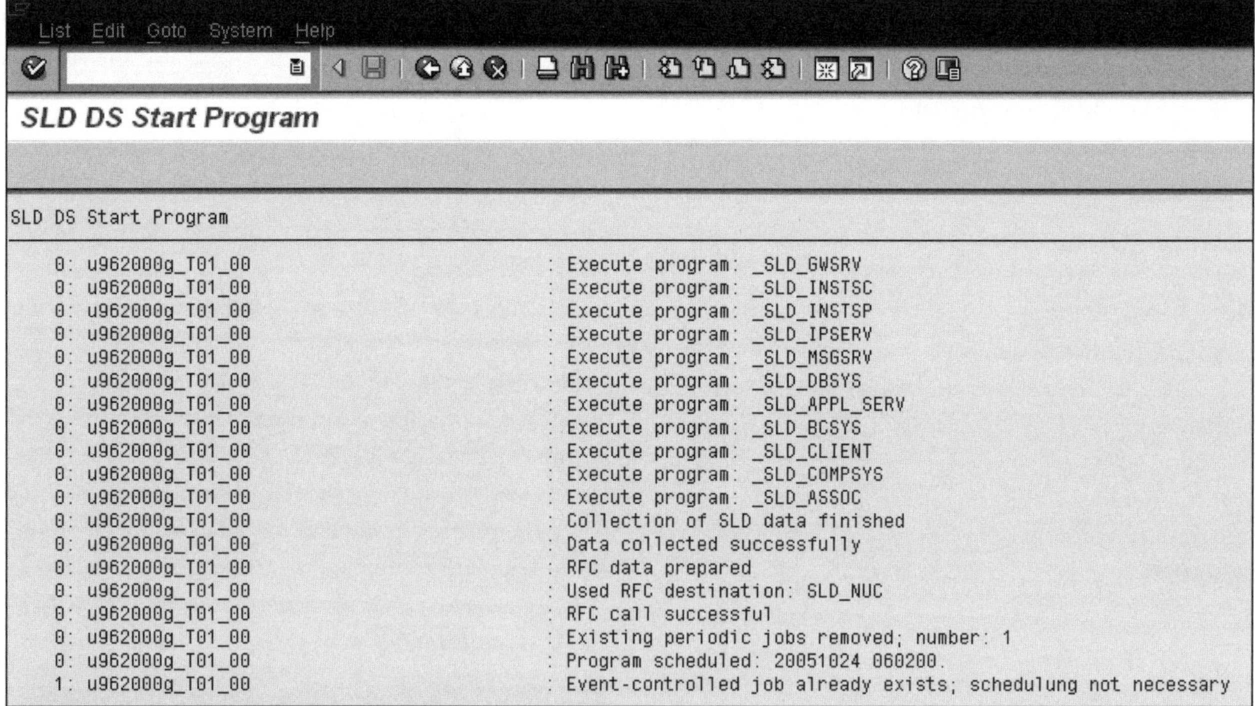
```
SLD DS Start Program

SLD DS Start Program

0: u962000g_T01_00      : Execute program: _SLD_GWSRV
0: u962000g_T01_00      : Execute program: _SLD_INSTSC
0: u962000g_T01_00      : Execute program: _SLD_INSTSP
0: u962000g_T01_00      : Execute program: _SLD_IPSERV
0: u962000g_T01_00      : Execute program: _SLD_MSGSRV
0: u962000g_T01_00      : Execute program: _SLD_DBSYS
0: u962000g_T01_00      : Execute program: _SLD_APPL_SERV
0: u962000g_T01_00      : Execute program: _SLD_BCSYS
0: u962000g_T01_00      : Execute program: _SLD_CLIENT
0: u962000g_T01_00      : Execute program: _SLD_COMPSYS
0: u962000g_T01_00      : Execute program: _SLD_ASSOC
0: u962000g_T01_00      : Collection of SLD data finished
0: u962000g_T01_00      : Data collected successfully
0: u962000g_T01_00      : RFC data prepared
0: u962000g_T01_00      : Used RFC destination: SLD_NUC
0: u962000g_T01_00      : RFC call successful
0: u962000g_T01_00      : Existing periodic jobs removed; number: 1
0: u962000g_T01_00      : Program scheduled: 20051024 060200.
1: u962000g_T01_00      : Event-controlled job already exists; schedulung not necessary
```

Figure 3.8 Local Administration—Connection Log

Data Collection Program	Data Contents reported to the SLD
_SLD_APPL_SERV	Application server/instances
_SLD_BCSYS	SAP system
_SLD_CLIENT	System clients
_SLD_COMPSYS	Hosts
_SLD_DBSYS	Database
_SLD_INSTSC	Installed software components
_SLD_INSTSP	Installed support packages
_SLD_MSGSERV	SAP message server
_SLD_RFC	RFC destinations
_SLD_ASSOC	CIM dependencies between generated objects

Table 3.1 Data Collection Programs

After saving and executing the transaction, a short status report is displayed (Figure 3.8).

This figure shows that the start of the selected data selection programs is confirmed and the used RFC destination is displayed. Additionally, you are informed about the automatic job scheduling of these data selection programs. You will also be notified if problems occur during execution or job scheduling.

System Message

Using the **System Message** menu item, you can write a system message, which is displayed on every user screen at logon. This function is comparable to the familiar R/3 system Transaction SM02 (system messages).

Administration of the SLD Namespace

To simulate or test future SLD scenarios, or to build up multilevel SLDs, you can create several logical areas in the SLD, provide them with individual settings, and switch between these areas. To create a new namespace for the SLD, from the administration main menu of the SLD, change to the **Namespaces** submenu.

This brings you to the configuration menu shown in Figure 3.9, where you can either create a new namespace or delete existing ones.

As illustrated in Figure 3.9, click on the **Add...** pushbutton and add a new namespace named *sld/new* to your SLD. You will now see a new namespace called *sld/new* in the selection overview (see Figure 3.10).

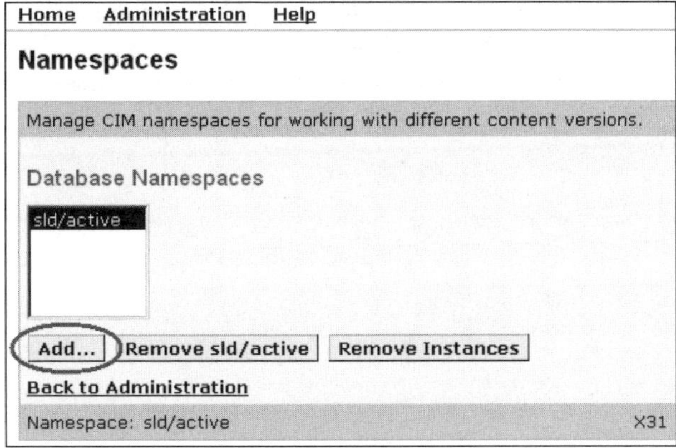

Figure 3.9 Namespace Administration

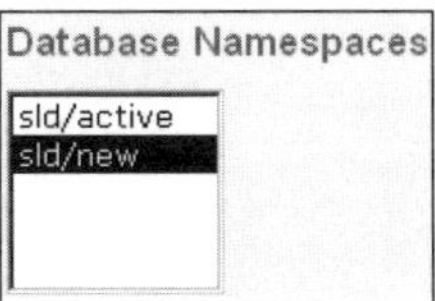

Figure 3.10 SLD Namespaces Overview

You can now export your settings from the original namespace and import them into the new namespace.

To switch between the two namespaces, you can click on the small link called **Namespace** at the bottom of your browser at any time (see Figure 3.11).

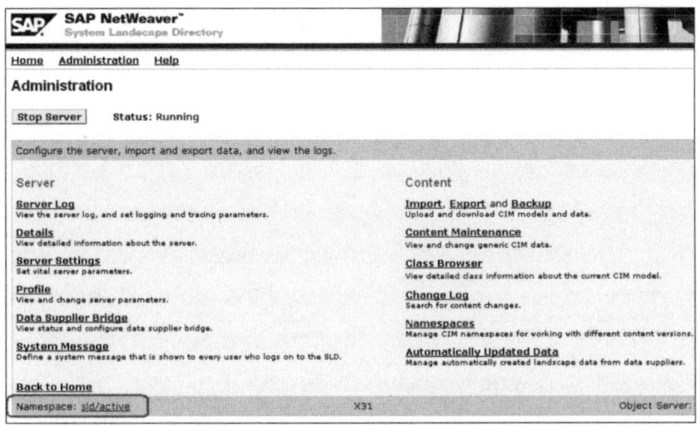

Figure 3.11 Switching Between Namespaces Within the SLD

For your information, the link always displays the current namespace. You can also access the namespace by using the **Namespaces** menu item (as described above) and, by double-clicking, go to the **Namespaces** menu to select an active namespace.

To delete a namespace, go to the **Namespaces** menu again, select the entry to be deleted, and click on the **Remove <NamespaceName>** pushbutton (see Figure 3.9 above).

3.2 Customizing the System Landscape Directory

The System Landscape Directory (SLD) contains an overview of all technical systems involved in the process, including the installed software components and versions. From the technical definition, an abstraction level called business system is defined. The business system reflects the individual clients of a technical system. A technical system is defined using the IP address, the server name, the dispatcher, and so forth. This technical system (an R/3 system in our example) uses a two-client structure. Both clients are to be provided with different data by the Exchange Infrastructure in future. Therefore, two business systems are created in the SLD for the technical system. In the following example, we assume that our technical system is T20 and the server is *sapt20*. The system is a 46C system functioning as a central vendor management system for a corporate group. Therefore, we call the system *CVM* (Corporate Vendor Management). In our example, this CVM system has the clients 100 and 131. To set up this technical system, we first have to log onto the R/3 system using SAP GUI. Call Transaction SXMB_IFR. Your locally installed web browser will open and display the XI home page as shown in Chapter 2. Click on the relevant link to change to the SLD. The overview is displayed as shown in Figure 3.12.

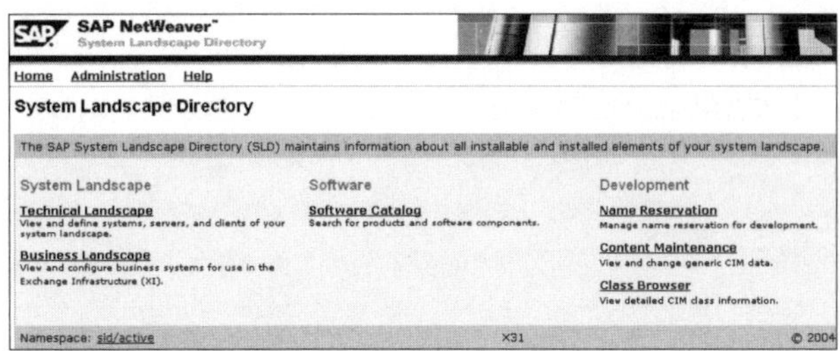

Figure 3.12 Main Menu of the System Landscape Directory

Main Menu of the SLD

As shown in Figure 3.12, the SLD menu enables you to maintain technical systems, business systems, and software catalogs. Another part is the **Development** category, which is not covered in detail in this book.

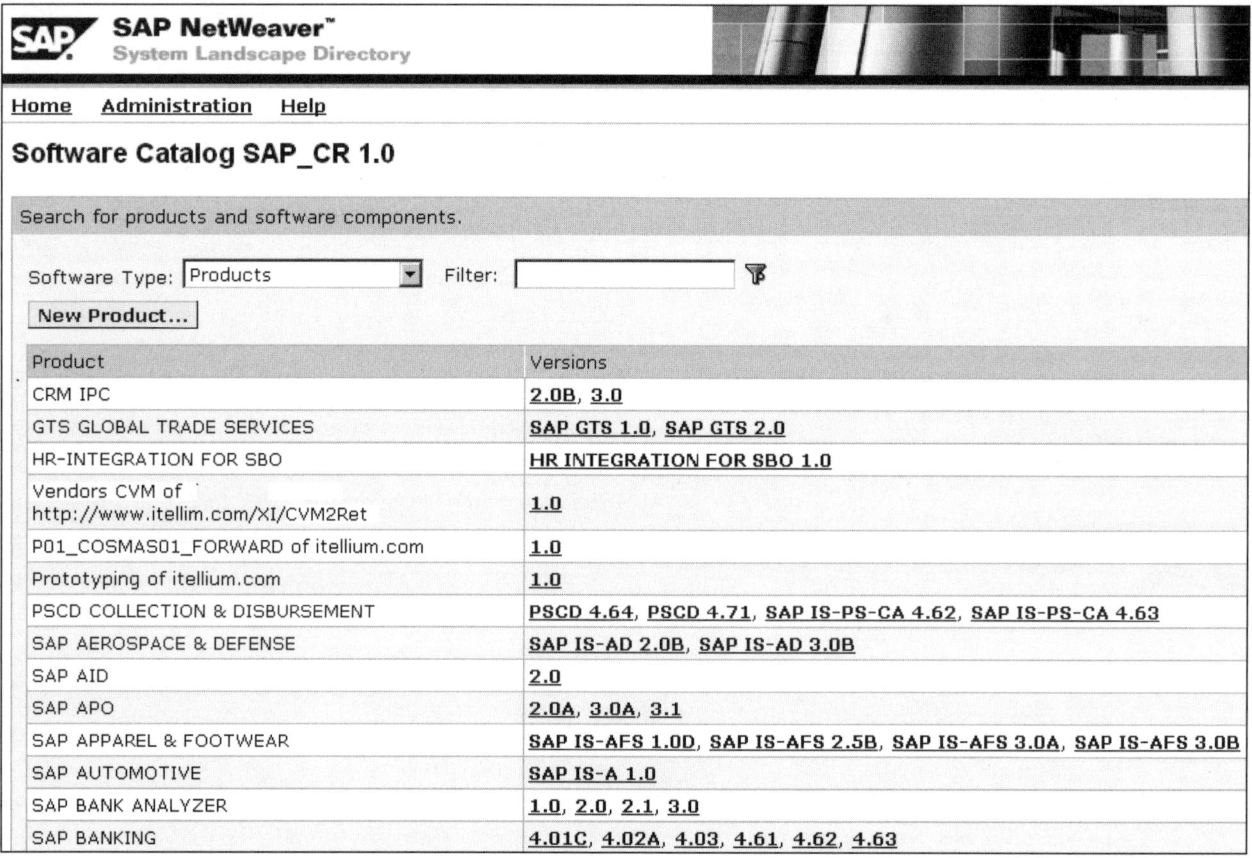

Figure 3.13 System Landscape Directory Software Catalog SAP_CR 1.0

In this category, too, the SLD can be called directly via a URL and a browser.

In our example, the URL would read as follows:
http://[Hostname]:[Port]/sld/index.jsp

Software Catalog

In the **Software Catalog** category, in addition to the information about the technical and business systems, the software components involved in an interface or a business transaction are maintained. A software component is then regarded as a modular unit that can be implemented in different products of a software vendor. A product is a composition of software components and can exist in different versions. In the SLD, the link between product versions and the component versions is mapped using objects of the *software feature* type.

For the first interface, you should consider that software component versions are required during namespace creation and are therefore a prerequisite for creating all dependent objects such as interface structures in the Integration Repository.

From the main menu, we therefore go first to the **Software Catalog** category to define the necessary settings. The web page shown in Figure 3.13 is displayed.

In the selection, you can now decide whether you want to create a new project or a new software component. After the selection, click on the **New Product** or **New Component** pushbutton to create a new entry. We want to create a new product and therefore select **Products** in the **Software Type dropdown box**. The **New Product** pushbutton creates a new product, and the dialog shown in Figure 3.14 is displayed.

After you entered the relevant information in the dialog, click on the **Create** pushbutton to create the product with its individual name. After creating the product, a dialog for entering a software component for this product is automatically displayed (Figure 3.15).

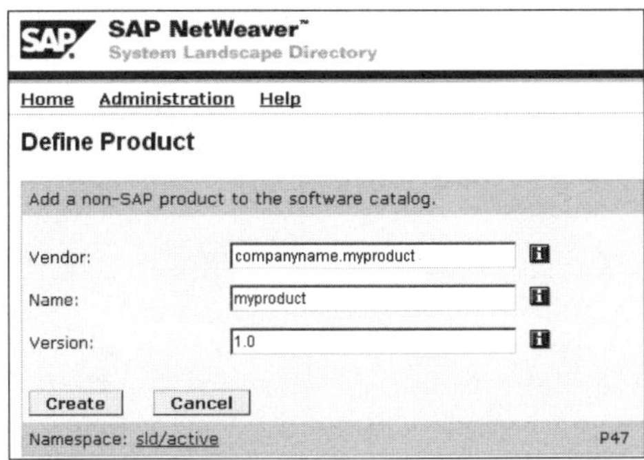

Figure 3.14 System Landscape Directory—Define Product

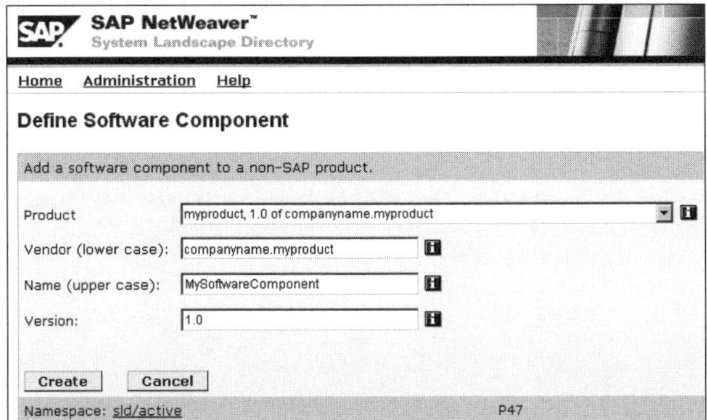

Figure 3.15 System Landscape Directory—Define Software Component

Here you can define the name of the software component to be created as well as the version you want to store. By clicking on the **Create** pushbutton, the software component is automatically assigned to the previously created product. The **Name** and **Version** fields are initialized again after saving. Now you can assign any number of software components to the product *myproduct* (see Figure 3.14).

If you want to assign a software component to an existing product at a later stage, instead of choosing **New Product** in the main menu you can directly select **New Component** and then proceed as described above.

In order to model or display dependencies between different software components, you can use the **New Component** option in the main menu. Navigate to the software component to be changed by clicking on its name. The screen shown in Figure 3.16 is displayed.

Via the **Usage Dependencies** link (see Figure 3.16), you can now display existing dependencies or delete them, or maintain new dependencies on other components.

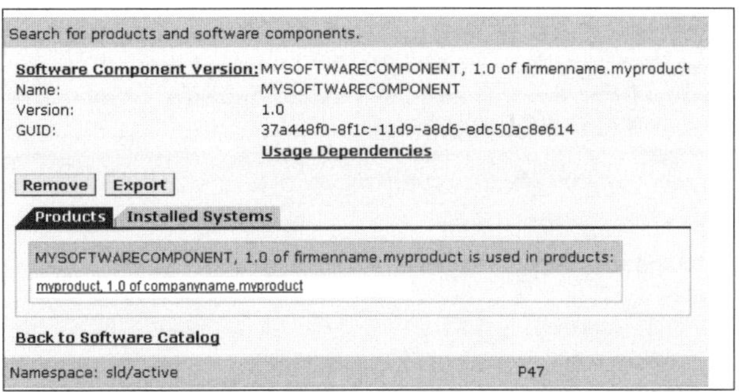

Figure 3.16 System Landscape Directory Products

To assign the newly created products or software components to a technical system, go to the **Technical System Browser** of the SLD and select the corresponding system. Under the **Installed Products** category, you will find the **Add**... link, which enables you to assign the information previously created in the system (see Figure 3.17).

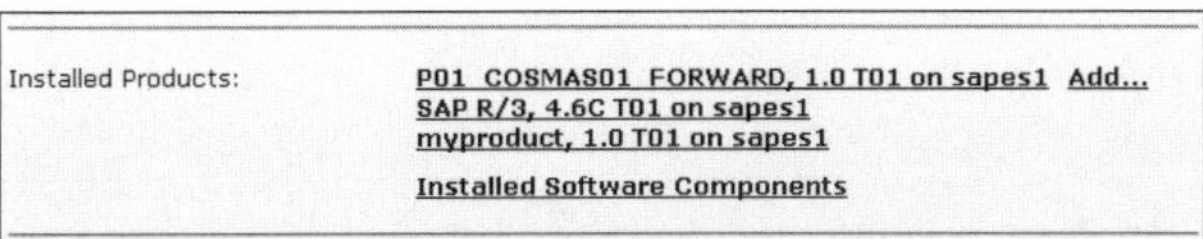

Figure 3.17 Installed Products of a Technical System

Technical System

The link **Technical Landscape** from the SLD main menu (see Figure 3.12 above) opens the Technical System Browser, which displays a list of configured technical systems of the landscape (see Figure 3.18).

All systems involved in a business transaction or an interface must be added as technical systems to the technical landscape. It would be ideal if the SLD was globally catalogued as a map of all systems existing in a company, including their software versions and inventories. To make our first interface work, however, it will suffice to maintain the systems involved.

The creation of a new technical system is conducted via the **New Technical System** pushbutton (see Figure 3.18). When it is created, the system is registered under a technical system name with all relevant technical attributes. A technical system is registered in several small dialog steps. We will describe these individual steps and show our new technical system in Figure 3.21 below.

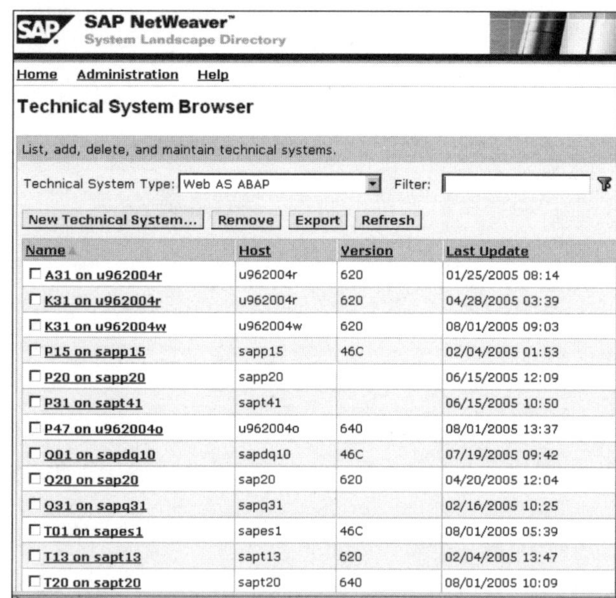

Figure 3.18 System Landscape Directory—Technical System Browser

In the first step, you define the corresponding type of the technical system. The following types are available for selection:

- Web AS ABAP
- Web AS Java
- Standalone Java
- Third-Party
- System Landscape Directory

For our example, we select the **Web AS ABAP** technical system type. You are now taken to a second dialog in which you must enter the SID, the installation number, and the host name of your database server. After you have entered these values, a dialog is displayed in which you must register your message server (host name + port and logon group), as well as information about your application server (host name + instance number). After you have entered these values, you can register the clients of the system in another dialog so that you can assign them to a business system later on. In our example, we will again use the two clients previously described (100 and 131). In the last dialog of this creation wizard, from the existing products of your SLD, you select those entries that describe which software components/versions are installed on this system.

In our example, the technical system is called T20. After the previously described creation of the technical system, you can change to the detail view as shown in Figure 3.19 to specify or correct additional settings.

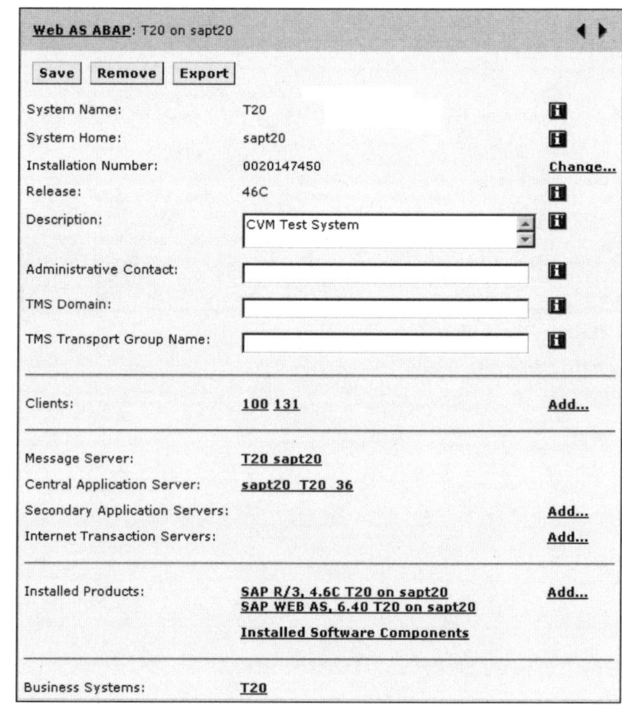

Figure 3.19 System Landscape Directory—Detail View of the Technical System

Now we'll explain each maintenance option shown in Figure 3.19:

- **Description**
  A short description of the system. In our example, this would be our *CVM test system*.
- **Administrative Contact**
  A possibility to store a contact person for the technical system. This field is not mandatory and is for information purposes only. In our example, we'll leave this field empty.
- **TMS Domain**
  Here you store the TMS domain of the R/3 system.
- **TMS Transport Group Name**
  Name of the transport group to which the system is assigned in the landscape. Its meaning will be explained later.
- **Clients**
  Here you can add other clients after creation, or delete obsolete information.

- **Message Server**
  Here you can change or correct the message server settings.
- **Secondary Application Servers**
  If there are any secondary application servers, they're stored with their host name. In our example, we use only one application server.
- **Internet Transaction Servers**
  If an Internet Transaction Server (ITS) is installed, it can be stored here. In our example, we don't use an ITS.
- **Installed Products**
  Here you can change the specified settings and add new products.
- **Business Systems**
  Here the business systems that are related to this technical system are listed. If you already created a business system for the technical system, you can go directly to the business system configuration via a link.

You just created your first technical system in your SLD. We will now proceed with the creation of a business system.

Business System

Since the technical system T20 in our example has two clients, we want to create an appropriate business system for each client.

Setting up a business system takes place within the **Business System** category in the SLD main menu. The link **Business Landscape** opens the overview of the business landscape. As in the Technical System Browser, a list of previously configured business systems of your system landscape is displayed (see Figure 3.20).

Note Please note that on SAP systems a business system always reflects a client of the technical system.

Similar to the creation of a technical system, you start a creation wizard using the **New Business System** pushbutton shown in Figure 3.20. In the first dialog step, you select the type of the technical system to be referenced by your business system. The selection of the type is identical to the selection options for the creation of a technical system as described above. For our example, we select the **Web AS ABAP** type again.

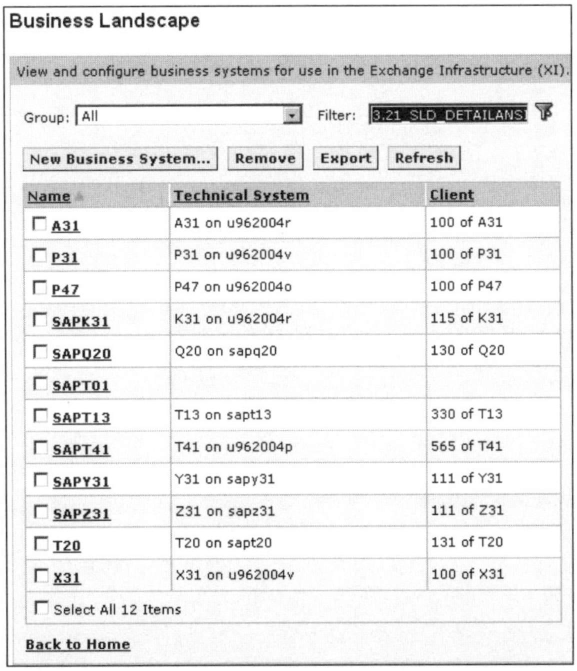

Business Landscape

View and configure business systems for use in the Exchange Infrastructure (XI).

Group: All   Filter: 3.21 SLD DETAILANS

New Business System... | Remove | Export | Refresh

Name	Technical System	Client
A31	A31 on u962004r	100 of A31
P31	P31 on u962004v	100 of P31
P47	P47 on u962004o	100 of P47
SAPK31	K31 on u962004r	115 of K31
SAPQ20	Q20 on sapq20	130 of Q20
SAPT01		
SAPT13	T13 on sapt13	330 of T13
SAPT41	T41 on u962004p	565 of T41
SAPY31	Y31 on sapy31	111 of Y31
SAPZ31	Z31 on sapz31	111 of Z31
T20	T20 on sapt20	131 of T20
X31	X31 on u962004v	100 of X31

Select All 12 Items

Back to Home

Figure 3.20 System Landscape Directory—Technical System Browser (Overview of Existing Business Landscape Systems)

In the next dialog step, you can select an existing technical system. After the technical system to be referenced has been selected, you choose the client to be mapped to this system. In our example shown in Figure 3.21, we chose client 131. Then you select the products of the technical system that are relevant to your business system.

The last dialog step lets you define the role of the business system. The roles **Application System** and **Integration Server** are available for selection. Since our example is dealing with an application server, we select the **Application System** role. When selecting the **Application System** role, the wizard asks for the integration server to which this business system should be assigned. If you choose the **Integration Server** role, the pipeline URL of the XI system is requested in the following format: *http://[Hostname]:[Port]/sap/xi/engine?type=entry*.

You have just created a business system and assigned it to a client of a technical system. As is the case with the creation of a technical system, you can now change to the detail view of your business system and correct or enhance the values you just entered. The detail view of our example business system is shown in Figure 3.21. We'll define the transport target and the business group in the next section.

To be consistent with our example and for you to get some practice creating these systems, we recommend that you create another business system with the aforementioned target system K31, including a business system. Which company server you use or which names you select is not relevant to this example. In our example, we didn't combine the name of the business system with an individual specification based on the clients to be mapped. If we stick to our example and define two clients as business systems for our technical system T20, a more effective naming for the business system would be advisable. To simplify the example, we refrained from doing so.

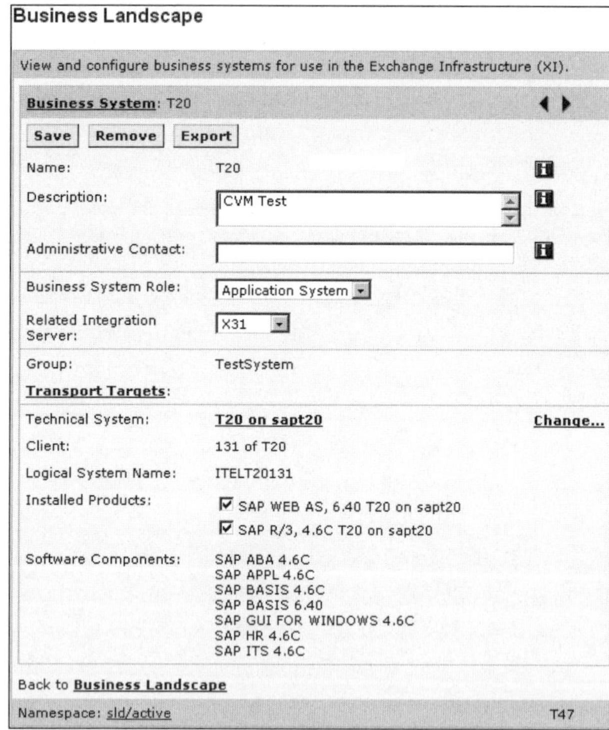

Figure 3.21 System Landscape Directory—Detail View of the Business System

In our example shown in Figure 3.22, we defined two groups. One group contains all test systems. The other group includes all quality and production systems because the example is based on a two-way landscape. In order to create a new group, click on the dropdown box in the upper left corner labeled **Group** (Figure 3.22) and select the **Edit Groups...** entry. This opens the configuration dialog shown in Figure 3.23.

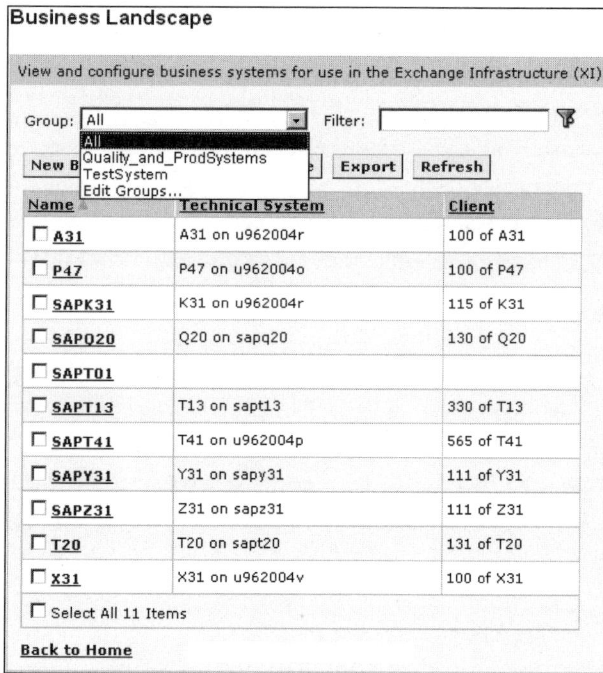

Figure 3.22 System Landscape Directory—Business System Groups

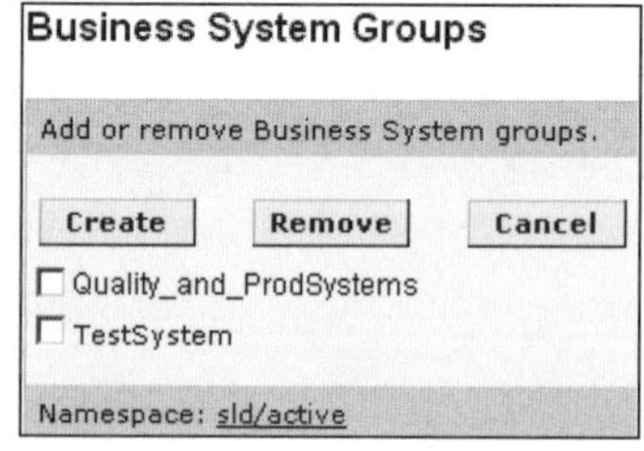

Figure 3.23 System Landscape Directory—Edit Business System Groups

Transport Groups

As soon as your landscape includes more than one XI system and more than one SAP system, you should assign appropriate transport groups to your systems in the SLD. Go to the overview of your business systems as described above.

You can now create a new group or delete existing groups. We want to create a new group called **Special-cases**. For this purpose, click on the **Create** pushbutton. A dialog with the corresponding values is shown in Figure 3.24.

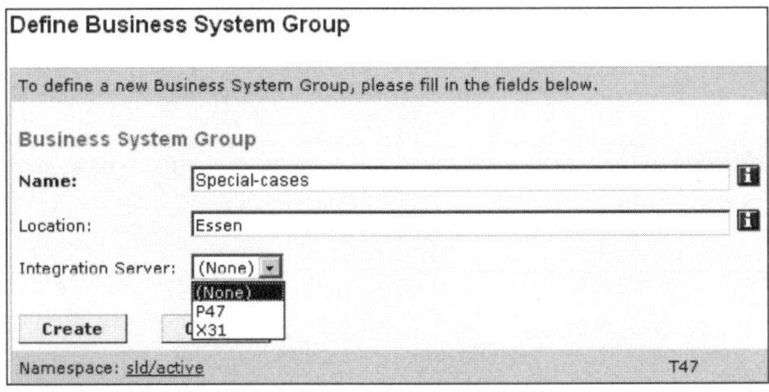

Figure 3.24 System Landscape Directory—Define Business System Group

If you previously specified an assigned integration server for each business system that you created, you can now automatically assign these business systems to a group by selecting the integration server. In this case, we select X31 and are presented with the test systems in the **Special-cases** group (see Figure 3.25).

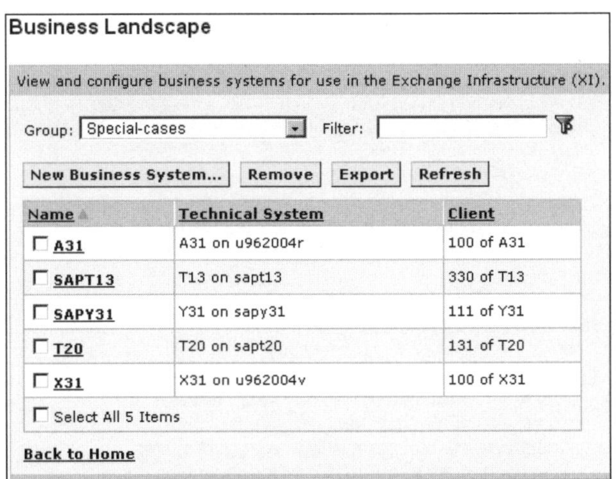

Figure 3.25 System Landscape Directory—Business Landscape

We now assume that you divided your own R/3 systems into the two groups **TestSystems** and **Quality_and_ProdSystems**, as described above. To define transport targets we have to go back to the individual business systems as shown in Figure 3.26.

The example presented in Figure 3.26 shows that our test system T20 is assigned to the integration server X31 (XI test system) and has thus been added automatically to the **TestSystems** group. Via the **Transport Targets** link, you can now specify the settings shown in Figure 3.27.

You can select groups from which you can choose a target system. In our example, the T20 (vendors test system) should have Q20 (vendor quality assurance system) as a target system. We therefore select **SAPQ20** and confirm this selection with **OK**. As far as transports from the test XI to the production XI are concerned, the Exchange Infrastructure now implements the target or source systems of your interface in the same way as it does the transport (in this example from T to Q). Therefore, you no longer need to change these values manually. Instead, we recommend that you ensure you have a clean configuration of these parameters.

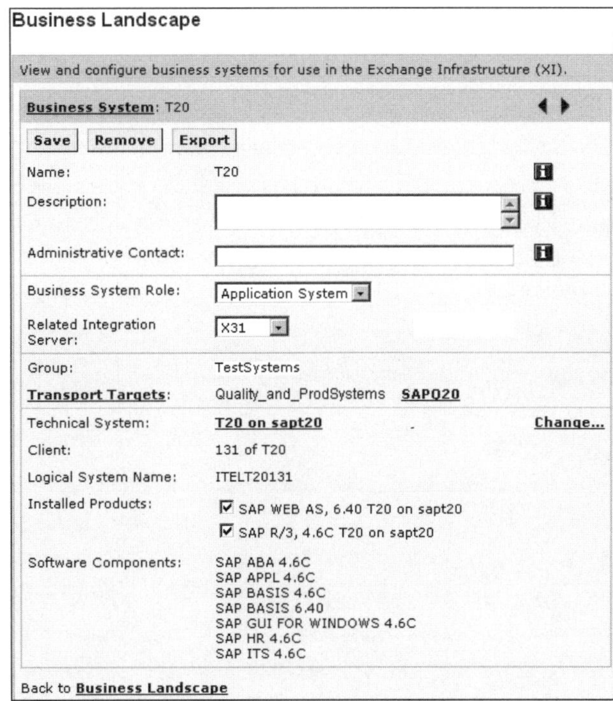

Figure 3.26 System Landscape Directory—Business Landscape

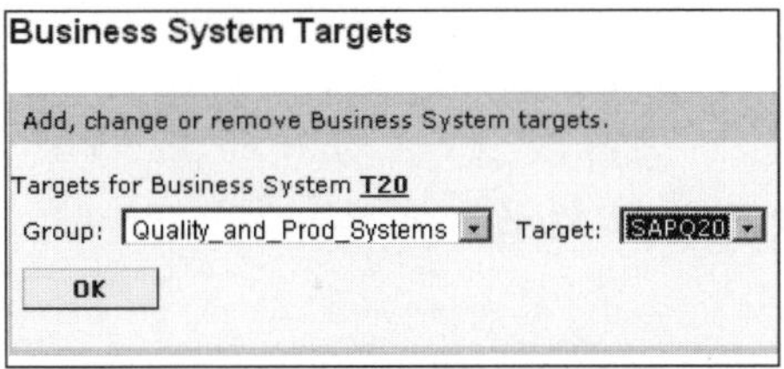

Figure 3.27 System Landscape Directory—Business System Targets

3.3 Change Management Service

In our example, the Change Management Service (CMS) is used as a transport studio to transfer our changes in the repository or in the directory from our T to the Q or P system.

CMS Architecture

Among other things, the CMS connection depends on the selected SLD architecture. You can choose between different architectures:

- A central SLD for your XI system and a separate one for your CMS
- One SLD for every XI system and a separate one for the CMS system
- One SLD for every XI system; the CMS uses one of the existing SLD installations
- A central SLD for your XI system and central CMS system

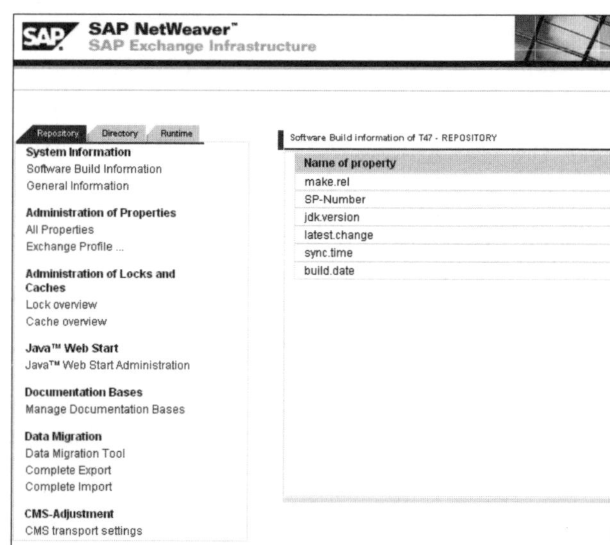

Figure 3.28 Administration of Exchange Profiles

In order to centralize our SLD and our CMS system, we opted for the last architecture listed above. Because several namespaces can be stored in the SLD, you can also store customized configurations in the central SLD for testing purposes, if necessary.

We already addressed this subject in a previous section and described the available options. However, before we can enjoy using our newly set up CMS system for transports, we need to make some changes in XI and CMS.

In the standard version, the CMS is disabled for the installation for transports in XI. This means you can only carry out transports via the file system between your XI systems by performing exports and imports. To be able to use the CMS as a transport platform, you must first change some J2EE parameters in XI (we assume that you successfully deployed the relevant CMS files on your J2EE server first, according to the SAP installation manual).

Call the home page of your XI environment. On the upper right side, change to the administrator area. Now the screen shown in Figure 3.28 is displayed with the **Repository**, **Directory**, and **Runtime** tabs on the upper left side.

In this menu, you can display and, if necessary, change the individual parameter settings for XI repository, directory, and runtime. Additionally, you can obtain an overview of potential locks on objects and the cache contents. The specific setting options were discussed in detail in Section 2.2 under *Setting System Parameters*. To activate the CMS as your preferred transport system, in the repository, select the **Exchange Profile** category to go to the menu shown in Figure 3.29.

Figure 3.29 System Landscape Directory—Exchange Profile

This is the dialog for editing profiles. Since we simply want to activate our CMS system, the only relevant settings are those of *IntegrationBuilder.Directory* and *IntegrationBuilder.Repository*. Both menu items have the same parameters. Therefore, we just explain the required steps for activating the CMS for the repository. You can then perform the same steps for the directory.

First, we expand the *IntegrationBuilder.Repository* tree and immediately recognize the three relevant parameters shown in Figure 3.30. (We assume that these parameters were already entered during the installation with a value of *false*.)

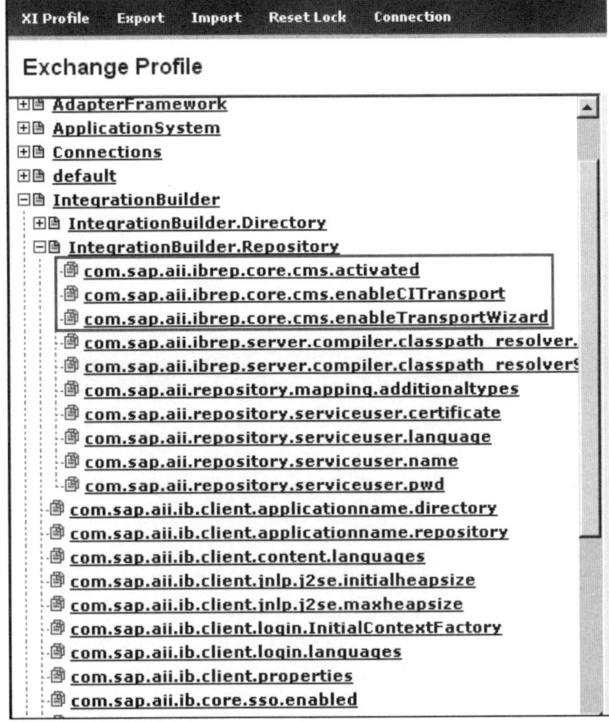

Figure 3.30 System Landscape Directory—Exchange Profile

We click on the first parameter *com.sap.aii.ibrep.core.cms.activated*. If the value is set to *false*, we change it to *true* to activate the CMS.

After activating the CMS, we also change the parameter *com.sap.aii.ibrep.core.cms.enableCITransport* to *true*, if it is set to *false*. To use the function of sending changes to the CMS as a selection option in our GUI, we change the last parameter to *true*. After we have performed the same measures for the directory, we can use the CMS for transports in our XI landscape. If the parameters don't exist yet (in contrast to what we assumed), you must create them with the previously described values. We recommend that you restart the J2EE server once after making changes to the profiles.

After a successful restart of the J2EE stack, you should now see a corresponding selection option **Transport Using CMS** under the **Tools • Export Design Objects** menu item in your repository or directory (as shown in Figure 3.31).

Setting Up the Change Management Service System

After we convince the XI to send its changes to the CMS system, we must configure the CMS system itself.

Calling the web page *http://[Hostname]:[Port]/devinf/* brings up the overview shown in Figure 3.32 (the presentation is based on SP10).

Click on the last link **Change Management Service**. This takes you directly to the CMS system. Another way to call it directly is via the URL *http://[Hostname]:[Port]/webdynpro/dispatcher/sap.com/tc~SL~CMS~WebUI/Cms*. The menu system is shown in Figure 3.33.

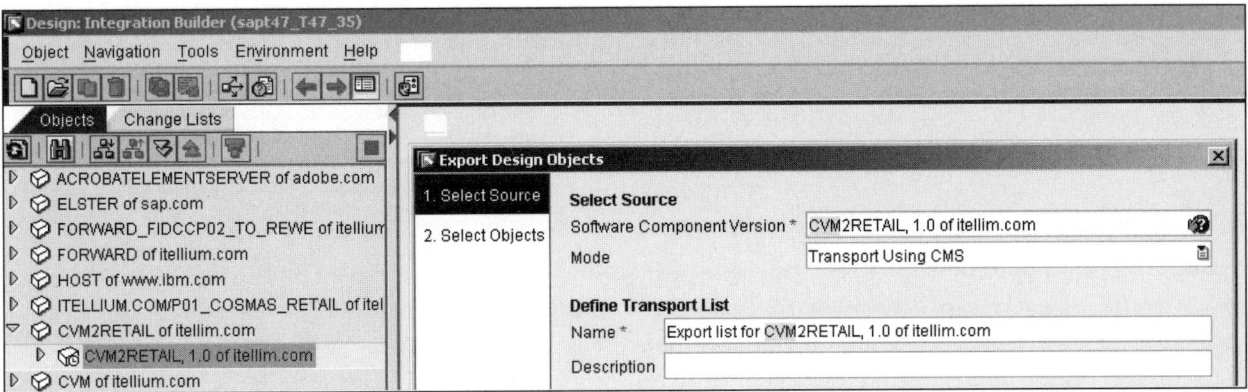

Figure 3.31 System Landscape Directory — Design Objects

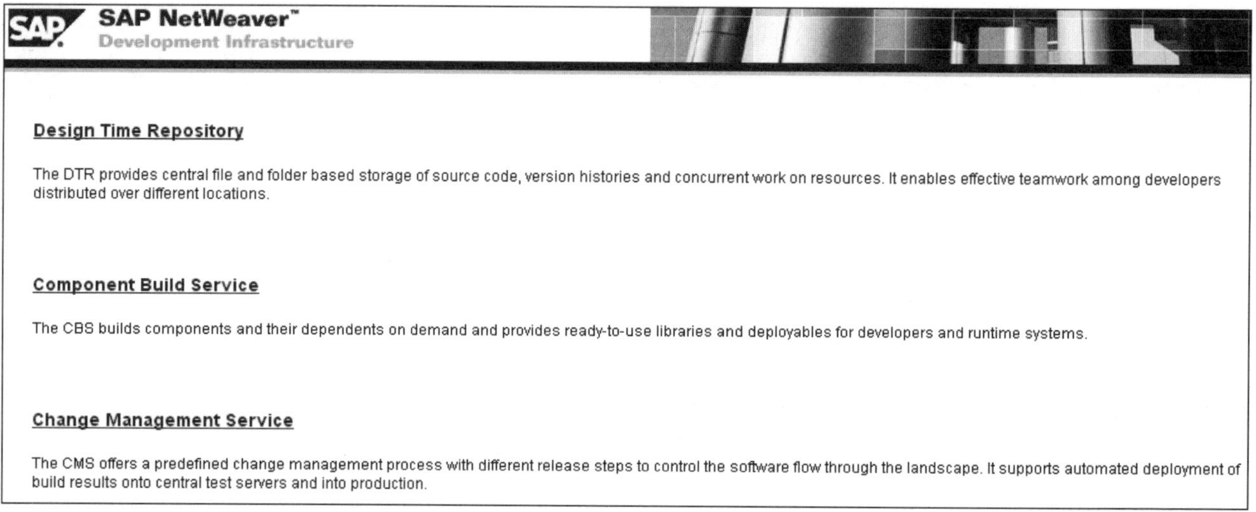

Figure 3.32 System Landscape Directory—CMS

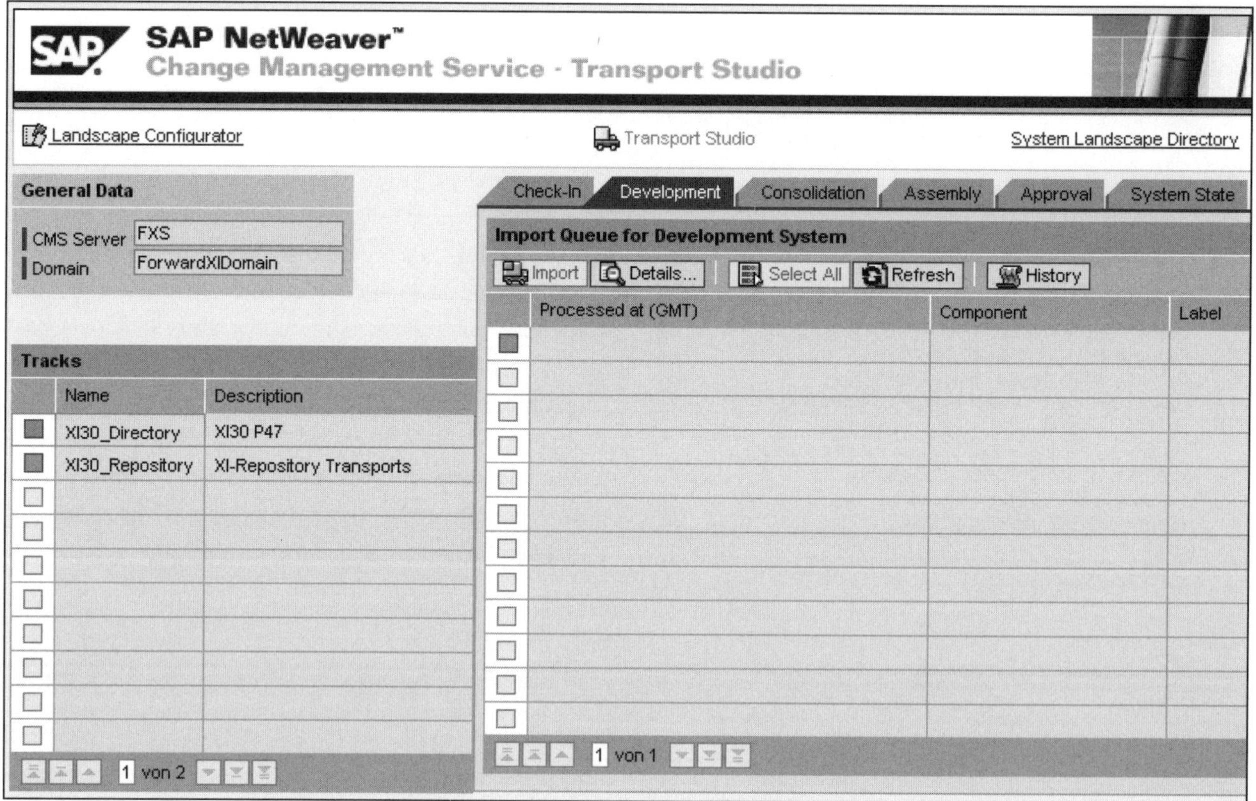

Figure 3.33 System Landscape Directory—CMS

If you are surprised by a red stop sign with an **AccessDenied** message in the middle of the screen, you should first assign the relevant roles to your user. If you have not done so yet, change to the user management of your J2EE server and create the two roles **CMSDeveloper** and **CMSAdministrator**. Assign the **CMS.Display** and **CMS.Export** actions to the **CMSDeveloper** role, and the **CMS.Administration** action to the **CMSAdministrator** role. Then, complete the authorizations of your user with the corresponding role.

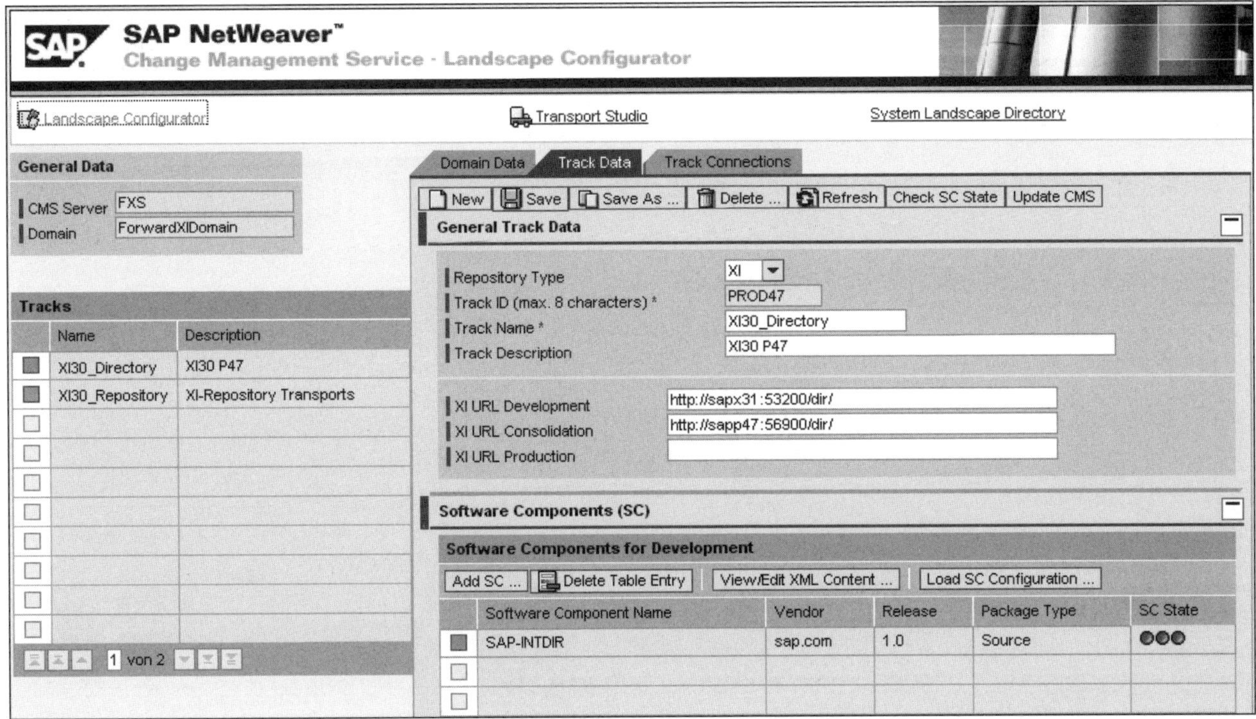

Figure 3.34 System Landscape Directory—CMS

The CMS main menu items are **Landscape Configurator**, **Transport Studio**, and **System Landscape Directory**. The latter is just a link to the familiar SLD and is therefore no longer discussed in greater detail here. To set up the CMS, we first need to go to the Landscape Configurator (see Figure 3.34).

Landscape Configurator

To specify or review the necessary basic settings, we change to the **Domain Data** view. You now see the basic configuration of the CMS service (see Figure 3.35).

In the Landscape Configurator, you store the name of your CMS server in the **CMS Name** field. For our example, we chose the name *FXS*. Additionally, you store a description of the server in the **CMS Description** field. In our example shown in Figure 3.35, we installed the CMS service on the server *sapx31*. Therefore, the **CMS URL** field was populated with the URL to the J2EE server of the *sapx31* system.

Therefore, this example deals with the URL *http://sapx31:53200*. As explained in the previous sections, this URL always consists of the server name and the port address derived from the value 50000 + number of the installation * 100. For our example, this translates to 50000 + 32*100 = 53200. After you entered the server URL, you must specify a user with the corresponding password for this server. You need to ensure that the user has been assigned the necessary roles on the server. The required roles and users are discussed in detail in Chapter 4. Here we only want to mention that this user should also dispose of the **CMSAdministrator** role described above and a **CBSAdministrator** role with the **CBS.Administrator** action.

Then you define the domain ID and the domain name, and store a domain description. Please note the **SLD URL** field where you store the SLD to which the CMS system is connected. In one of the previous sections, we mentioned the various architecture options. Since our example uses a central SLD on the *sapp47* system along with a central CMS system connected to this SLD, this field shows the following link to our central SLD: *http://sapp47:56900/sld*.

After you entered all the required information in the dialog, save the data using the **Save Domain** pushbutton. If you want to store another SLD, for example, at a later stage, you must click on the **Update CMS** pushbutton af-

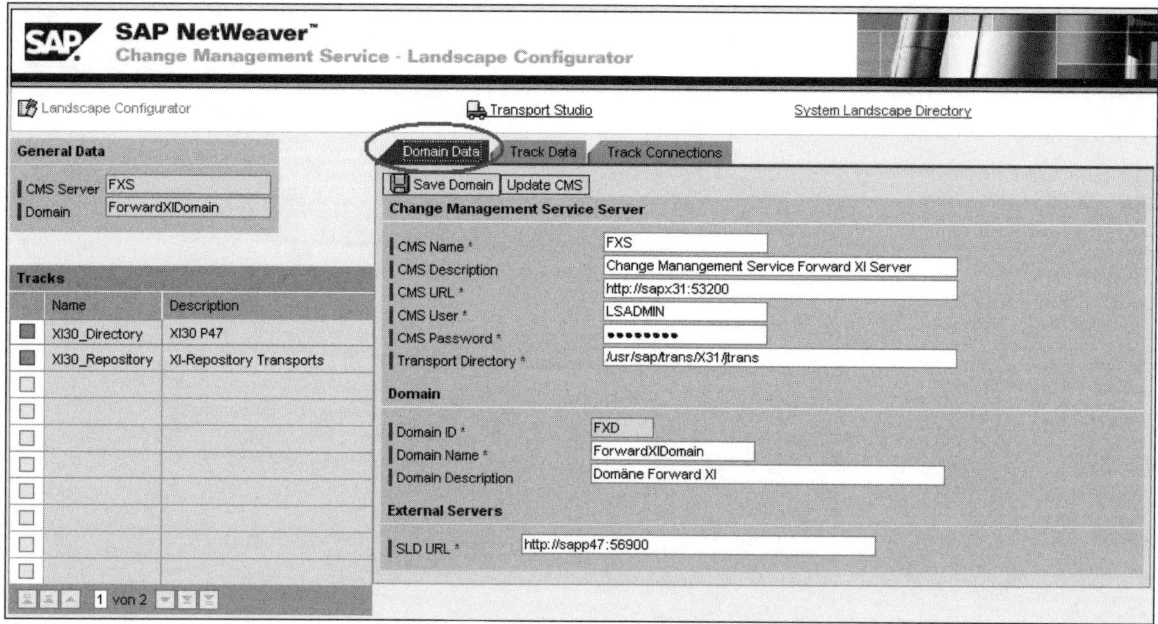

Figure 3.35 System Landscape Directory—CMS

ter making the change. Now that our CMS service is basically set up, we need to configure the corresponding transport tracks for transporting objects from our repository or directory, respectively.

For this setting, return to the **Track Data** tab and look at the options shown in Figure 3.36.

First, select the **XI** value as the **Repository Type**. The value **DTR** is also available for selection. If you want to

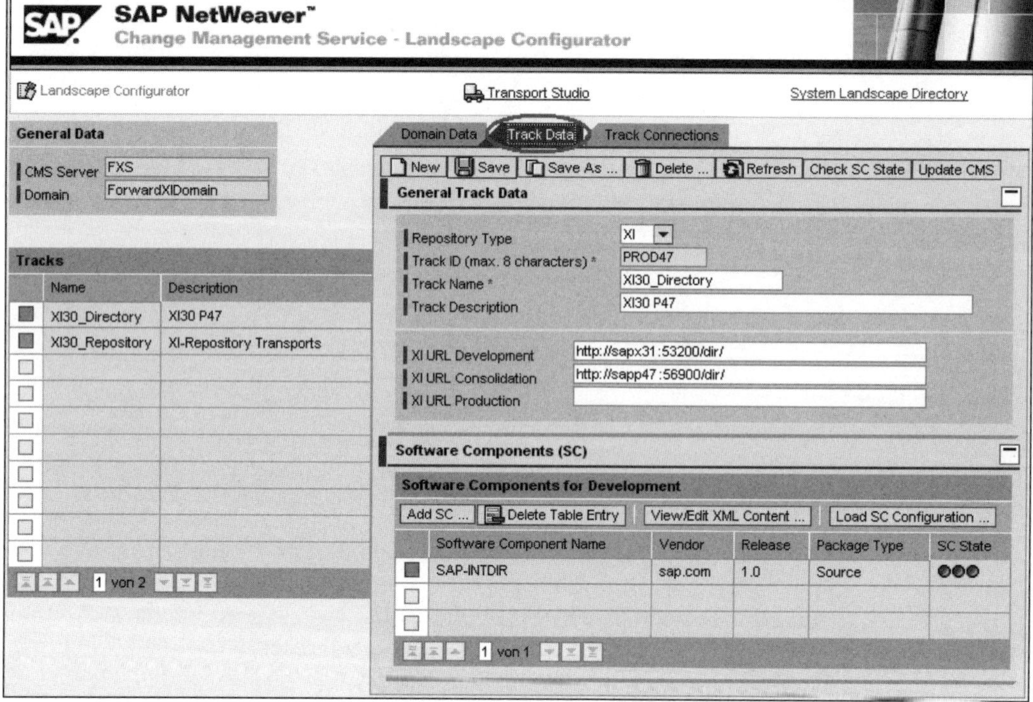

Figure 3.36 System Landscape Directory—CMS

use the SAP NetWeaver Developer Studio (NWDS) for Java developments with several developers, we recommend that you set a track for **DTR** here as well. However, for more information on the Java Developer Interface (JDI) subject, we suggest that you read *Java Programming with the SAP Web Application Server* (SAP PRESS 2005). Now specify the name of the track to be created in the **Track Name** field. Because we want to create a track for transports from the dictionary first, we choose the name **XI30_Directory**. A short description in the **Track Description** field is advisable. Afterwards, store the corresponding URLs for your multilevel landscape. If your landscape consists of only two levels, enter the URL of your production system under **Consolidation System**. Please note the URL structure—the server name with the specific port and the folder */dir/* at the end, which serves as a supplement or reference to your dictionary. Since the folder name can be changed within the J2EE parameters, you should first extract the correct name from the Exchange profiles. To do that, see Section 2.2 under *Configuring the System Parameters*. Click on the **Add SC ...** pushbutton (see Figure 3.37).

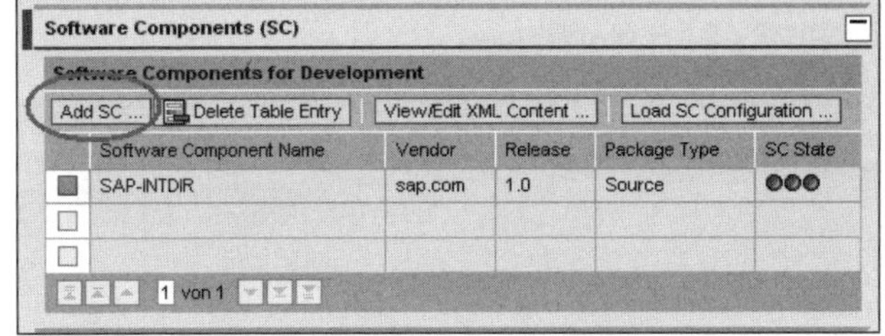

Figure 3.37 System Landscape Directory—CMS

Select the software component *SAP-INTDIR* and add this component to the dialog. This software component refers to all configuration objects of the Integration Directory. Now that you created a transport track for the dictionary, we want to create a track for the repository as well. For this purpose, click on the **New** pushbutton again and create a new track. We'll describe these settings shortly as you need to take into account some specific aspects.

Please note the change of the corresponding folder from the name */dir/* to the name */rep/* at the end of the URL (see Figure 3.38). Also notice the selection of the corresponding software components. In the Integration Repository, you need to store the individual software

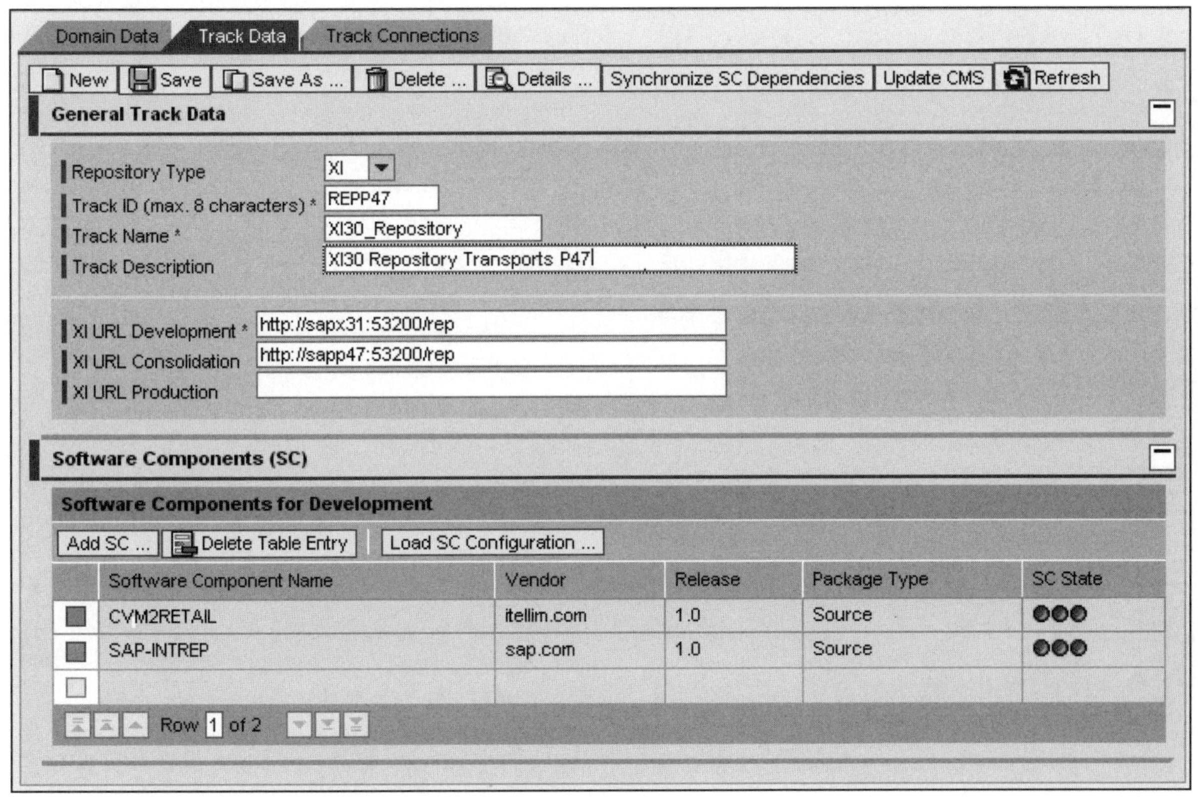

Figure 3.38 System Landscape Directory—CMS

components (contrary to the Integration Directory). In our example shown in Figure 3.38, in addition to the *SAP-INTREP* example, we added a separate software component called *CVM2Retail*. Naturally, the *SAP-INTREP* software component does not make much sense here and serves only as an example.

Since you always have to store your own software components in the Integration Repository, you should first click on the **Load SC Configuration** pushbutton to display new or changed components in the selection dialog.

After saving, do not forget to click on the **Update CMS** pushbutton. We won't discuss the option of connecting tracks to each other (in the **Track Connections** category) in detail, but will briefly describe the functionalities. Detailed information can be found in the comprehensive SAP online documentation under *help.sap.com*.

Using the **Track Connections** function, you can map two types or scenarios:

- **Transport Connection Type**
  This type defines a standard connection between two transport tracks. You can use this type to control the distribution of your software changes within your landscape.
- **Repair Connection Type**
  You define a repair connection type if you want to specify the next operations for further processing. These changes can then be imported back into a preceding track. This connection type makes sense, for example, for repairing software component versions.

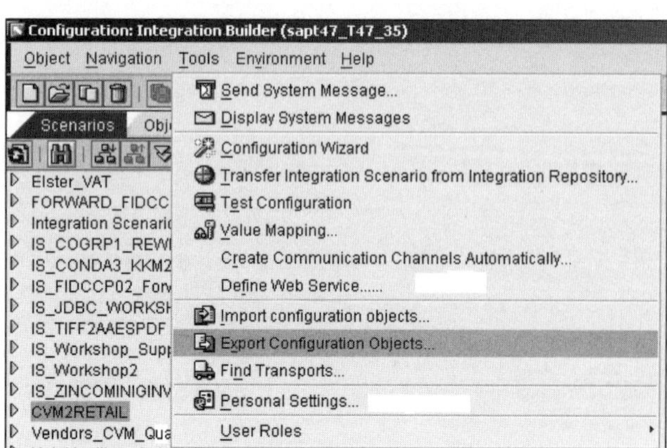

Figure 3.39 System Landscape Directory—CMS

You can now send transports to the CMS via the transport wizard in the repository and in the directory. For this purpose, in the repository go to the **Tools • Export Configuration Objects** menu and select **Transport Using CMS** (see Figure 3.39).

Transport Studio

After you transferred some objects from your repository to the CMS for transport purposes, change to the transport studio. The transport studio can be called by logging on to CMS and selecting the corresponding link called **Transport Studio**. The menu shown in Figure 3.40 is now displayed on your screen.

The lower left side of Figure 3.40 shows the tracks that you previously created. Since we sent a transport request in the repository, select the repository track with your mouse. After selection, the line selection box should be orange. To transport your transport request to the production system, select the **Consolidation** tab (see Figure 3.40). Because we are using a two-system landscape in our example, the consolidation system represents our productive platform in this case. You now see your transport request in the import queue of the consolidation system. After selecting the request, you can integrate it in the system using the **Import** function. If import errors occur, the import process is canceled and an error message is displayed. Using the **Details** function, you can display more information about the cause. A typical error in a multisystem landscape, which does not use a central SLD, is, for example, a missing software component or a missing technical or business system on the target system. But, because our example uses a central SLD, we reduced these import problems to a minimum.

To carry out transports for the directory, you proceed in the same way. Here, too, transport errors can occur if the target system is not synchronized with the source system. We recommend that you start with a central SLD for your XI landscape to minimize problems.

> **Note** Please look at the SAP OSS Note 827415. If you do not want to allow transports from change lists via the CMS, you can disable this function for selected software component versions.

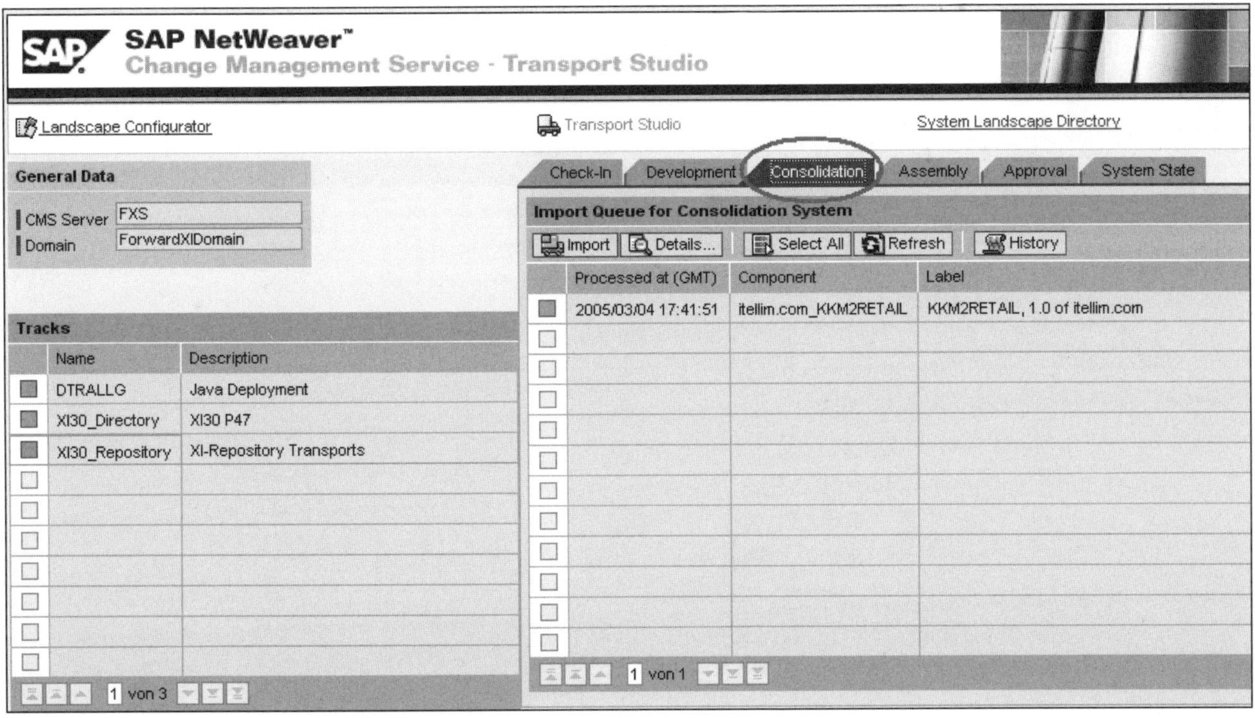

Figure 3.40 System Landscape Directory—CMS

CMS transports via transport lists or transports via the file system are not affected by this setting. The deactivation function is accessible via the XI home page (**Administration · CMS transport settings**).

Open change lists of the software component versions for which you set a value of *false* will then pass into the *closed* state immediately after release, without transferring the changes to the CMS.

If change lists of these software component versions had the *transportable* status before you made this change, you can either close them on the **Change Lists** tab without transporting them, or you can transport these remaining change lists via the CMS.

3.4 Minimum Configuration of the Transport System (without CMS)

If you don't want to use a CMS service for your XI transports, you can also choose the manual transport option. For this purpose, you simply need to create a directory at operating-system level which your test, quality, and production systems can access. In the repository and in the directory, you can then transport the individual design objects via flat file from A to B using export and import functions. After you set up an appropriate share in the repository or directory, select the **Transport Using File System** option from the menu under **Tools · Export Design Objects** or **Tools · Import Design Objects** (see Figure 3.41).

For importing design objects, you proceed in the same way as you did for exporting and select the corresponding menu functions. If you don't see an import queue, check the import paths stored in your parameter settings. Note that we discussed how to set or edit the parameters in the previous chapters.

For both transport options (with or without CMS), note that after importing into your Q or P system you might still need to perform some actions there, for example, when configuring your communication settings, because specific settings cannot be implemented automatically (e.g., RFC destinations/logins, etc.). These changes are listed in a change list on your system, for example, under the system user LSADMIN. When this list is activated, you're also notified of any missing settings.

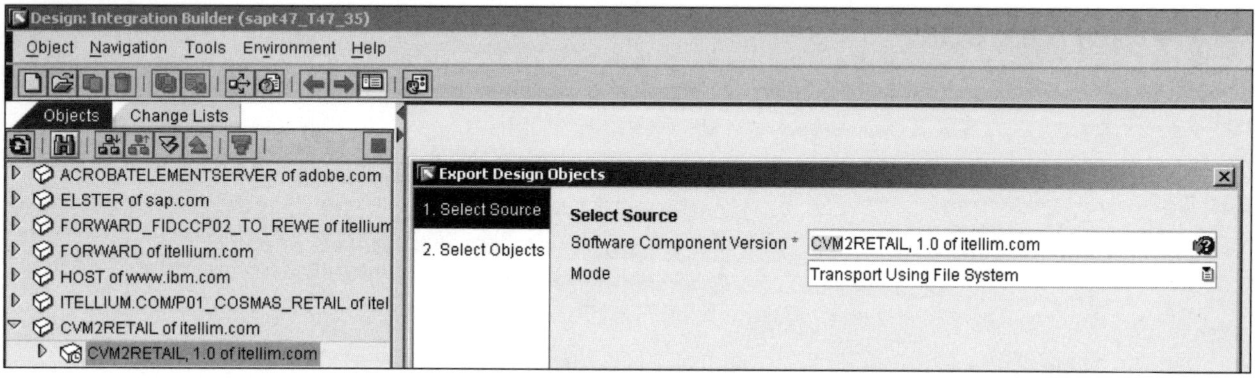

Figure 3.41 System Landscape Directory—CMS

4 Authorizations

4.1 Single Sign-On

Each time that you log on to a SAP Exchange Infrastructure (SAP XI) menu, you must enter your user name and password. As SAP Basis administrators, we would like to spare you this annoying and time-consuming task and introduce you to the Single Sign-On configuration. You then need to log on to your browser and access both the Java frontends (repository and directory) and the other web-based configuration options conveniently via a single mouse click.

First, log on to your Visual Administrator. From the main menu, change to the **Cluster · Server · Services** path and call the **Security Provider** service (see Figure 4.1).

In the **Components** menu (see Figure 4.2), you'll find the individual software elements in which you can set various authentication types. The following components are relevant to XI:

- *sap.com/com.sap.xi.repository*rep* (Repository)
- *sap.com/com.sap.xi.directory*dir* (Directory)
- *sap.com/com.sap.xi.services*run* (Runtime)

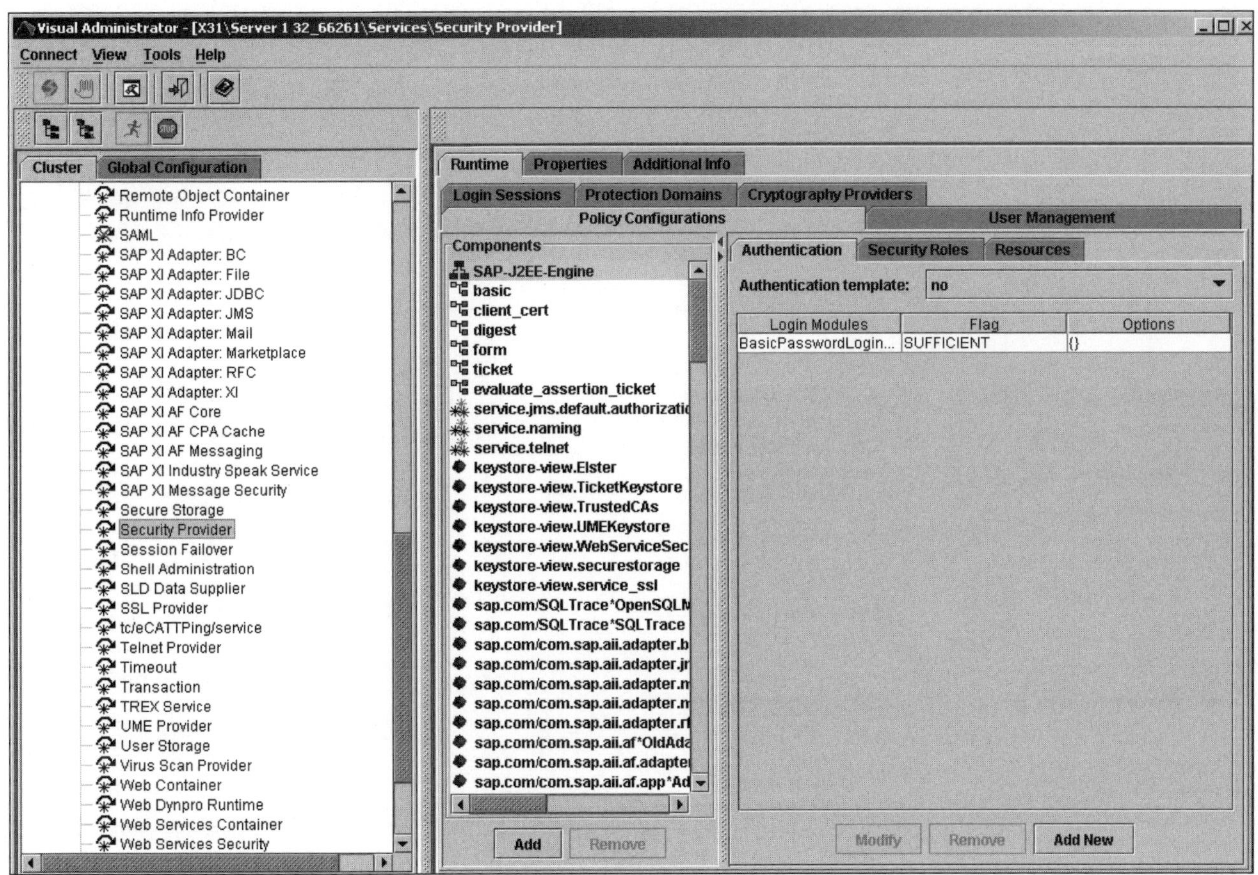

Figure 4.1 Single Sign-On Visual Administrator—Security Provider

- *sap.com/com.sap.xi.rwb*rwb* (RWB)
- *sap.com/com.sap.lcr*sld* (SLD)
- *sap.com/com.sap.rprof.remoteProfile*exchangeProfile* (ExchangeProfile)

We show the required settings for the *sap.com/com.sap.xi.repository*rep* component, which you can then transfer accordingly to the other components. Using your mouse, select the *sap.com/com.sap.xi.repository*rep* component and open the detail view. Figure 4.2 shows the detail view that should be displayed.

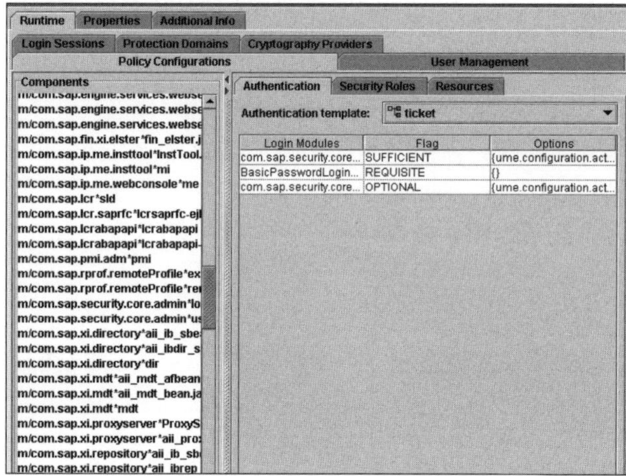

Figure 4.2 Single Sign-On Visual Administrator—Policy Configuration

From the **Authentication template** menu item select the **ticket** value. You thus enabled Single Sign-On for this software component. Repeat this procedure for all XI software components.

In the Exchange profile, you only need to set the *com.sap.aii.ib.core.sso.enabled* parameter to *true* to stop those tedious logon dialogs. After setting this parameter, we recommend that you restart the J2EE stack. You should now see the parameter in the overview shown in Figure 4.3.

4.2 XI Role Concept

Before you can start configuring, the XI administrators and developers must be given the corresponding authorizations.

SAP provides the authorization administrators with special composite roles that can be assigned to the XI administrators and developers, depending on the application and their requirements via Transaction SU01 or the User Management Environment (UME). The composite roles include the authorization for ABAP transactions, as well as for the Java tools of the Integration Builder.

Ensure that the SAP roles are copied to the customer-specific namespace (e.g., Z_*) before they are assigned to users. Table 4.1 lists the roles for the XI dialog and system users (Transaction SU01).

Tools | Admin
XI System: X31 u962004

Repository | Directory | Runtime

System Information
Software Build Information
General Information

Administration of Properties
All Properties
Exchange Profile ...

Administration of Locks and Caches
Lock overview
Cache overview

Java™ Web Start
Java™ Web Start Administration

Documentation Bases
Manage Documentation Bases

Data Migration
Data Migration Tool
Complete Export

com.sap.aii.ib.client.applicationname.repository	sap.com/com.sap.xi.repository/
com.sap.aii.ib.client.content.languages	EN,DE
com.sap.aii.ib.client.jnlp.j2se.initialheapsize	32m
com.sap.aii.ib.client.jnlp.j2se.maxheapsize	512m
com.sap.aii.ib.client.login.InitialContextFactory	com.sap.engine.services.jndi.InitialContextFac
com.sap.aii.ib.client.login.languages	EN,DE
com.sap.aii.ib.client.properties	com.sap.aii.ib.client.*, com.sap.aii.ib.core.*, com.sap.aii.util.xml.*, com.sap.aii.connect.*, com.sap.aii.repository.mapping.additionaltype com.sap.aii.docu.*, com.sap.aii.ibrep.core.cms.activated, com.sap.aii.ibdir.core.cms.activated, com.sap.aii.ibrep.core.cms.*, com.sap.aii.ibdir.core.cms.*
com.sap.aii.ib.core.sso.enabled	true
com.sap.aii.ib.server.anonymizedUser	
com.sap.aii.ib.server.concurrent_edit	false
com.sap.aii.ib.server.connect.webas.r3.ashost	u962004v
com.sap.aii.ib.server.connect.webas.r3.client	100
com.sap.aii.ib.server.connect.webas.r3.sysnr	32
com.sap.aii.ib.server.connect.webas.r3.useofootrfc	true

Figure 4.3 Single Sign-On Administration—Parameter Overview

Role (S=Single role; C=Composite role; M=Transaction menu)			Description
C S S S	 M 	SAP_XI_DISPLAY_USER SAP_SLD_GUEST SAP_XI_DISPLAY_USER_ABAP SAP_XI_DISPLAY_USER_J2EE	**Display role:** Mere display authorization for the entire Exchange Infrastructure functionality
C S S S S	 M M 	SAP_XI_DEVELOPER SAP_SLD_DEVELOPER SAP_XI_DEMOAPP SAP_XI_DEVELOPER_ABAP SAP_XI_DEVELOPER_J2EE	**Developer role:** Design of business scenarios, interfaces, and mappings in the Integration Repository using the Integration Builder, as well as imported existing interfaces from business systems
C S S S	 M 	SAP_XI_CONTENT_ORGANIZER SAP_SLD_ORGANIZER SAP_XI_CONTENT_ORGANIZER_ABAP SAP_XI_CONTENT_ORGANIZER_J2EE	**Organizer role:** Configuration and maintenance of Integration Repository/ Directory, SLD, and software components
C S S S S S	 M M M 	SAP_XI_MONITOR SAP_SLD_GUEST SAP_XI_BPE_MONITOR_ABAP SAP_XI_DEMOAPP SAP_XI_MONITOR_ABAP SAP_XI_MONITOR_J2EE	**Monitor role:** Authorizations for all activities within the entire Exchange Infrastructure that are related to monitoring
C S S S S S S S	M M M M M 	SAP_XI_ADMINISTRATOR SAP_ALM_ADMINISTRATOR SAP_ALM_CUSTOMIZER SAP_SLD_ADMINISTRATOR SAP_XI_ADMINISTRATOR_ABAP SAP_XI_ADMINISTRATOR_J2EE SAP_XI_BPE_ADMINISTRATOR_ABAP SAP_XI_DEMOAPP	**Administrator role:** Technical configuration and administration
S		SAP_SLD_ADMINISTRATOR	**SLD administrator role:** System Landscape Directory administration
S		SAP_SLD_CONFIGURATOR	**SLD configurator role:** System Landscape Directory configuration

Table 4.1 Roles for XI Dialog and/or System Users

The SAP roles delivered were only partially created with transaction menus. Many roles don't require calling transactions, because these applications are started via special XI Web applications.

The role authorizations make up both Web Application Server (Web AS) and pure SAP Basis transactions. Please make changes to existing predefined roles only after you have copied them to the customer-specific namespace.

Note If you want to change the authorizations of single roles that are already mapped to composite roles, you must copy the corresponding composite roles to the customer-specific namespace as well.

Additionally, in the Java Proxy Runtime in Visual Administrator under **Security Provider Service**, you should determine whether the J2EE Engine security roles are assigned to the designated user groups as follows:

Security role	User group
xi_jpr_register_bindings	SAP_XI_ADMINISTRATION_J2EE SAP_XI_DEVELOPER_J2EE
xi_jpr_list_bindings	SAP_XI_ADMINISTRATION_J2EE SAP_XI_DEVELOPER_J2EE SAP_XI_CONFIGURATOR_J2EE
xi_jpr_admin	SAP_XI_ADMINISTRATION_J2EE SAP_XI_CONFIGURATOR_J2EE

Table 4.2 Assignment of Security Roles to User Groups

Please check the availability of user groups on the J2EE page.

Via Transaction **PFCG · Tabstrip Description**, SAP briefly explains the purpose and authorization scope of the roles. For more information, please see *SAP Exchange Infrastructure Release 3.0* under *service.sap.com*, beginning on page 68.

The following service users are not dialog-enabled. They are automatically created during the XI installation and should not be changed:

Service user	Description	Assigned roles
XIREPUSER	Users for the Integration Repository	SAP_XI__IR_SERV_USER
XIDIRUSER	Users for the Integration Directory	SAP_XI_ID_SERV_USER
XIAP-PLUSER	Users for those sender application systems that are sender business systems	SAP_XI_APPL_SERV_USER
XIRW-BUSER	Users for the Runtime Workbench	SAP_XI_RWB_SERV_USER
XILDUSER	Users for the System Landscape Directory	SAP_BC_AI_LAND-SCAPE_DB_RFC
XIISUSER	Users for the Integration Server	SAP_XI_IS_SERV_USER_MAIN
XIAFUSER	Users for the Adapter Engine (communication between SLD, Integration Server, and adapter framework)	SAP_XI_AF_SERV_USER_MAIN
LSADMIN	Users for the Change Management Service (CMS) server	SAP_XI_CMS_SERV_USER

Table 4.3 Automatically Created Service Users

Passwords for these special background users are assigned during the installation. Please change the passwords only after you have read OSS Note 721584! This note gives a detailed description of the procedure.

We recommend that you define the passwords for the service users only once and change them as rarely as possible, that is, only in an emergency, or for special security reasons.

Please note the following:

- The new password is effective only after restarting the J2EE Engine.
- For sender applications, the password must be changed for the HTTP destinations as well.
- When copying clients, all roles must be copied as well.
- For the delivery roles, mass generation must be carried out via Transaction PFCG.

Using the User Management Environment (UME), important authorization roles, groups, and users are set up for Java applications. These can be displayed via the Visual Administrator.

You can access the UME via the start page of your J2EE server (not XI!) under the link *http://[Hostname]:[Port]/index.html*. To the right side of the browser, click on User Management. You now need to log on with your user ID and your password. Figure 4.4 shows the User Management Environment.

Here you can create, change, delete, and lock users, as well as create, change, delete, and assign authorization roles, roughly like you can do with Transaction SU01.

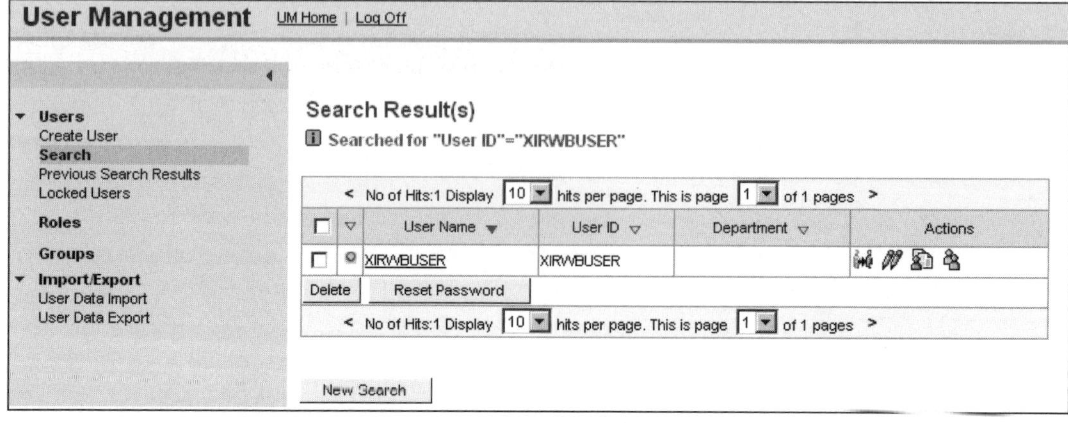

Figure 4.4 User Management Environment

The following roles are available by default in the User Management Environment:

UME Role	Meaning of the Roles
Administrator	General administration authorizations
CBSDeveloper	Component Build Services (CBS) are a part of the SAP NetWeaver Java development infrastructure. Components are created using this service, and their offshoots are provided with complete libraries, deployable data, and the runtime workbench, if required. With this role, you can assign the required authorizations needed by a developer for his or her daily work.
CMSAdministrator	Setup and configuration of the Change Management Services (transport system for the repository and directory components)
CMSDeveloper	CMS developer
XiDir_AllButValueMapping	Denies access to the values of mapping objects
XiDir_OnlyValueMapping	Allows access to values of mapping objects
XiDir_Unrestricted	Allows full access to all directory objects (including values for mapping maintenance)
XiMdt.ExtendedMonitor	Extended monitor
XiMdt.StandardMonitor	Standard monitor
XiMdt.StandardViewer	Standard viewer
XiRep_Unrestricted	Allows full access to all repository objects

Table 4.4 UME Roles

Role authorizations are maintained via the Visual Administrator.

For authorization, the roles listed above are stored for the various functions of the building blocks. The SAP NetWeaver Java Development Infrastructure consists of three building blocks, the Design Time Repository (DTR), the Component Build Server (CBS), the Change Management Server (CTS). In addition to these three building blocks, it contains the System Landscape Directory (SLD), which provides comprehensive information on all systems involved. Therefore, you can control the entire available functionality by simply assigning the user the functions of the relevant building block using the groups in the UME. This is necessary when you want to divide the XI team into specific user types (e.g., administrators, developers, and auditors). Before performing an action, look at the authorizations for each role. Create mnemonic group names in the UME with the required roles. If the predefined authorizations for a building block are not sufficient for the authorization concept, you must take the necessary action regarding role authorizations in the Visual Administrator.

In the Visual Administrator, you call the relevant screen via **Cluster • Server * • Services • Security Provider • Runtime • Policy Configurations • Security Roles**. Here, for example, a newly created group with the corresponding roles is stored for the respective node (component). For existing users in this group, any authorization changes take effect immediately because they represent one and the same application.

To avoid having to log on over and over again, every time with a different password, user management can be immensely simplified via a central user management (CUM). This can be implemented either via the LDAP directory service or via an R/3 system. The UME of Web AS supports both procedures. For the development and quality assurance system, you should also enable Single Sign-On via the Visual Administrator. This also handles tedious password requests, which saves a lot of time. The parameter settings for activating Single Sign-On were already described in Section 4.1.

4.3 Web Administrator

If you use several workstations or you cannot make any local installations on a customer workstation, you can still use the Visual Administrator.

SAP provides a small tool for this very purpose that enables you to access the individual parameters of the J2EE stack via a web interface similar to the Visual Administrator. To use this web interface, first, you must deploy the program on the J2EE stack. Then, you must go to the start page of your J2EE instance and call the link *http://[Hostname]:[Port]/*. Next, click on the link **J2EE Engine Examples**. An overview of various J2EE example programs is displayed (see Figure 4.5).

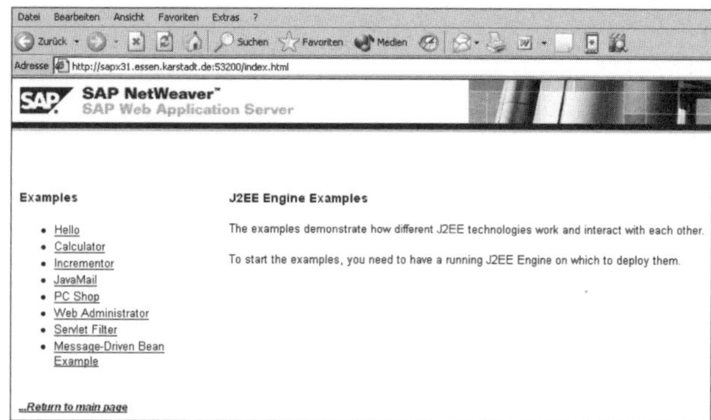

Figure 4.5 Overview of J2EE Engine Examples

Call the **Web Administrator** example and click on the **Run** pushbutton. When you run this example for the first time, the following dialog asks you to first deploy the Web Administrator example. Click on the **Deploy** pushbutton to make the application available on your J2EE stack.

Now that you deployed the Web Administrator tool on your J2EE stack, you can enter the logon dialog of the application using the link *http://[Hostname]:[Port]/admin/LoginForm.jsp*, that is, for our example *http://sapp47:56900/admin/LoginForm.jsp*. After logon you can access the J2EE parameters just like you did in the Visual Administrator. You can stop or start services and view their settings in a convenient Web dialog. Figure 4.6 shows the graphical interface.

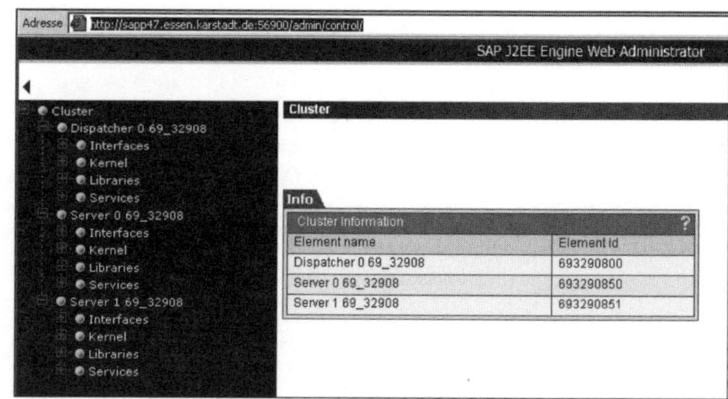

Figure 4.6 Web Interface SAP J2EE Engine Web Administrator

Please note the significant functional restriction as compared to the Visual Administrator, which is definitely the preferable option.

5 Performance Optimization Measures

Within the SAP Exchange Infrastructure (SAP XI), there are many ways in which to improve the performance of individual interfaces, or even the whole system. Naturally, the available measures depend on the specific hardware used and the corresponding operating system of your application server, as well as on the installed patch levels. In this chapter, we'll share tips and tricks that are platform-independent and are therefore applicable in most architectures. The topic structure is based on the existing SAP documents (especially the *SAP Exchange Infrastructure Tuning Guide* from *sdn.sap.com*), which we enhanced with examples from our own experience. Here we address only those topics that are most relevant to the subject matter.

5.1 Adapting Web AS 6.40 for XI 3.0

Since the Exchange Infrastructure uses Remote Function Call (RFC) connectivity extensively, we will focus on the optimization of RFC settings on both the R/3 side and the new J2EE side. Thereafter, we will discuss the individual parameter settings for the RFC and the Gateway parameterization on the R/3 side.

Because configuring the RFC quota and the Java Connector (JCo) service provider requires specific configuration steps, we describe these steps individually in the following two sections before we specifically describe each parameter setting in detail.

RFC Quota on the R/3 Side

Depending on the number of existing CPUs and the main memory, the ABAP side of the XI server can be optimized by different parameterizations. Examples include the number of work processes that are available in the R/3 basis stack for processing the queues. You should note that the J2EE stack logs on to the R/3 basis stack per RFC dialog user. This means that you don't need to increase the number of batch processes, as you might expect, just the dialog processes. The number of dialog processes can be controlled using the *rdisp/wp_no_dia* profile parameter.

One important configuration factor is the RFC quota, which defines the maximum number of dialog processes that can be occupied by RFC users on a system. The purpose of this quota is to prevent all dialog processes from being occupied by RFC users from other systems so that the actual dialog users can no longer log on to the system. You can retrieve the RFC quota using Transaction RZ12 (see Figure 5.1)

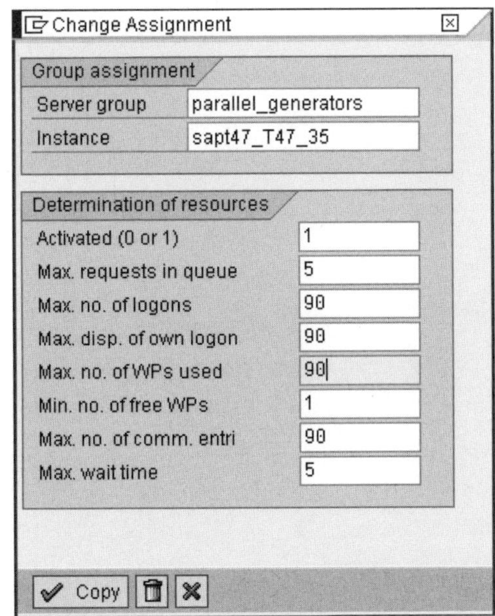

Figure 5.1 Settings—Computing Center Management System (CCMS) RFC Server Group Maintenance

We recommend that you use a maximum value for the **Max. no. of WPs used** depending on the available work processes. You need to consider the associated system parameter *rdisp/rfc_max_own_used_wp*. The default value is 75%. This parameter value indicates the maximum percentage of dialog work processes that may be occupied by an RFC user. Since XI logs on to the R/3 system with a service user, this value needs to be set accordingly. For most of our projects, we increased this value to 90%. Transaction RZ10 sets this parameter in the instance profile. If the parameter is not set, a default value of 75% is used automatically. After setting the parameter, you must restart the application server.

Additionally, if you really want to operate the XI server as an integration platform only, we recommend that you set the **Min. no. of free WPs** field to a value between 1 and 2 to optimally use the set dialog processes for batch operation.

You should also consider that every work process that is additionally set and cannot be used effectively reserves a certain amount of main memory on the server.

The settings within the instances are just as important as planning the number of actual instances, depending on the CPUs and the main memory.

The number of available work processes can be set using Transaction RZ04, as shown in Figure 5.2. Note that the maximum number is defined in the profile parameters. If it is necessary to change this maximum, a restart is required.

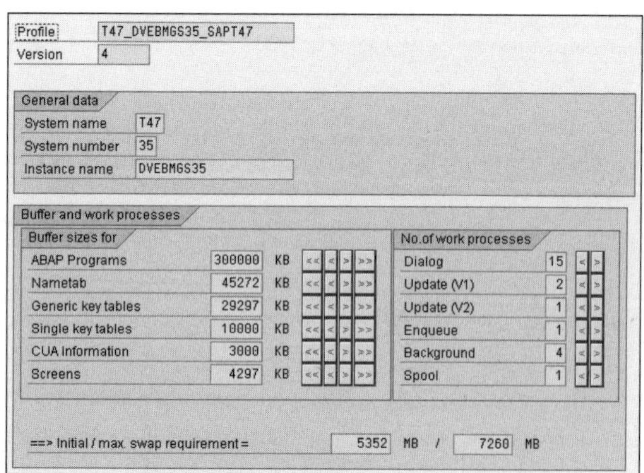

Figure 5.2 Setting Work Processes—Transaction RZ04

Now that we looked at the number of instances and the number of processes per instance, don't forget to check the number of existing queues per basis instance as well. The number of queues that accept incoming data in parallel and then send it simultaneously (qRFC queues) is hard to configure and depends largely on the average parallel requests and on the size of the messages to be processed, which must be dealt with by the XI system. We will later discuss in detail the necessary parameterizations and some recommended values based on our project experience.

JCo Service Provider on the J2EE Side

Now that we looked at the settings within the ABAP instances and at the number of ABAP instances, we should also consider the "new" SAP world—J2EE instances.

The first aspect to clarify is the number of J2EE instances to be installed. A good initial value is two J2EE instances, however, the actual number of J2EE instances depends largely on the number of activities to be carried out simultaneously (e.g., mappings) and the used adapters on your J2EE stack. In our implementations, we did quite well with two initial instances, even for high-performing interfaces. But, for more intense activities and parallel operations on the J2EE stack, a scaling according to the J2EE instances is recommended. Because this is a very singular characteristic that depends on the used interfaces and systems, there is no general formula that we can recommend you apply.

As we did for the ABAP stack, here, also, we must consider the number or processes running within a single instance on the J2EE side as well. You should note the number of processes required for the individual RFC destinations of the *JCo RFC Provider* service. Our experience values in this regard are between 15 and 20 processes for this service per instance.

Conversely, if you're using multiple J2EE server nodes and find that there is no effective load distribution, the reason might be that the number of RfcEngine threads per server is set too high. In this case, reduce the number of threads for the RFC destination AI_RUNTIME_* depending on the number of parallel mapping requests. This problem exists because the SAP gateway does not know the J2EE configuration. To achieve an effective load distribution, you should observe this information and configure your system accordingly.

The settings on the J2EE side can be checked as follows: First, open the Visual Administrator. This software is located in the XI installation directory under *c:\usr* *sap\....\j2ee\admin* (example of a Windows installation). From there, you can start the Visual Administrator under UNIX or Windows derivatives by calling the *go* batch file (see Figure 5.3)

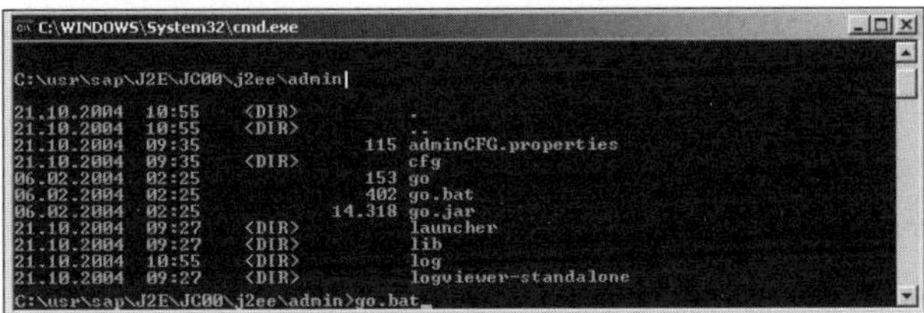

Figure 5.3 Calling the Visual Administrator

After you logged on to the system, the interface of the Visual Administrator is displayed as shown in Figure 5.4, where you can display and change the individual parameters online.

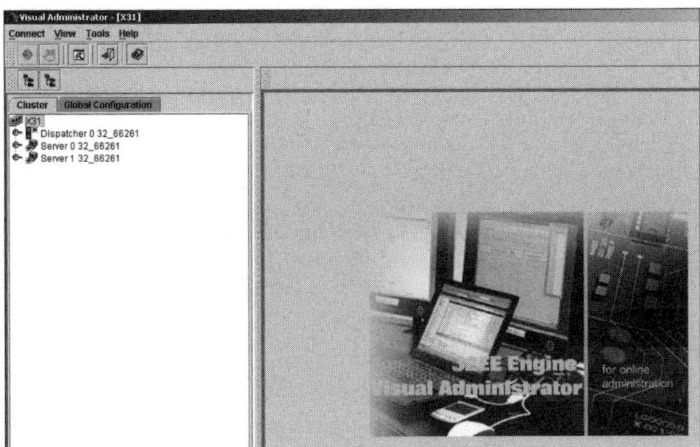

Figure 5.4 Main Menu of the Visual Administrator

In our example shown in Figure 5.4, there are two J2EE instances and a dispatcher instance in the cluster on system X31. Every instance provides a separate configuration option to set the number of processes available for this service. Therefore, these services need to be run separately for both J2EE instances. We will now explain the setting possibilities using the example of the first instance of the system X31 shown in Figure 5.4. We expand the first instance and then the **Services** node in the Visual Administrator. The individual services of this instance are now displayed, as shown in Figure 5.5.

To set the available processes for each RFC connection, call the *JCo RFC Provider* service. The setting options are shown in Figure 5.6.

On the left-hand side, there is a list of the individual available RFC connections in use. By selecting these RFC

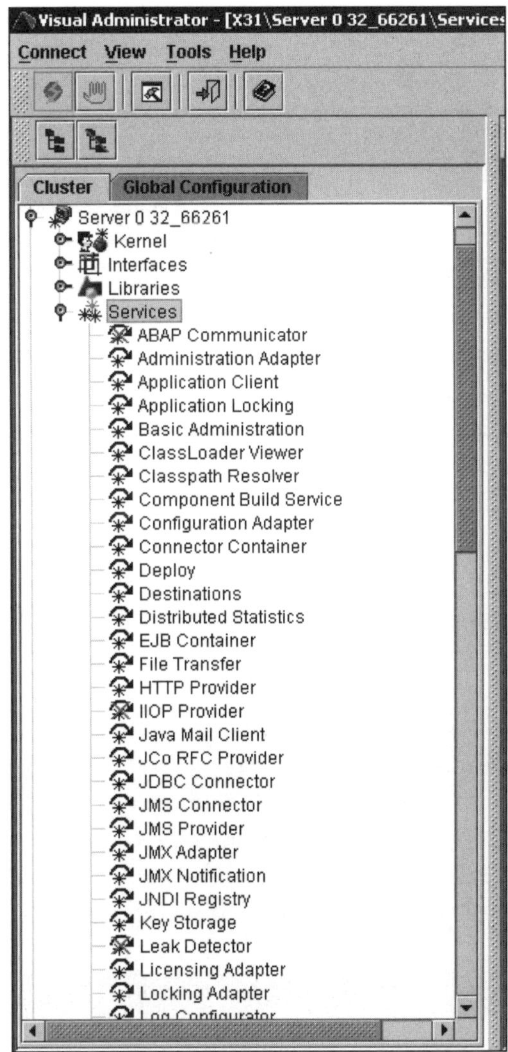

Figure 5.5 Visual Administrator—Services Overview

connections using your mouse, you can change the corresponding parameters on the right-hand side. You can tell from the example in Figure 5.6 that within this instance there are 10 processes for this RFC connection that are available for the directory. If this parameter is set to the same value on the second instance, there are 20 processes available altogether. You must always take into account that on the R/3 side of the XI system, the RFC quotas and the work processes need to be set accordingly. If there are enough work processes available on the R/3 part of your XI system, we recommend that you set a value of 20 threads here for the directory and the runtime. Naturally, you should adapt the *MaxConnection* and *MaxProcesses* parameters accordingly if you increase the number of processes.

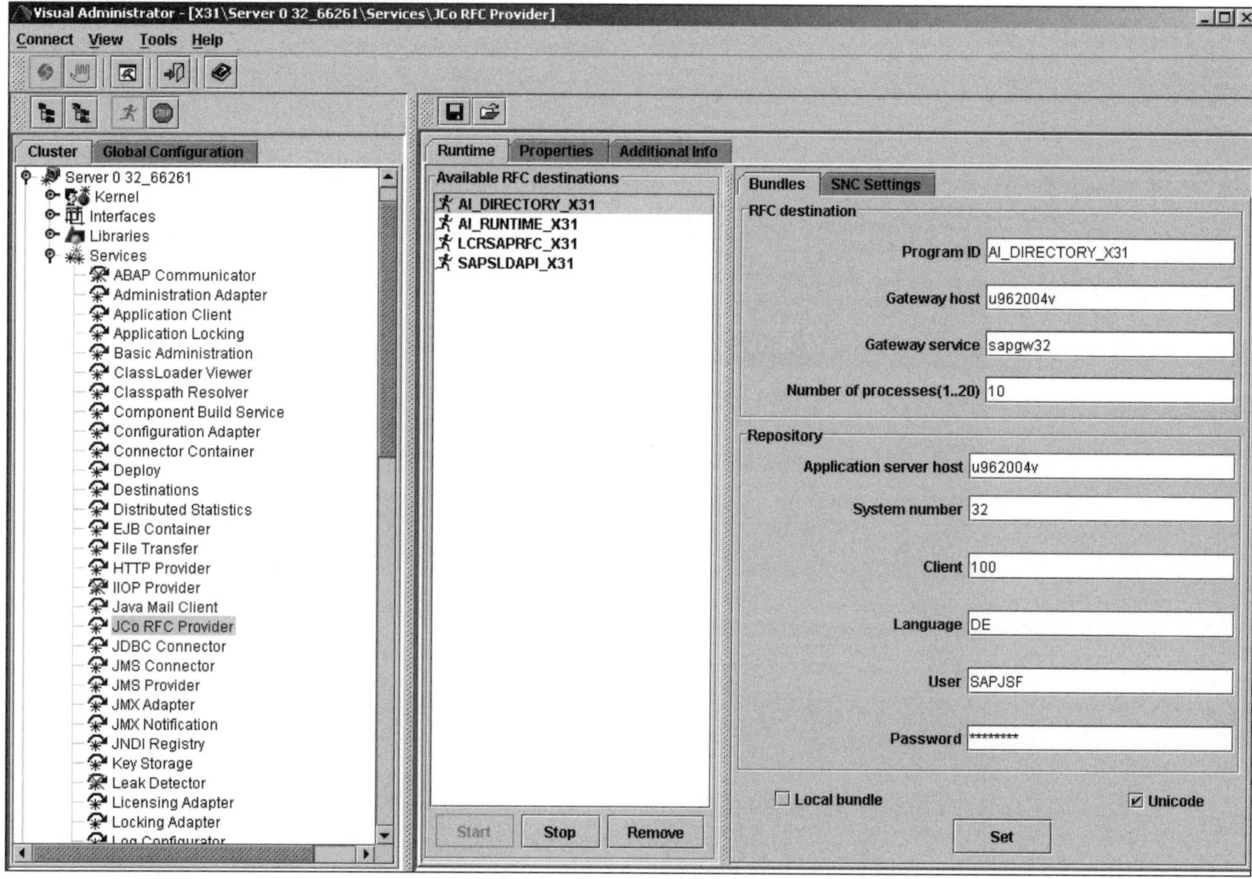

Figure 5.6 Settings in the JCo RFC Provider

Name	Value	Description
gw/max_conn	2000	Sets the maximum number of active connections (gateway).
gw/max_overflow_size	10000000	Sets the size of the local main memory area for the gateway in bytes
gw/max_sys	2000	Maximum number of gateway clients. Please note that an R/3 server is a single client for the gateway.
gw/max_shm_req	400	Reflects the maximum number of Common Programming Interface Communication (CPIC) requests in the gateway that should be stored in the shared memory.

Table 5.1 Parameter Settings for the Gateway

5.2 Parameter Settings on the R/3 Side

Web AS 6.40—Gateway Parameters

As mentioned previously, the optimum configuration of the system for a high RFC load is significant. Therefore, we will now describe the most important R/3 profile parameters for the optimum configuration of the R/3 stacks for XI 3.0. First, we will focus on the settings of the gateway parameters (see Table 5.1).

Web AS 6.40—Communication Parameters

This section, too, focuses on the configuration of the system for an increased amount of parallel communication. Therefore, in combination with the gateway parameters described above, you should set or change the following values:

Name	Value	Description
rdisp/force_sched_after_commit	No	Sets the automatic rollout of the context after the work commit.
rdisp/max_comm_entries	2000	Sets the maximum number of connection entries.
rdisp/rfc_max_own_login	90	Sets the RFC quota for its own login.
rdisp/rfc_max_own_used_wp	90	Sets the RFC quota for the self-used work process.
rdisp/rfc_max_wait_time	5	Sets the maximum wait time in seconds for RFC after the load check.
rdisp/wp_ca_blk_no	1000	Sets the block buffer size for WP communication (integer value)
rdisp/tm_max_no	2000	This value sets the maximum number of connections for an instance, including both dialog users and interfaces.
rdisp/max_comm_entries	2000	Number of communications from and to an instance (without dialog users).
rdisp/max_arg	2000	This parameter limits the maximum amount of asynchronous messages used for making information known throughout the system. Please note that this parameter must be identical to the *rdisp/max_comm_entries* parameter.
rdisp/appc_ca_blk_no	2000	Buffer for TCP/IP communications (integer value). Note that this parameter allocates space in the shared memory.
zta/max_mem-req_MB	2048	Limitation value for a single memory allocation request (in MB, default: 64), important for processing particularly large messages.
ABAP/arfcrstate_col_delete	X	This entry deletes the log data ARFCSTATE in the background. Every two to five minutes, this parameter starts the ABAP program `RSTRFCEU` in the background.

Table 5.2 Advisable Parameter Settings regarding RFC, Communications or Other Aspects

Note Since the ABAP side in particular will be exposed to massive parallel RFC requests, you should place the highest priority in your optimization measures on the configuration of gateway and communication parameters.

XI 3.0 Parameter Settings—Tuning Category

The number and type of queues available in Web Application Server (Web AS) for processing the messages can be set via Transaction SXMB_ADM using various parameters. Within this transaction, select the **Tuning** category. This category allows you to add or change various parameters. We should point out, however, that the number of queues depends on the number of work processes on the instance, as well as the parallelization required, the threads available on the J2EE stack, and the message size of the individual messages to be processed by the queues.

Additionally, note that the principle "the more, the faster" is definitely not applicable here. The qRFC scheduler algorithm works more effectively with fewer queues and with a greater amount of data per queue, than it does with a high number of queues containing a very low number of messages the reason being that the scheduler can process a queue only every 60 seconds. Fortunately, this parameter (60 seconds) can be manipulated, if necessary, to have the queues processed faster and to effectively increase the number of queues and thus the amount of parallelization. The ideal value is very hard to find because it depends on extremely different factors. Within our processes, we calculated an initial value using the existing CPUs to start with the fine-tuning described above. We recommend that you set two queues per CPU as an initial value, but you should also take into account the simultaneous adaptation of work processes on the R/3 side.

The optimum configuration of the queues requires a certain flair. This configuration clearly influences the system performance. In fact, the performance for some interfaces can be improved by up to 50%. Therefore, you should focus primarily on a setting that is customized to reflect your environment. We suggest that you carefully document every change of the settings and their individual impact on system performance.

Transaction SXMB_ADM brings you to the administration dialog of the XI parameters (see Figure 5.7).

Here you can adjust the parameter settings of your XI system in different areas. We'll start with the **Tuning** category and describe how you can increase the speed of your XI system. As a category, select the **Tuning** value and

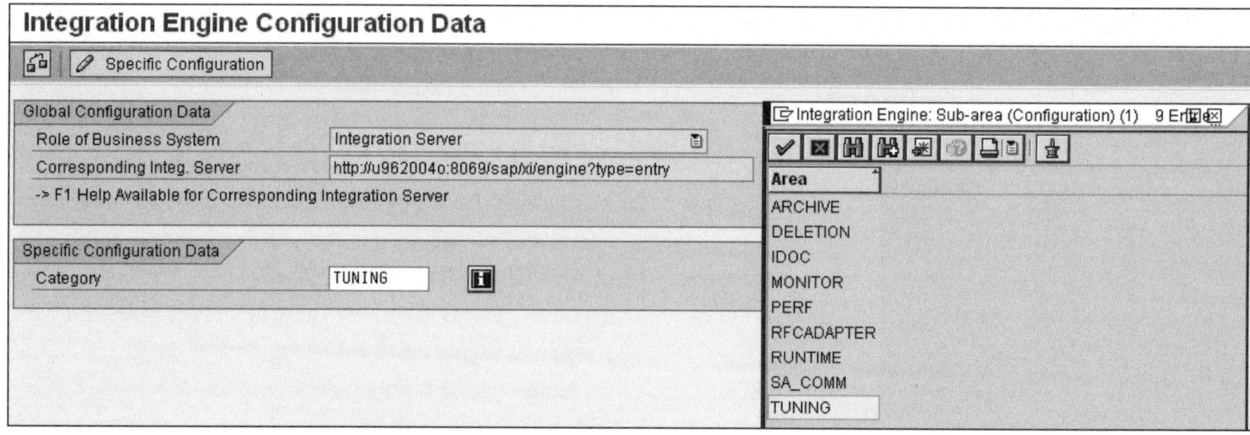

Figure 5.7 Administration of Configuration Data (Subareas Overview)

click on the change mode. This will take you to the menu shown in Figure 5.8.

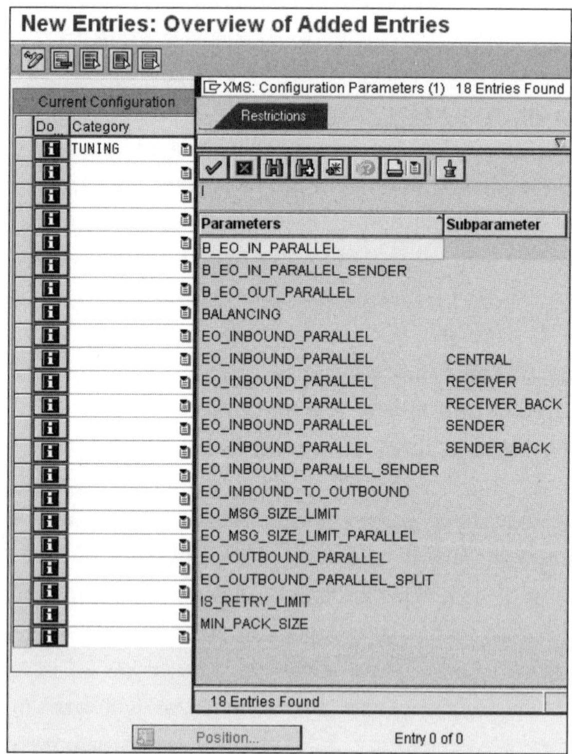

Figure 5.8 XI Configuration Parameters—Tuning Category

As you can see in Figure 5.8, you can configure the queues with the following parameters:

- EO_INBOUND_PARALLEL
- EO_INBOUND_PARALLEL_SENDER
- EO_INBOUND_TO_OUTBOUND
- EO_OUTBOUND_PARALLEL
- IS_RETRY_LIMIT
- EO_MSG_SIZE_LIMIT
- EO_MSG_SIZE_LIMIT_PARALLEL
- B_EO_IN_PARALLEL
- B_EO_OUT_PARALLEL
- B_EO_IN_PARALLEL_SENDER
- BALANCING

We will now describe the individual parameters and their impact on your system:

- **EO_INBOUND_PARALLEL**
  This parameter determines the extent of parallelization for processing messages in the inbound and outbound areas with the quality of service *Exactly Once*. The queues affected have the namespace XBTI (I = Central). For the value of this parameter, *n* queues are created in the system by attaching the prefix *n* to the name of the queue. Therefore, if the parameter is set to four queues, the following queues are created: XBTI0, XBT1, XBT2, XBT3. If on a system both the central integration server and the local sender and receiver client are installed on different clients, the degree of parallelization can be set individually for each queue type (S = Sender, I = Central, R = Receiver, B = Sender and Receiver Acknowledge Queues) using the subparameters *Sender*, *Central*, *Receiver*, *Sender_Back*, and *Receiver_Back* as supplements to the main parameter.
- **EO_INBOUND_PARALLEL_SENDER**
  This is a more detailed version of the previous parameter. The meaning is the same with the addition that

we can explicitly indicate the sender for which we want to specify the setting. Thus, we can override the general previous settings for individual interfaces and redirect the data in separate prioritized queues. To be able to do so, however, we must define a sender/receiver ID via Transaction SXMSIF, which specifies the identification schema, the partner, and the service of the sender (normalized to the integration server). This sender ID will be attached to the main parameter as a subparameter.

- EO_INBOUND_TO_OUTBOUND
  This parameter explains how to place messages received with the quality of service *Exactly Once* directly after there is receiver determination in dedicated outbound queues for output processing. You can force this behavior by setting this parameter to 1. If you keep the default parameter value of 0, these messages are processed during inbound processing. Depending on the type of messages to be processed, you can increase the performance by having the respective messages processed in separate queues.
- EO_OUTBOUND_PARALLEL
  This parameter is very significant with regard to the sending speed of your messages, with the quality of service *Exactly Once*, because it defines the degree of parallelization of outbound processing for the messages on the integration server. An outbound message with this attribute is placed by the integration server in a separate internal queue named "XBTO+<Receiver ID>+<Number>" or "XBTB+<Receiver ID>+<Number>" for the confirmation of receipt. The number is a four-digit value generated at runtime. To fine-tune individual interfaces, you can define an individual degree of parallelization specifically for this key using a subparameter by combining the values of an identification schema, the partner, and the service. However, we recommend that you don't set this degree of parallelization too high (even if your XI system could handle it), because you might cause problems on your target system. The processing speed of your target system should therefore determine the degree of parallelization that is defined. The default value is 3. On average, we increased this value to 10 and did quite well with this setting in our SAP landscape. Possible values for this parameter are between 1 and 10,000.
- IS_RETRY_LIMIT
  The parameter *IS_RETRY_LIMIT* defines the maximum total number of retries when the asynchronous processing finds a retrievable error and the integration server sets the retry status during queue processing. This parameter will only be effective if a bigger retry value was set within the affected qRFC queue. If not, the value of this parameter will be ignored and overridden by the queue parameter. Possible values for this parameter are between 0 and 100. We recommend that you choose a value between 10 and 15.
- EO_MSG_SIZE_LIMIT
  This parameter defines a threshold for the size of a message. If this threshold is exceeded by a message, this message is processed serially in its own special queue named XBTL. If several larger messages must be processed simultaneously by the integration server, you can increase performance considerably with this parameter, because there might not be enough main memory for processing several bigger messages concurrently. Furthermore, your system produces a higher I/O rate due to paging, for example, which might affect the whole system. Serial processing within this special queue ensures that only one bigger message can impact the main memory at a time. The integration server can then continue to process the smaller messages in parallel. If this situation occurs in your integration scenarios, we recommend that you enable this parameter and set it to reflect the size of your messages.
- EO_MSG_SIZE_LIMIT_PARALLEL
  This parameter enables you to adjust the parameter described above even further in order to fine-tune the main memory load. All messages exceeding the threshold value of the *EO_MSG_SIZE_LIMIT* parameter are edited serially. Via this parameter, you can still determine a user-defined parallelization. The messages are processes in the special queue XBTL with a counter. Possible values for this parameter are between 1 and 10,000. Depending on the main memory of your integration server and the size of your messages, you should choose this value very

carefully so as not to achieve the opposite effect for your performance.

- **B_EO_IN_PARALLEL**
  This parameter is dependent on the *EO_INBOUND_PARALLEL* parameter described previously. It ensures an even distribution of the individual messages to the queues defined in the *EO_INBOUND_PARALLEL* parameter. The value of this parameter represents the maximum number of messages per queue. Activate this parameter if you previously increased the number of parallelizations in the *EO_INBOUND_PARALLEL* parameter in order to force a redistribution of messages to the individual queues. Thus, a quicker processing of these queues can be achieved. However, please note that the value of the *EO_INBOUND_PARALLEL* parameter multiplied with the value of the *B_EO_IN_PARALLEL* parameter should be bigger than the number of entries in the corresponding queues because otherwise a sensible redistribution of messages is not possible. Possible values for this parameter are between 1 and 100,000 messages. The parameter will be activated only via the *BALANCING* parameter. If this parameter is not active, these settings will not take effect.
- **B_EO_OUT_PARALLEL**
  This parameter is the counterpart of the parameter described previously. It defines the message distribution for the sender process, that is, for outbound queues. The definitions are identical to the parameter described above. Note that this parameter is activated only by setting the *BALANCING* parameter. Possible values for this parameter are between 1 and 100,000 messages.
- **B_EO_IN_PARALLEL_SENDER**
  Like the two parameters described above, this parameter refers to a redistribution or equal distribution of messages to specific queues. In this case, equal distribution refers to the queues defined in the *B_EO_INBOUND_PARALLEL_SENDER* parameter. This parameter can take values between 1 and 100,000 and is dependent on the BALANCING parameter
- **BALANCING**
  The *BALANCING* parameter activates the parameters described above and ensures an equal distribution of messages to the individual queues, which were described in the respective parameters. If the redistribution of queues was successful, the parameter is disabled automatically so that the messages are processed normally again. Since the customizing table is locked by the transaction in which you set the parameter, we recommend that you leave the transaction immediately after setting this value so that the integration server can change the value accordingly after a successful redistribution of queues.

XI 3.0 Parameter Settings—Runtime Category
Within the previously described transaction, you can maintain various parameters under the **Runtime** category as well. The following parameters can affect the performance of your system in a positive or negative way:

- ENGINE_TYPE
- HTTP_TIMEOUT
- ERROR_ON_NO_RECV_FOUND
- ACK_SYSTEM_FAILURE
- CACHE_DIRTY_READ
- CACHE_REFRESH_PACKAGE_SIZE
- ENTRY_LOCK
- LOGGING
- LOGGING_SYNC
- TRACE_LEVEL

The purpose and impact of these parameters are as follows:

- **ENGINE_TYPE**
  With this parameter, you define the type of your XI server depending on the current client. If you do not set the parameter, the client is configured as a non-XI engine by default. The HUB value causes the client to be configured as an integration server. If you enter the value LOC, the client is configured as a sender/receiver system.
- **HTTP_TIMEOUT**
  This parameter defines the timeout for an HTTP connection between two data packages in your network. Note that when you set this parameter, the *icm/server_port_n* profile parameter is overridden. If you want to prevent this from occurring, you should set its value to 0 to use the profile setting. If the network connection of your company is slow, we recommend that you increase the value accordingly. Otherwise, a

timeout between 700 and 1000 should suffice in most instances. If a faster termination is needed, you can reduce this value to improve the response time of your system.

- ERROR_ON_NO_RECV_FOUND
  This parameter determines the two qualities of service—*Exactly Once* and *Exactly Once in Order*—if the queue should be stopped when an error occurs and no receiver can be detected, or, if the processing should be finished and considered to be accurate. If you want to mark the processing as faulty and stop the entire qRFC queue, you must set this parameter to 1. Otherwise, you need to set this parameter to 0. With regard to performance, the respective queue is stopped and error-free messages are not processed until you manually intervene.
- ACK_SYSTEM_FAILURE
  This parameter defines whether your system should report system errors for asynchronous messages expecting an acknowledgement. Enabling this parameter results in a slight overhead on your system. The value 1 enables the reporting of system errors. The value 0 disables the reporting of errors.
- CACHE_DIRTY_READ
  The Exchange Infrastructure uses a cache to optimize message processing. This cache needs to be updated on a regular basis. It can be done either manually or automatically. If there are messages being processed at the time, the system can choose between two options:
  - It can either interrupt processing messages and wait for the cache refresh, or
  - It can use the old cache contents and continue processing.

  This parameter controls these two options. If you set it to 0, the system waits until the cache has been refreshed. If the parameter is set to 1, processing is not interrupted and the old cache contents is used. This parameter thus influences the performance during data processing. You should understand that messages are not necessarily affected by a change in the cache. If, for example, a target system that was not involved in processing current messages was changed, the old contents of the cache can be used free of problems. Therefore, if you can implement changes that do not affect interfaces in productive operation or that are currently being processed, you can set this parameter to 1 in order to improve performance. If you cannot ensure that the interfaces will not be adversely affected, we recommend that you use a value of 0.
- CACHE_REFRESH_PACKAGE_SIZE
  When setting this parameter, you should reduce the default value of 10 MB to a value of 7 MB. The Exchange Infrastructure copies the configuration files per HTTP from the Integration Directory into the XI cache. This parameter defines the package size that is used to transfer this data. Our test series showed an increased transfer speed for a smaller package size. Possible parameter settings are between 1 and 500 MB. You should consider the dependency on the speed and usage of your network connection, as well as the configuration size in your Integration Directory.
- ENTRY_LOCK
  Although this parameter does not impact the performance of your Integration Engine, we must mention it briefly here. By setting a value of 1, you can lock the entire inbound processing of your Exchange Infrastructure. This is recommended especially for extensive changes to or updates of your system. A value of 0 reactivates data reception in your inbound queues.
- LOGGING
  To enable the logging function for asynchronous messages, set this parameter to a value of 1. Logging leads to a reduced performance. Note that deactivated logging is automatically reactivated whenever the logging tag in the diagnostics header of a message is set to 1. For that reason, we recommend that you deactivate the logging function since you can activate it, if necessary, via the diagnostics header and therefore ease up on the average I/O rate of your system.
- LOGGING_SYNC
  This parameter is identical to the *LOGGING* parameter described above with the difference that this parameter affects synchronous messages. Here, too, we recommend that you deactivate logging by default and enable logging only individually through the diagnostics header of the relevant messages, if necessary. Valid values are 1 for enabling and 0 for disabling the logging function.

▶ TRACE_LEVEL

As the name of this parameter implies, it enables you to define the trace level for message processing. The higher the setting of the trace level, the lower the system performance when processing messages. You can set the following values:

Values	Meaning
0	Tracing is deactivated.
1	Important processing steps are documented.
2	Important processing steps and details are documented.
3	All processing steps and details are documented.

5.3 Archiving and Deletion Procedures in XI 3.0

In this section, we introduce you to archiving and deleting messages in XI. A reasonable planning of these two activities is part of an effective and sensible configuration of every XI system. Failure to do so can result in a degradation of performance.

Archiving

In order not to jeopardize performance due to legacy items in your system, you should run a regular archiving job in your system. You can schedule this job in Transaction SXM_ADM (see Figure 5.9).

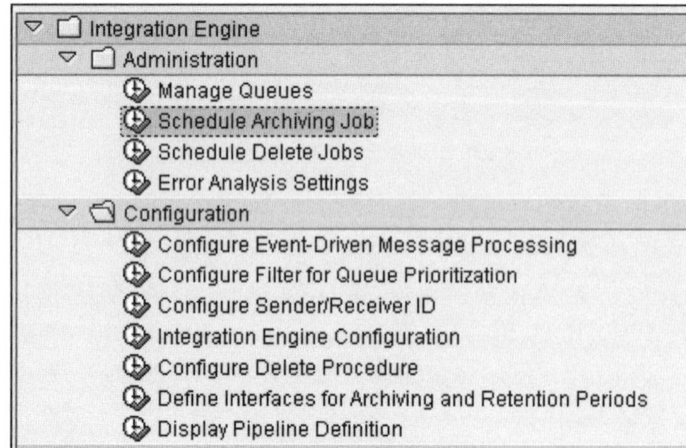

Figure 5.9 Scheduling an Archiving Job

Start the **Schedule Archiving Job** function as shown in Figure 5.9. You can now define the desired degree of parallelization and the user name that should be used by the jobs for archiving your XML messages.

Note that you can specify the number of parallelizations. Archiving jobs will not use dialog processes, which used to be the norm in XI, but instead will use batch processes. Therefore, you should select the possible number of 1–99 based on the available batch processes. With a number of x available batch processes, we recommend that you don't choose the number x, but a maximum of x-1. After scheduling the archiving process, a background job named *SAP_BC_XMB_ARCHIVE* is run that starts the actual archiving sessions.

The possible individual parameters can be set using Transaction SXMB_ADM (**Integration Engine Configuration** category) as described above. For this purpose, select the **Archive** category as shown in Figure 5.10.

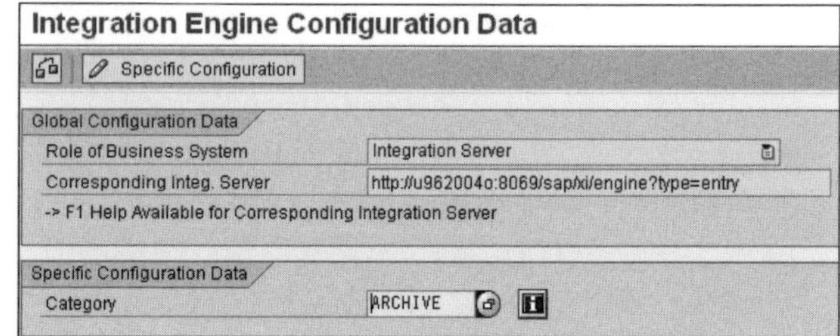

Figure 5.10 Specific Configuration Data—Archive Category

Here you can maintain the following parameters:

▶ PERSIST_DURATION

With this parameter, you define the maximum retention time of your XML messages in your system. SAP defines the retention time as the time during which an asynchronous message is kept in the database after it was successfully processed. If this time is exceeded, this message is archived during the archiving session described above. Via the sending or receiving interface, you can define the messages to be archived. However, please note that all messages that are not marked for archiving will be removed by the deletion job described in the next section. Possible values can be between 1 and 999 days (SP11).

▶ ARCHIVE_PARALLEL

This parameter controls the number of archiving sessions to be started simultaneously. As described above, you can override this value in the dialog. It is

advisable, though, to properly store this value in the parameter. Note that the parameter also controls the number of archives that are written to in parallel. The messages marked for archiving are then distributed among these archives according to this parameter. With regard to performance, this leads to significant improvements the more messages you process with your XI system. As described above, we recommend that you don't use all available batch processes for archiving jobs, because no other batch activities can run on your system during this time.
Possible values can be between 1 and 99.

- **PERSIST_ARCH_MANUAL_CHANGES**
  This parameter is rather interesting for optimizing the archiving behavior for your development or quality assurance systems. If, in a productive system, the processing of a message is terminated for a specific reason or a message is edited manually, you can use this parameter to control the respective behavior. But, this is not really necessary in a test or quality assurance system and would only compromise performance. Therefore, you can influence the behavior of archiving using this parameter. It can take a value of 0 (no) or 1 (yes). A value of 0 means that messages changed manually in a non-productive system will be archived or deleted according to the settings described previously. A value of 1 causes messages that were changed manually, that is, also messages the processing of which was terminated, to be archived.
  In a test and quality assurance system, we recommend a value of 0 and, naturally, a value of 1 for your productive environment.

Deletion Procedure

Similar to scheduling archiving jobs, you can schedule a deletion job (as shown in Figure 5.11), which is controlled using the parameters of Transaction SXM_ADM as well.

After selecting the **Schedule Delete Jobs** node, you can specify the relevant settings for the deletion job as shown in Figure 5.12.

As in normal job scheduling, you determine the start date, the start time, and a periodic limit that specifies the interval in which the deletion job is to be run on your system. This can be days, hours, or even minutes. The default setting is 10 days.

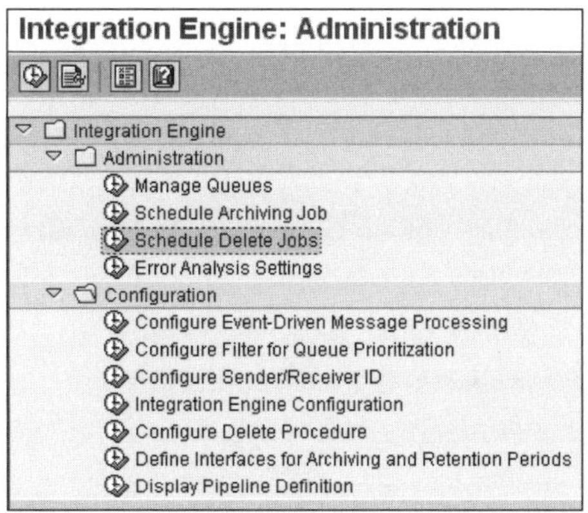

Figure 5.11 Schedule Delete Jobs Menu Function

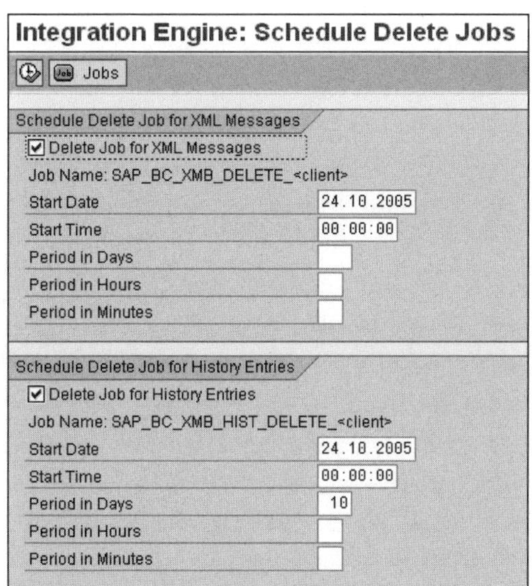

Figure 5.12 Scheduling a Deletion Job

Using the parameter settings of Transaction SXMB_ADM (**Integration Engine Configuration** category) you can set various parameters (like for archiving) in the **Deletion** subcategory to control the deletion behavior. The parameters are used as follows:

- **PERSIST_DURATION (ASYNC and SYNC)**
  Similar to the archiving parameter of the same name, this parameter controls the retention time for synchronous or asynchronous messages, which are processed without errors until they are removed from the system by the deletion job. Otherwise, this parameter is identical to the archiving parameter.

Possible values are 1 to 999 days for asynchronous messages and 0 to 999 days for synchronous messages.

- PERSIST_DURATION (HISTORY)
  This parameter defines the retention time of history entries until the data is eventually deleted. This retention time includes the time during which a history entry of a deleted or archived message is kept in the database after the message has been deleted. The history entry will then be removed by the next session of the history deletion job. Note that history entries are only needed for the IO log (Exactly Once).
  Possible values are between 7 and 999 days.
- PERSIST_DURATION_ERROR
  This parameter defines the maximum retention time for messages that were not properly processed, until they were deleted from the system by the scheduled deletion job. In this case, the retention time is defined as the time during which a message that was processed synchronously is kept in the database after it was incorrectly processed.
  Possible values are between 1 and 999 days.
- DROP_MAX_TABLE_LOAD
  This parameter must be seen in the context of the switch procedure. If you have a rather high number of data to be deleted or archived, SAP allows you to use the switch procedure that affords an improved performance. For every database table involved, SAP delivers an identical table in the standard version. At first, the original tables are the sources of data storing. If messages are scheduled for deletion or archiving, the entry is not deleted from the original table. Instead, just an indicator is set, which marks this message for deletion or archiving, respectively. After a certain fill level defined by the *DROP_MAX_TABLE_LOAD* parameter, the deletion or archiving job determines that a reorganization (switch) is necessary. The table copies are then made the active tables. New data is now written directly to these table copies. Subsequently, the original table is used to determine which data is not marked with a deletion indicator. This data is then taken over into the table copy. After this copy process is finished, the original tables are permanently deleted from the database and then immediately recreated on the system.
  The maximum fill level defined in this parameter refers to the SXMSPMAST table. In the standard version, the "normal" deletion procedure is enabled. This means that the messages are always deleted directly in the original table, which can significantly impact the performance for very high data volumes. To activate the switch procedure, go to Transaction SXMB_ADM (**Integration Engine Configuration** category) and select the **Configure Delete Procedure** entry. This will bring up the dialog shown in Figure 5.13.

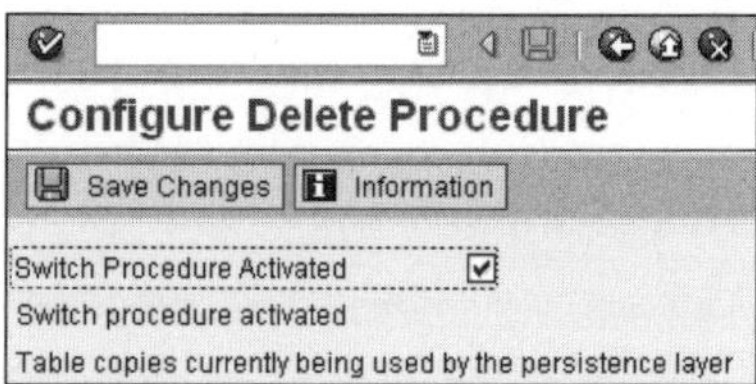

Figure 5.13 Configure Delete Procedure (Switch Procedure)

To enable the switch procedure, you can simply select the option **Switch Procedure Activated**. But, note that the deletion or archiving of messages depends on the clients. This means that you must specify archiving and deletion settings individually for each client. In the switch procedure, however, this is a cross-client parameter. Additionally, although the switch procedure can be easily activated, in order to disable it, you must ensure that the counter for the number of deleted records in the original table is set to 0 if the original tables are active. If this is not the case at that time, the XI system adheres to the administrator's request and will not carry out the changes until the next copy procedure.

The *DROP_MAX_TABLE_LOAD* parameter controls this process by defining the maximum fill level for the master table in %. This behavior can be calculated by multiplying the expected number of entries with the *DROP_MAX_TABLE_LOAD* parameter and dividing it by 100. If this value is smaller than the actual number, a table switch is carried out with a subsequent drop of the original tables. For example, if we expect 1,000 entries and the parameter is set to 50%, a table switch would be carried out as soon as the table reaches a number of 500 entries.

Possible values are between 0 and 100.

- ROWS_PER_LOOP (DELETE, SWITCH)
  Within the XI system, there are two function modules that manage the deletion of messages—one for standard deletion and one for the switch procedure. These modules affect the deletion process via loop control. This parameter specifies how many messages are deleted in one loop. You can set the respective module using the **DELETE** or **SWITCH** subparameters.
  Possible values are between 1 and 999 messages per loop.

5.4 Parameter Settings on the J2EE Side

In this section, we explain two interesting settings on the J2EE side or for the Java Virtual Machine (JVM) of your Exchange Infrastructure, respectively.

J2EE ApplicationThreadManager

The adapter framework running on the J2EE stack requires a fixed number of threads on the J2EE side. The effective number of threads required on the configuration is in your Integration Builder or Integration Directory, respectively. The RFC sender channels and the file adapter channel, for example, need their own threads on the J2EE stack. Therefore, you should proactively increase the number of application threads to a minimum of 250. For this purpose, you must change the *ApplicationThreadManager* parameter value accordingly using the Visual Administrator as shown in Figure 5.14.

Tuning the Java VM

Please ensure that you're using the current version 1.4 of JVM. Another important aspect to consider is setting the correct heap size. In Note 723909, SAP recommends that you start the server nodes with 1 GB each, which, we can attest is accurate, based on our experience. In the performance tests, we ran the server nodes between 512 MB and 1 GB. The tests below 1 GB were not particularly successful.

Furthermore, the maximum and the initial heap sizes should be identical. You can set this using the *-Xmx1024m* and *-Xms1024m* parameters. According to Note 723909, higher values can cause problems. It is therefore recommended that you use additional server nodes instead of an even higher heap size.

The Java Dispatcher can be run at a smaller heap size without incurring problems. We ran the dispatcher with a size of 256 MB in our landscape and didn't encounter any problems. In the note mentioned above, SAP even recommends a size of 170 MB only. It is also recommended that you increase the dispatcher heap by 50 MB per server process if the instance includes more than three server processes. Naturally, your machine should dispose of a sufficient amount of physical main memory to load the heap specifications in the physical area. If you defined specifications that are too high, you strain your system with increased paging activities that result in a re-

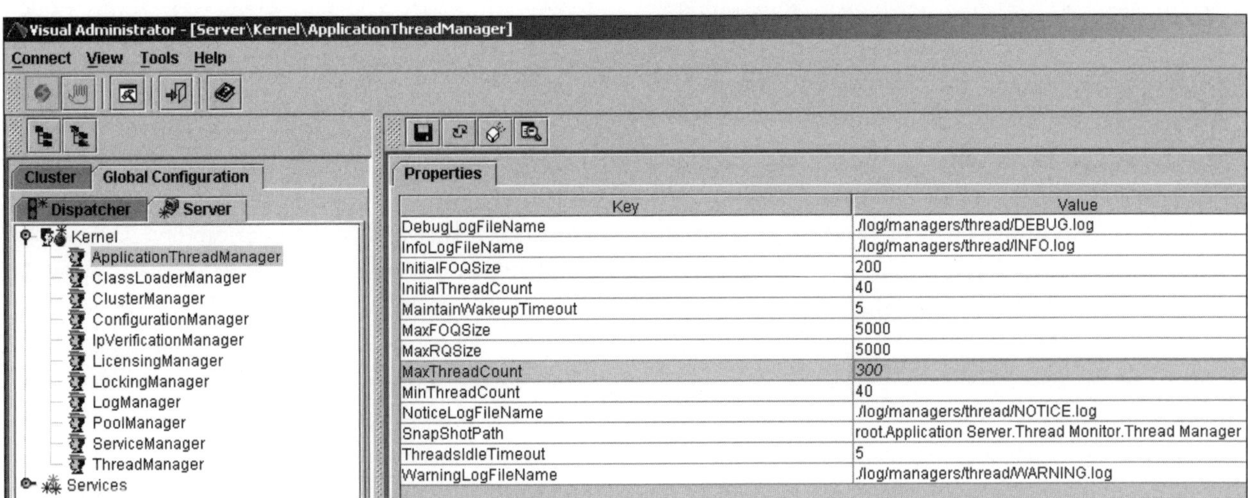

Figure 5.14 ApplicationThreadManager Parameters

ally bad I/O rate. For every JVM on the server, the entire Java memory should fit completely into the physical memory.

Please note that your OS system partially reserves a substantial amount of main memory for monitoring tools. This value should be taken into account when calculating the ideal heap size.

According to SAP, you should also always set the *–verbose:gc* parameter as your default. Since we worked with an HP Itanium server in our scenario, we will now describe the parameter settings based on this hardware. These parameters can be slightly different from other hardware platforms. Please take this into account. The use of a server JVM is definitely recommended. SAP does not recommend using the *–server* or *–client* parameter, respectively, because the J2EE 6.40 startup framework does not accept these parameters. On demand, the JVM type must therefore be entered in the instance profile via the *jstartup/vm/type* entry. The R/3 profile maintenance transaction is not aware of this parameter and therefore it needs to be set manually.

You should also consider that the startup framework loads the server JVM by default if this parameter has not been changed manually beforehand.

The JDK 1.4 also includes several implementations of the garbage collector. The performance of your system on the J2EE side depends to a great extent on the garbage collector. For accelerating the garbarge collections (GCs), SAP recommends their parallelization using the *–XX:+UseParNewGC* parameter. Additionally, the *–XX:+UseConcMarkSweepGC* parameter could improve the performance. After consulting SAP, we did not use this parameter, though, because it caused the JVM to crash according to the note mentioned above (even if it refers to older versions only).

Especially for HP hardware, SAP Note 716926 recommends the following Java parameters:

- *XX:PermSize=192m*
- *XX:MaxPermSize=192m*
- *XX:NewSize=32m*
- *XX:MaxNewSize=64m*

Please note the following: The *–Djava.compiler=NONE* parameter should be removed from the configuration.

Note If you have already installed SP11 on your system and you want to use the XI platform as SAP's NetWeaver Development Infrastructure (NWDI) platform as well, we recommend that you also increase the number of JDBC connections. The default value is 10. A value between 60 and 80 is explicitly recommended in Note 840524 for installations from SP11 onwards.

5.5 Application Tuning

We recommend that you package the messages you're sending to the XI system in chunks of approximately 7 MB, if possible. The package size, however, depends on the hardware and the configuration of your XI system. Therefore, you should carry out performance measurements to determine your ideal package size.

From SP11 onward, XI also supports packaging IDocs within the XI landscape. The problem with systems prior to SP11 was that although IDocs could be sent in packages from the source systems, they were not sent as individual, compiled packages within XI. Now this is possible with SP11 and higher. It increases performance and should definitely be implemented. Therefore, we recommend a timely upgrade of your system to SP11 or more current SP versions so you can use the new packaging functions.

Additionally, you must consider that the XSLT mapping requires more memory for XI mappings than the generated mapping classes of the XI mapping toolkit.

We also recommend that you keep self-developed Java objects as small as possible. The smaller the individual Java objects, the fewer CPU resources are required during garbage collection (GC). As we mentioned in the previous sections, the GC is an important performance indicator for your J2EE platform. For that reason, you should examine the optimum configuration. Detailed information about tuning possibilities for your GCs can be found on the SUN website under *http://java.sun.com/docs/hotspot/*.

Because the tuning measures (finding an ideal parameterization of the GC and the optimum heap size) depend on your version and platform, we will not go into further detail here and suggest instead that you refer to the helpful SUN documentation (see URL above).

6 Central Monitoring in the XI Runtime Workbench

SAP Exchange Infrastructure (SAP XI) monitoring consists of the systemwide monitoring of all components and distributed processes at runtime. That includes the monitoring of the message flow (e.g., with regard to the data throughput) and the analysis and postprocessing for status tracking. Monitoring the processed IDocs and RFC connections for the adapters involved is also part of XI monitoring.

6.1 Types of XI Monitoring

In this chapter, we can only provide you with an overview of the different types of XI monitoring. Figure 6.1 illustrates the structure of XI monitoring, which should help you get an idea of the components it comprises.

XI monitoring provides several types of monitoring. These monitoring types are specific SAP transactions, the Computing Center Management System (CCMS), the web-based applications for message monitoring, component monitoring, alert monitoring (the entire alerting framework), and the performance analysis. The process monitoring infrastructure (PMI) is based on the message monitoring and performance analysis data. The basis for the performance analysis consists of the statistical data of the integration server and the PMI information for message processing. Component monitoring for the runtime itself is part of the CCMS. All this may sound rather confusing, but the purpose of XI monitoring is simple: to monitor all areas of the runtime workbench (RWB), such as engines, applications, adapters, tools, and settings,

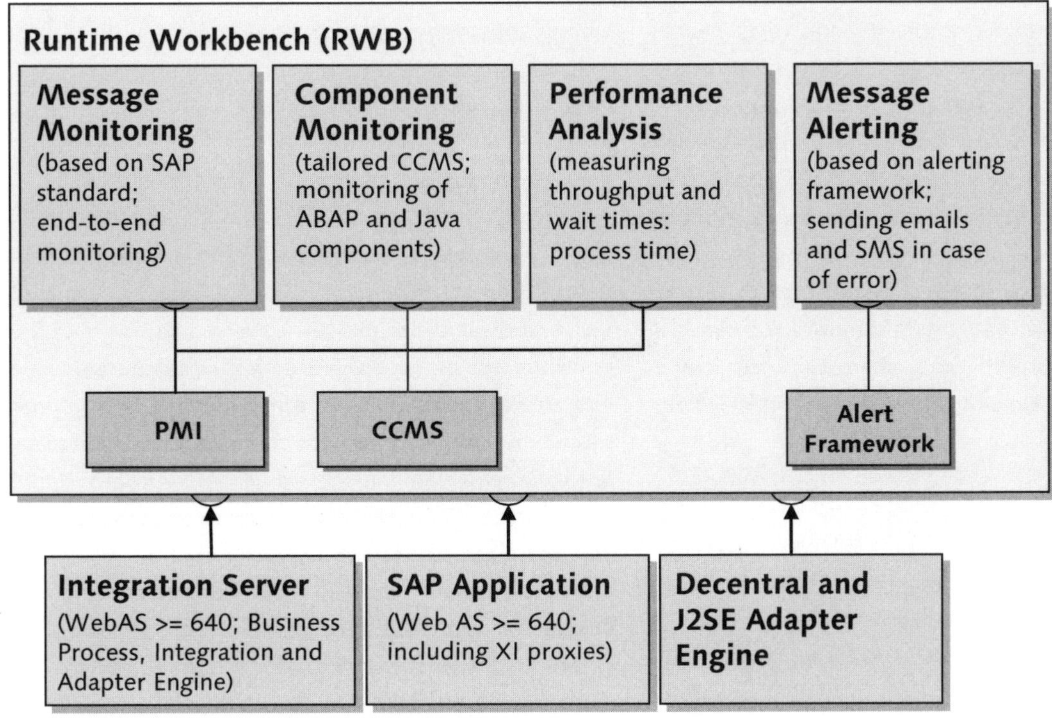

Figure 6.1 Central XI Monitoring

and to analyze the RWB for troubleshooting and performance.

For the activation and configuration of the alerting framework and end-to-end monitoring, you must make various settings in the XI system so that system monitoring is carried out in an event-driven mode and you can ensure that the notification about erroneous statuses actually works.

6.2 Monitoring Requirements and Options

The following parameters must be activated in the exchange profile (administration) for the CCMS monitor, the PMI server, and the alert server:

- *com.sap.aii.rwb.server.centralmonitoring.r3.aashost*
- *com.sap.aii.rwb.server.centralmonitoring.r3.client*
- *com.sap.aii.rwb.server.centralmonitoring.r3.sysnr*
- *com.sap.aii.rwb.server.centralmonitoring.r3.httpport*

For the technical user XIRWBUSER, you must set the following additional parameters for the RWB:

- *com.sap.aii.rwb.serviceuser.name*
- *com.sap.aii.rwb.serviceuser.pwd*
- *com.sap.aii.rwb.serviceuser.language*

Moreover, the Internet Transaction Server (ITS) plug-in must run on the integration server and the central monitoring server so that you can call CCMS Transaction RZ20 via ITS from the web-based message monitoring. You can check the service status via Transaction SICF.

SAP also points out that the profile parameter *em/global_area* must be set to 128 for the ITS operations to function properly. To check the current values, call Transaction SA38 and view the `RSPARAM` report. You can easily determine the currently set system profile parameter by using the search function in that report.

Note The relevant services for end-to-end and alert monitoring can be automatically started using the RSXMB_ACTIVATE_ICF_ SERVICES report. Start this program via Transaction SE38/SE80 and make the settings listed in Table 6.1.
You can also start the services manually via Transaction SICF.

Function	Path to service
ITS plug-in	/sap/bc/gui/sap/ist/webgui
End-to-end monitoring	/sap/bc/bsp/sap/spi_monitor /sap/bc/bsp/sap/spi_admin /sap/public/bsp/sap/public/graphics/jnet_handler /sap/public/bsp/sap/public/graphics/mimes /sap/bc/bsp/sap/public/graphics /sap/bc/graphics/net /sap/bc/bsp/sap/graph_bsp_test /sap/bc/bsp/sap/graph_bsp_test/mimes
Alert monitoring	/sap/bc/bsp/sap/alertinbox /sap/bc/bsp/sap/sxms_alertrules /sap/bc/bsp/sap/system /sap/bc/bsp/sap/public/bc /sap/public/bsp/sap/public/bc /sap/public/bsp/sap/system /sap/public/bsp/sap/htmlb /sap/public/bc/icons /sap/public/bc/icons_rtl /sap/public/bc/ur

Table 6.1 Services for End-to-End and Alert Monitoring

Note You can easily find the services by using the search help (above the tree structure).

SAP Note 768456—*Troubleshooting Runtime Workbench XI 3.0*—contains a list of known error sources and provides information on the following topics:

- Configuration Guide
- Settings in the Exchange Profile
- Service in Transaction SICF
- Login Modules

Please assign the relevant authorizations to your monitoring users. All the monitoring programs, transactions, and web applications described in the following sections are integrated in the predefined authorization roles (see Chapter 4). It is advisable to assign all those roles to your monitoring users. Later, you can restrict the authorizations at any time.

Transaction SLDCHECK verifies the consistency of the Service Landscape Directory (SLD) and generates a comprehensive log file. You should call this program on a regular basis to monitor the current status of your SLD.

The XI system contains various monitoring programs. A very important transaction is SXMB_MONI, *Integration*

Engine Monitoring, which provides several useful tools for analyzing the message flow.

Once you have executed Transaction SXMB_MONI, you can start several analysis, check, and correction programs (see Figure 6.2).

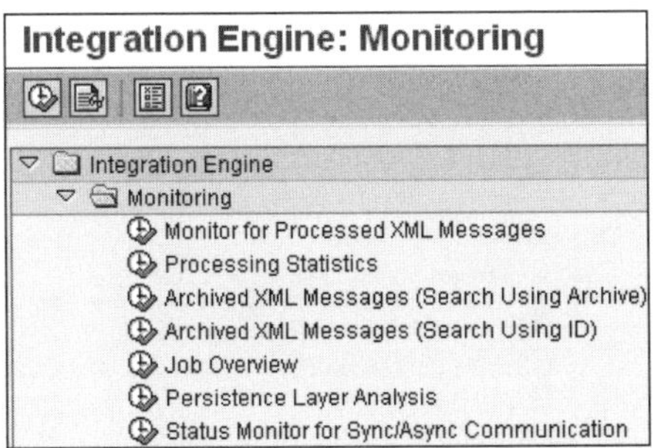

Figure 6.2 Integration Engine: Monitoring

For example, Transaction SXI_MONITOR, which can be executed via the **Monitor for Processed XML Messages** tree node, enables you to analyze messages precisely, troubleshoot errors, and restart the processing after you have completed the corrective action.

Run the program by double-clicking on the tree node **Monitor for Processed XML Messages**. In the selection screen that opens, enter an earlier date so that a hit list of processed messages can be created.

Figure 6.3 displays the processed messages and the corresponding status.

Figure 6.3 Monitor for Processed XML Messages

To analyze the occurring errors, you must accurately check the relevant status icons for the message confirmation and the acknowledgement of receipt. These icons are displayed in the first two columns of the list.

Figure 6.4 shows an excerpt from the status icon legend.

Status Icon Legend

Message Status

Icon	Meaning
	Message processed Message already processed Message with errors canceled Message Recorded (Commit Missing) Branching: Multiple receivers found
	System Error (Restart Possible) System Error - Restart Not Possible Application Error (Restart Possible) No receiver found
	Message Recorded (Commit follows) Scheduled for outbound processing Message is in automatic retry mode Manual Restart for Version Message changed manually
	Acknowledgment message stopped
	Message transferred to Process Engine
o	Log Version

Figure 6.4 Legend: XI Message Status

In most cases, the status helps you to identify the cause of the problem, that is, to find out which problem caused the message processing to abort. For some status icons, the corresponding short description even provides information on how to proceed from that point forward. A double-click on a message row (beginning with the third column) provides detailed information on the message processing for analysis.

For this purpose, SAP has developed a specific maintenance and display interface that enables you to analyze the individual steps of the pipeline per message (message sequence flow) in a screen that's divided into several separate areas. In addition, SAP provides you with an option to correct errors. If you click on the **Restart** button, you can restart the message processing (see Figure 6.5). Additional options for checking and analysis are provided by Transactions SXMB_MONI_BPE (Business Process Engine Monitoring), S_B6A_52000011 (CCMS: Exchange Infrastructure), and IDX5 (Adapter Monitoring).

For the runtime workbench (integration monitoring), SAP provides the following web-based options:

- Component monitoring
- Message monitoring
- Configuration/end-to-end monitoring

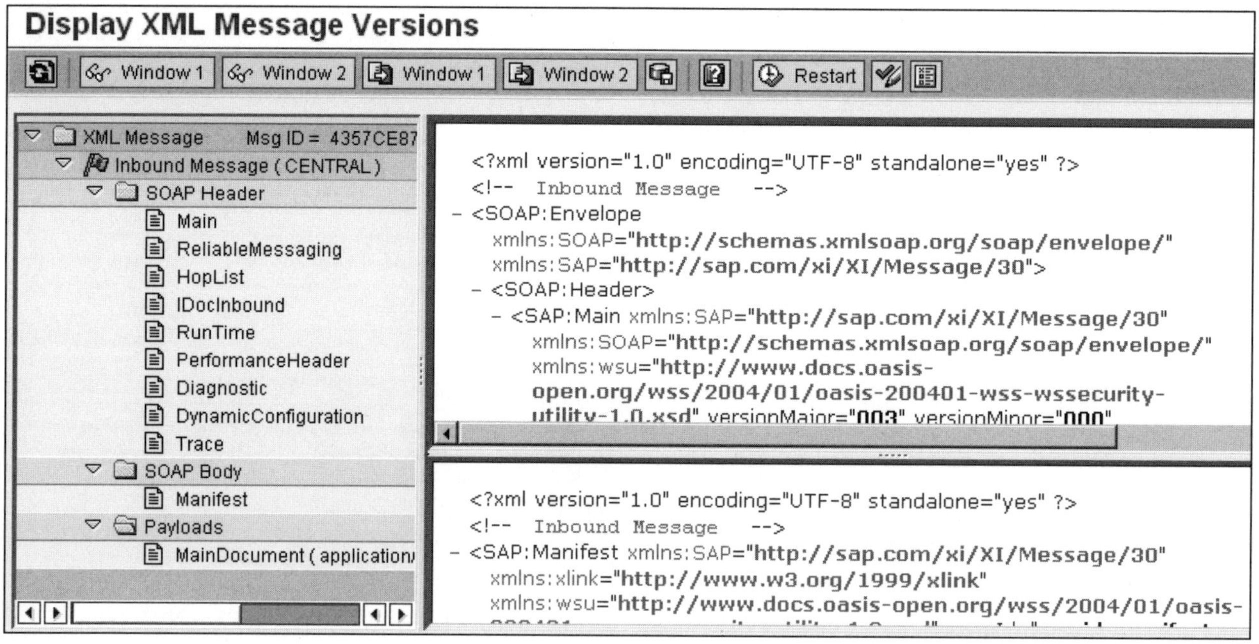

Figure 6.5 Message Sequence Flow Analysis and Correction

- Performance monitoring
- Alert configuration/alert inbox
- Cache monitoring

You must always start the integration monitoring (*http://[Hostname]:[Port]/rep/start/index.jsp*) from the runtime workbench (see Figure 6.6).

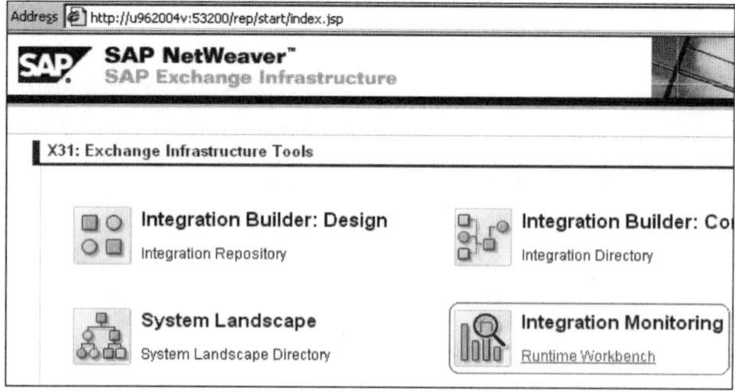

Figure 6.6 Runtime Workbench—Initial Page (Monitoring)

6.3 Component Monitoring

Figure 6.7 displays the web-based component monitoring in the runtime workbench.

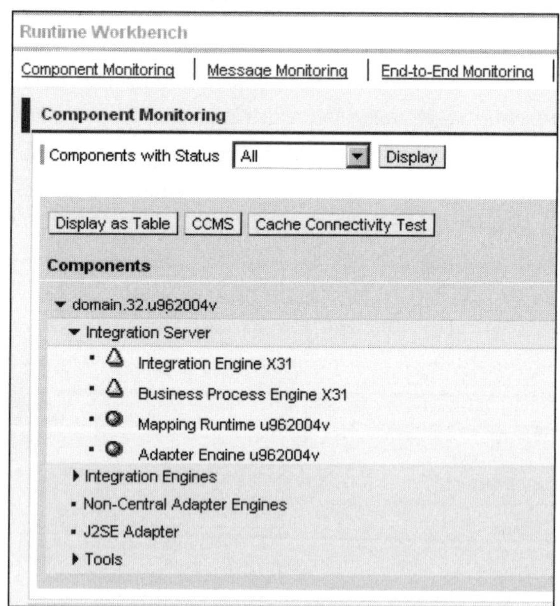

Figure 6.7 Component Monitoring

Component monitoring is used to perform the following checking activities:

- You can check the status of individual XI components of the SAP Exchange Infrastructure Runtime Workbench (integration server, integration engines, decentral adapters, J2SE adapters, and tools) and perform a "dead-or-alive" test.

- You can check the component settings (archive, deletion, IDoc, monitor, RFC adapters, RFC system information, runtime, SA_COMM, and tuning).
- You can send a test message to check the functionality of the XI runtime environment and to verify whether the message flow is functioning.
- You can check whether the SLD can be accessed and you can display the consistency of roles in SXMS_CONF_ITEMS and in the SLD.
- You can check whether the integration engine knows its business systems and whether the web service security has been properly configured.

CCMS monitoring can be operated either via Transaction RZ20 or as a web-based service via the RWB. In the latter case, Transaction RZ20 is called via the ITS and Web GUI. To be able to call the integrated CCMS, you must activate the relevant services for the ITS and Web GUI in Transaction SICF—*Service Maintenance*.

For the CCMS of the Exchange Infrastructure, you must then set up the specific configuration data via Transaction SXMB_ADM—*Integration Engine: Administration*.

When you start Transaction SXMB_ADM, the system displays a selection list of configuration tools for the integration engine. Click on the tree node **Configure Integration Engine** to configure the CCMS monitoring.

Figure 6.8 displays the corresponding configuration application.

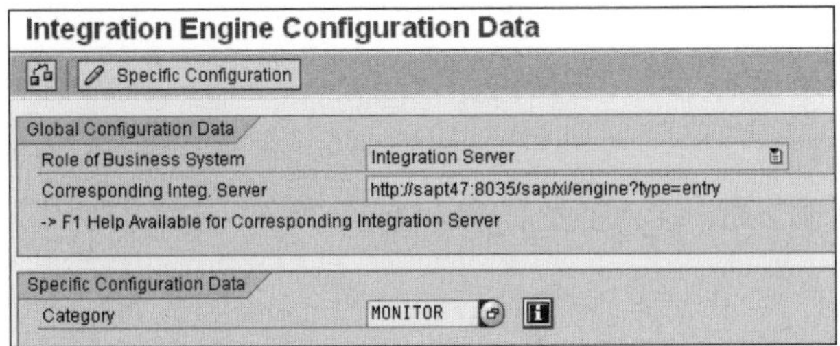

Figure 6.8 Configuring Exchange Infrastructure Monitoring

First, you must check the currently existing integration engine by clicking on the **Check** button. The check result shouldn't contain any information on errors. In the **Category** field of the selection screen, you must select the relevant configuration. In our example, this is the **Monitor** configuration.

Note The **Information** button next to the **Category** field provides important information on the parameters to be set.

Then click on the **Specific Configuration** pushbutton. A table is displayed, as shown in Figure 6.9.

Change View "Configuration of the Integration Engine"...

New Entries

Current Configuration

Do	Category	Parameters	Subparameter	Prefix	Current Value	Default Va
	MONITOR	CCMS_APPLERROR_ALERT			3	7
	MONITOR	CCMS_MONITORING			1	1
	MONITOR	PMI_MONITORING				1
	MONITOR	QRFC_RESTART_ALLOWED			0	0

Figure 6.9 Activating Exchange Infrastructure Monitoring and Maintaining the Parameters

Enter the possible values by using the category information and set the CCMS_MONITORING parameter to the value 1. This completes the CCMS monitoring activation.

There are several views available for selecting the check functions. You can display the status in the tree or table view.

6.4 Message Monitoring

In the XI system, this type of monitoring can be performed either via Transaction SXMB_MONI or as a web-based service via the integration monitoring RWB (see Figure 6.10).

The integration engine connects different application systems via the XML data transfer (messaging). XI uses an SAP-specific implementation of the Simple Object Access Protocol (SOAP) protocol. Messages received on the integration server run through a defined sequence of individual steps, which is called the pipeline service. When the integration server receives a message, these messages are checked, and all valid configurations are carried out for them, including those that are maintained in the Integration Directory.

Message monitoring is used to perform the following checking activities:

- To trace the status of a message (XML messages)
- To find the causes of errors
- To check the message throughput rate

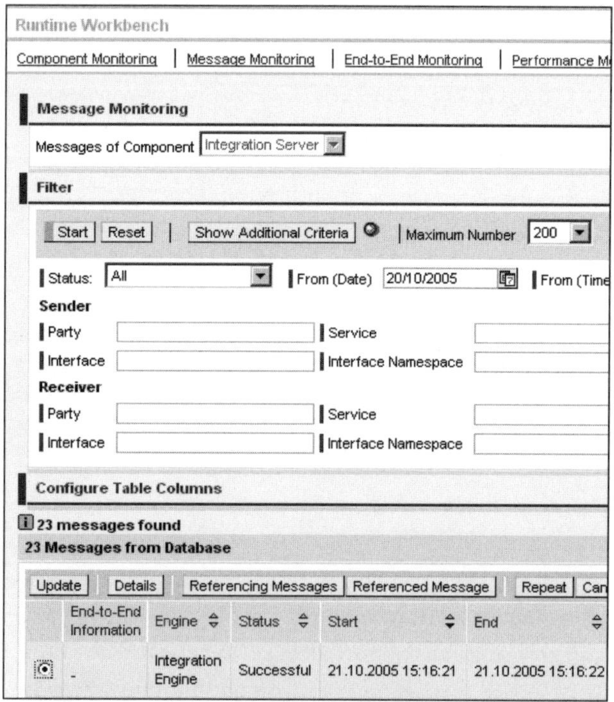

Figure 6.10 Message Monitoring

- To obtain an overview of archived and deleted jobs (integration engine)
- To analyze the persistence layer
- To obtain an overview of synchronous and asynchronous communications

Thus, this type of monitoring focuses extensively on the XML message flow. The monitor identifies and evaluates all XML messages that have been processed by the integration engine, and generates flow statistics based on that information. The messages can be selected and displayed according to specific criteria.

Here too, you can use Transaction SXI_MONITOR—Monitor for Processed XML Messages—to display the message data in short form in the XI system and, if necessary, to restart the message processing. You can also navigate through the detail screen to end-to-end monitoring.

6.5 End-to-end Monitoring

This type of monitoring is also a web-based service and is performed through the integration monitoring runtime workbench (see Figure 6.11).

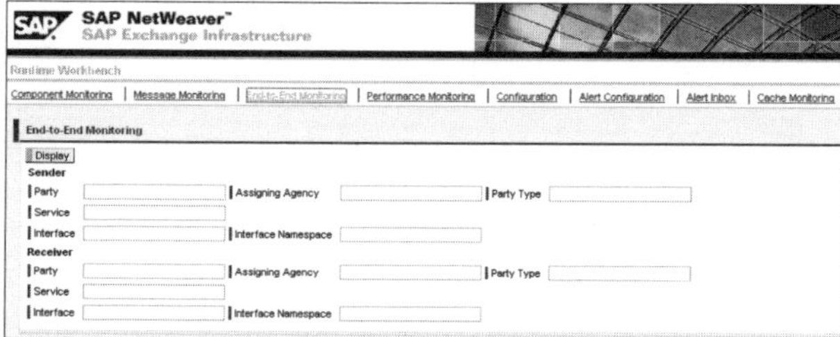

Figure 6.11 End-to-End Monitoring

End-to-end monitoring is used to perform the following checking activities:

- To monitor the message process step-by-step per component (i.e., to determine the status of IT components and processes)
- To observe the path of individual messages through the components (from start to end)
- To locate the origin or responsible cause of errors precisely within the process chain
- To reduce the response times
- To achieve an improvement in the software quality
- To determine performance bottlenecks as quickly as possible

For monitoring, you must activate the http service required for the CCMS and the process monitoring infrastructure (PMI) in the XI system via Transaction SICF or by using the specific program `RSXMB_ACTIVATE_ICF_SERVICES`. When the program is called again, all traffic lights in the log should be *green*.

The section on component monitoring contains a description of the necessary configuration via Transaction SXMB_ADM. Please make the settings in accordance with the provided descriptions, if you haven't already done that.

On the home page of your XI system, go to the **Runtime Workbench** category and select the menu item **Configuration**. The system now displays the configuration menu, as shown in Figure 6.12.

In the configuration menu, you can activate the different component types that you want to monitor in end-to-end monitoring, and you can set the relevant monitoring levels. For ALE-based components, you must also set the corresponding receiver port.

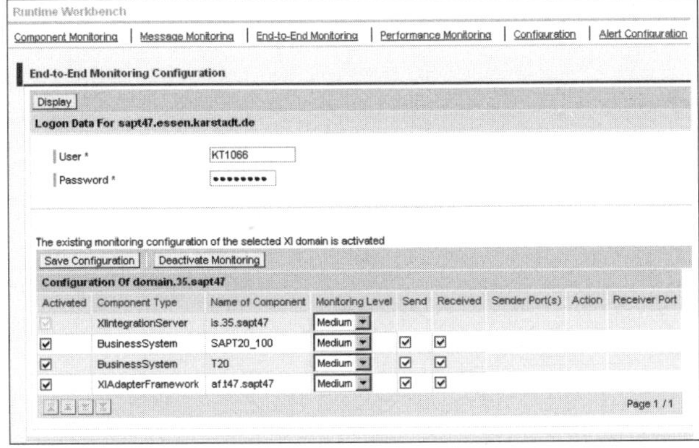

Figure 6.12 Configuring End-to-End Monitoring

The monitoring level defines tracking agents that must be active for each component and what kind of monitoring data the active agents are supposed to provide. You can find detailed descriptions of the agents and the configuration in the SAP PRESS Essentials books *Conception and Installation of System Monitoring Using the SAP Solution Manager* and *Java Monitoring Infrastructure in SAP NetWeaver '04* (SAP PRESS 2005).

Please note that if you have already activated Single-Sign-On (SSO) in your system, you can ignore the logon data displayed in Figure 6.12. For this figure we explicitly deactivated SSO to display the **User** and **Password** fields at this stage.

After selecting the components to be monitored we navigate to the **End-to-End Monitoring** function. The dialog contains the **Further Settings...** function, as you can see in Figure 6.13.

Click on the link to execute that function. The system now displays a new dialog where you can specify the update frequency of your process monitoring data.

Figure 6.14 displays a sample dialog.

As you can see in Figure 6.14, you can directly trigger monitoring by clicking on the **Start now** button. On the other hand, you can also deactivate monitoring by using the **Deactivate Monitoring** button. The **Details** tab contains information on the following subjects:

1. Resource management (maximum number of dialog processes)
2. Orientation values for the process (e.g., number of process instances)

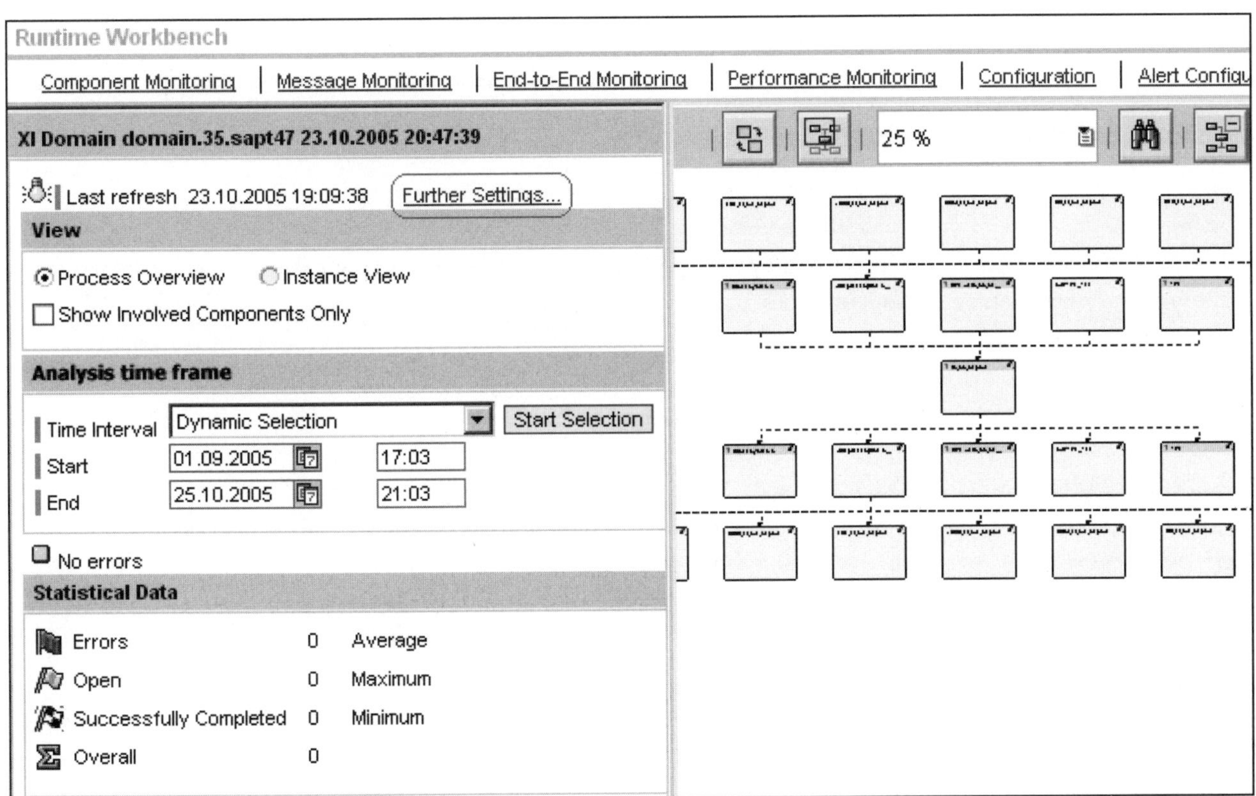

Figure 6.13 End-to-End Monitoring—Further Settings

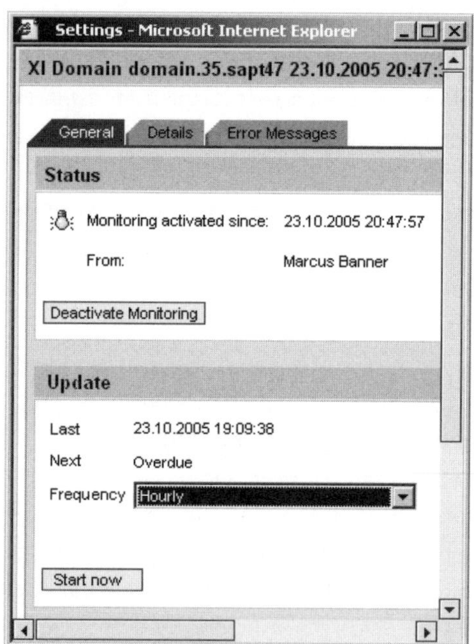

Figure 6.14 End-to-End Monitoring—Settings Dialog

3. Settings for the reorganization (e.g., minimum retention period for processes)

The **Error Messages** tab provides an overview of the latest error messages. The **Logging** function enables you to navigate to further details.

Figure 6.15 displays a sample dialog for the **Details** function.

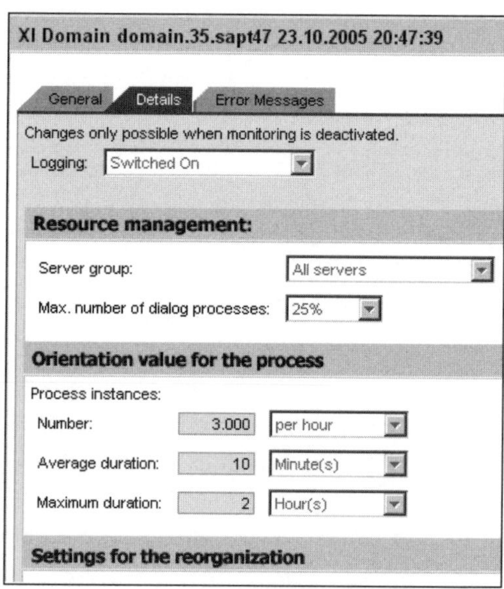

Figure 6.15 End-to-End Monitoring—Settings Dialog, Details

Moreover, in the runtime workbench, you must explicitly define a destination called *pmistore* for each adapter engine. Normally, this should have happened during system installation. The installation guide of SAP NetWeaver '04 contains a brief step-by-step description of how you can

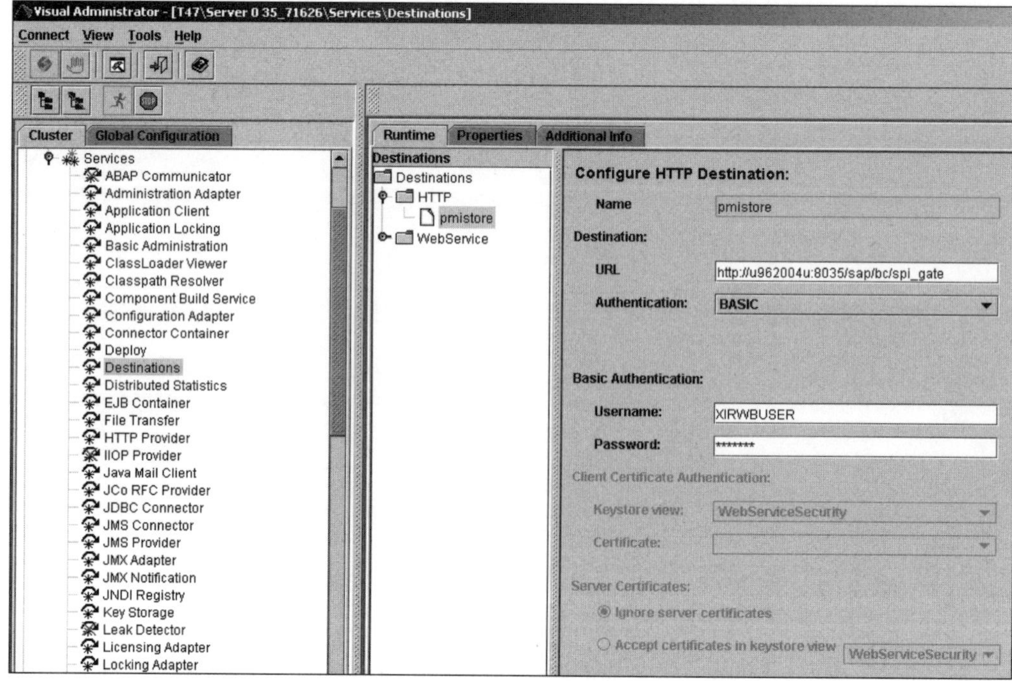

Figure 6.16 End-to-End Monitoring—pmistore in Visual Administrator

create the *pmistore* destination using the Visual Administrator. For this reason, we'll only touch on the necessary steps.

First you must use the Visual Administrator to log on to your J2EE server. Change to the **Destinations** service in the left-hand pane of the screen. The system now displays the dialog shown in Figure 6.16.

Then create a new http destination called *pmistore* in this dialog. Select the **BASIC** value as **Authentication** and enter XIRWBUSER in the **Username** field. The destination URL has the following structure: *http://<yourserver>:<ABAP-Port>/sap/bc/spi_gate*. If you don't know the ABAP port of your system, you can use Transaction SMICM in R/3 to call the **Services** function. Now you can determine the http port of your system (see Figure 6.17).

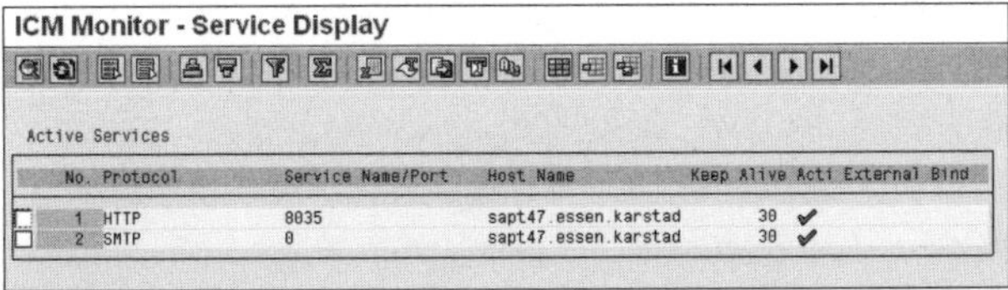

Figure 6.17 End-to-End Monitoring—Displaying the HTTP Port in R/3

The runtime workbench receives the end-to-end monitoring data from the process monitoring infrastructure. The PMI is another SAP option that enables you to monitor technical end-to-end processes that involve several components. You can also perform PMI monitoring via CCMS Transaction RZ20. Based on the PMI data for the individual process steps, end-to-end monitoring provides the following views:

- Process overview
- Instance view

In the process overview, all processed messages as well as all erroneous messages are displayed for each component with a corresponding status indication in different colors. Conversely, the instance view displays the path of a specific message through the involved components. For each process step, the administrator obtains detail data. Figure 6.18 displays a sample dialog.

6.6 Performance Monitoring

In the XI system, performance monitoring can either be launched via Transaction RZ20 or as a web-based service

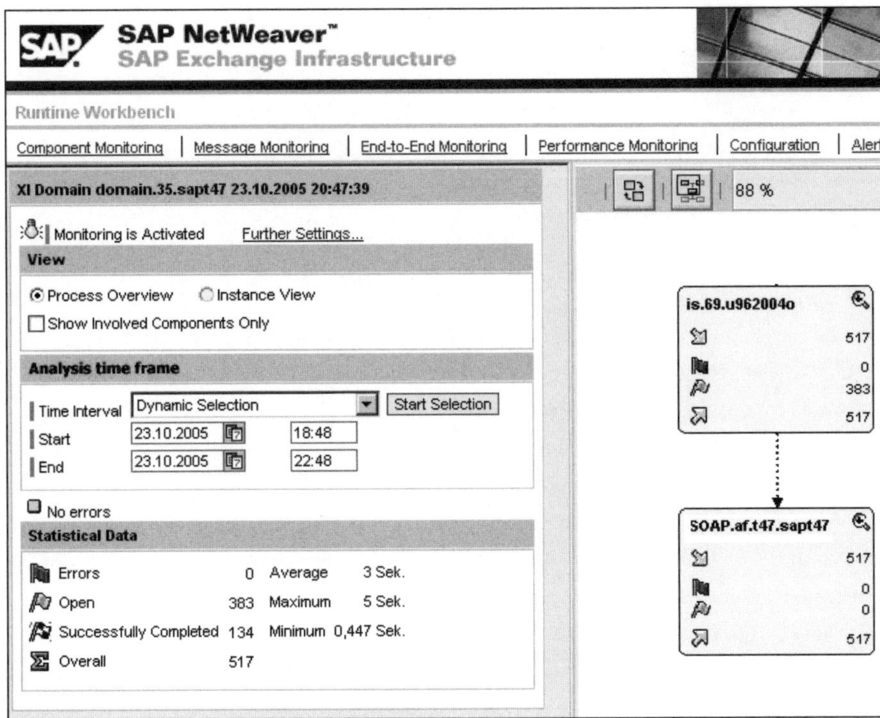

Figure 6.18 End-to-End Monitoring Configuration

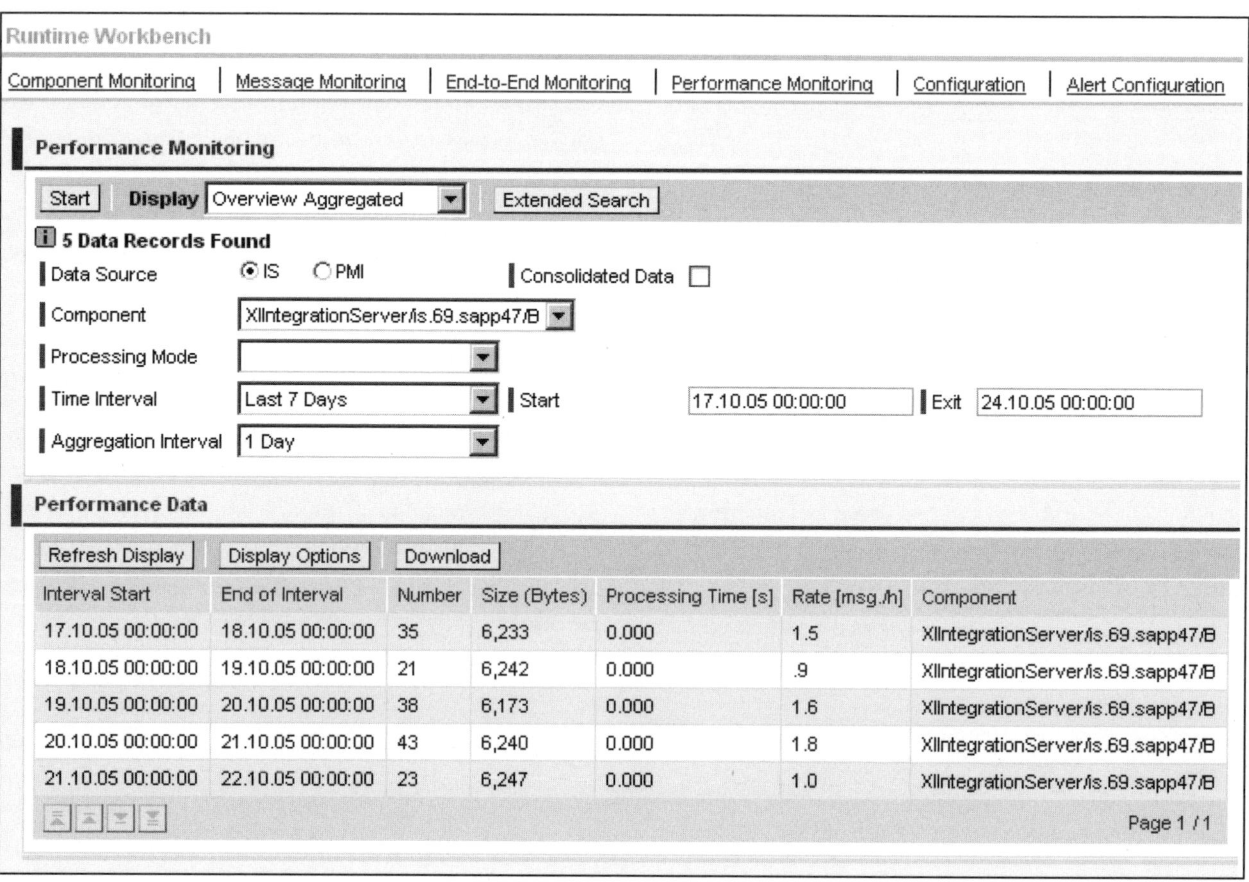

Figure 6.19 Performance Monitoring

via the integration monitoring runtime workbench (see Figure 6.19).

Performance monitoring is used to perform the following checking activities:

- To obtain an aggregated overview of the message process data
- To obtain an overview of individual message process data
- To obtain an aggregated overview of the message process detail data on the performance (throughput)
- To obtain an overview of individual message process detail data on the performance (throughput)

The statistical data provided by the integration server, or the data provided by the PMI for message processing, forms the basis for the performance process analysis.

Table ALXMBPFALERT provides additional monitoring options. You can maintain this table via Transaction SM30 and store alert threshold values for the interface processing performance measurement in it. Store the necessary technical details and specify the threshold value for triggering yellow and red alerts in milliseconds. SAP Note 730193 contains detailed information on this table.

6.7 Alert Monitoring

A web-based alert configuration and receipt of alert messages is possible. Figure 6.20 shows the web-based access to alert messages.

Alert monitoring is related to all other monitoring types described so far and it is used to display defined error statuses, to send alert messages to the alert inbox, and via email and SMS (Alert Inbox Transaction ALRTINBOX).

SAP provides excellent documentation to support the installation of alert management (ALM) on your XI system. You can find a detailed description of alert management in the document *Forwarding Alerts to Alert Manage-*

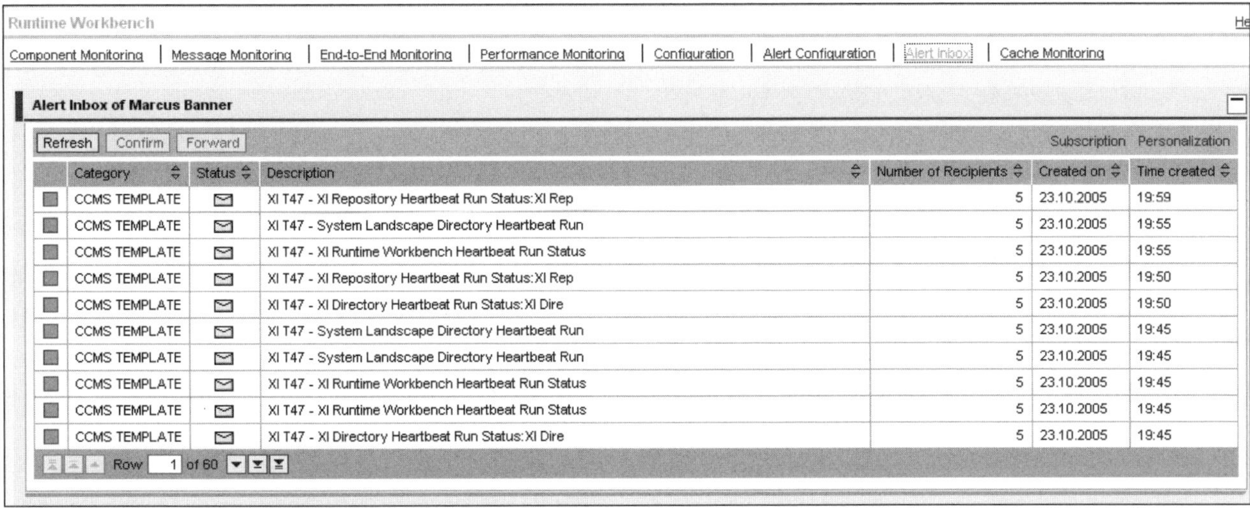
Runtime Workbench

Component Monitoring | Message Monitoring | End-to-End Monitoring | Performance Monitoring | Configuration | Alert Configuration | Alert Inbox | Cache Monitoring

Alert Inbox of Marcus Banner

Refresh | Confirm | Forward — Subscription Personalization

	Category	Status	Description	Number of Recipients	Created on	Time created
	CCMS TEMPLATE		XI T47 - XI Repository Heartbeat Run Status:XI Rep	5	23.10.2005	19:59
	CCMS TEMPLATE		XI T47 - System Landscape Directory Heartbeat Run	5	23.10.2005	19:55
	CCMS TEMPLATE		XI T47 - XI Runtime Workbench Heartbeat Run Status	5	23.10.2005	19:55
	CCMS TEMPLATE		XI T47 - XI Repository Heartbeat Run Status:XI Rep	5	23.10.2005	19:50
	CCMS TEMPLATE		XI T47 - XI Directory Heartbeat Run Status:XI Dire	5	23.10.2005	19:50
	CCMS TEMPLATE		XI T47 - System Landscape Directory Heartbeat Run	5	23.10.2005	19:45
	CCMS TEMPLATE		XI T47 - System Landscape Directory Heartbeat Run	5	23.10.2005	19:45
	CCMS TEMPLATE		XI T47 - XI Runtime Workbench Heartbeat Run Status	5	23.10.2005	19:45
	CCMS TEMPLATE		XI T47 - XI Runtime Workbench Heartbeat Run Status	5	23.10.2005	19:45
	CCMS TEMPLATE		XI T47 - XI Directory Heartbeat Run Status:XI Dire	5	23.10.2005	19:45

Row 1 of 60

Figure 6.20 Alert Inbox

ment (ALM) under the *Monitoring* link in SAP Service Marketplace (*http://service.sap.com/monitoring*, *Monitoring in Detail* folder).

Figure 6.21 provides a relatively simple and clear overview of alert management.

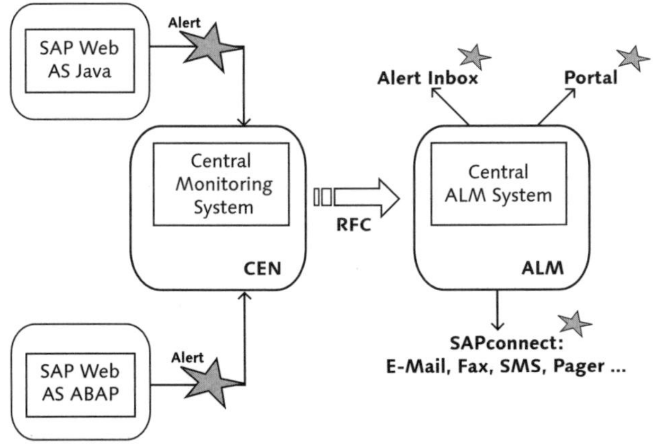

Figure 6.21 Central ALM System

All alerts are centrally collected and triggered in the CEN (client 000), and then sent via RFC to the central ALM system (work client). The ALM system client then sends the alert data for instance to the alert inbox, the portal, and via email to the specified administrators.

For a functioning ALM, the following configuration steps must be performed upfront (without using the CCMS agent):

1. Check the status of your support package: CEN or central monitoring is only possible from support package status SAPKB64009 of the SAP Basis component. For Basis release 6.20, you need support package status SAPKB62030.
2. Activate the central system dispatching via Transaction RZ21 on client 000. Call Transaction RZ21 and carry out the activation via the following path: **Technical Infrastructure • Configure Central System • Activate Central System Dispatching**.
3. Activate background dispatching for all systems to be monitored and for the CEN on client 000. Call Transaction RZ21 and carry out the activation via the following path: **Technical Infrastructure • Local Method Execution • Activate Background Dispatching**.
4. Activate the *alert inbox* service via Transaction SICF (**Default_host • sap • bc • bsp • sap • alert inbox**).
5. Create an RFC user with the role assignment SAP_BC_ALM_ALERT_USER in the XI work client (in our example, client 100) via Transaction SU01. Possibly the SAP role wasn't previously generated. In that case, you must first create it via Transaction PFCG.
6. Create an RFC connection on client 000 via Transaction SM59. Enter the previously created RFC user in the **Logon/Security** tab. Check the remote connection to the work client and the authorizations in the connections maintenance menu (path **Test • Authorization**).

7. Enter the previously created RFC connection to the work client in client 000 via Transaction SALRT1, *RFC Dest. of Alert Server*. The RFC destination must be specified even if the CEN and the alert management (ALM) are located in the same client.
8. In order to be able to send e-mails, faxes, and SMS, you must perform the SAPconnect configuration on the work client (Transaction SCOT etc.). You can find information on that configuration in SAP Support Portal (*http://service.sap.com*) in the **SAP Notes Search** web interface under the topic BC-SRV-COM.
9. Call Transaction RZ21 in the work client. Go to the **Methods** group box and select the radio button **Method definitions**. Click on the **Overview** button. Search for the `CCMS_Send_Alert_to_ALM_V2` method (up to and including support package status 11, you must search for the method `CCMS_Send_Alert_to_ALM`). Copy the method into the customer-specific namespace (e.g., `ZXI_CCMS_Send_Alert_to_ALM_V2`).
10. Double-click on the copied method. Check whether the **Any server** radio button is activated. If it isn't, activate it now.
11. Go to the **Parameters** tab, where we have specified the following values:

Parameter name	Parameter value
CATEGORY	CCMS TEMPLATE
TIME_ZONE	CET
REACT_ON_ALERTS	<optional>
SUBJECT_ALERT	XI-$SID–$NODENAME
SUBJECT_ALERT_CONT	XI-CCMS error message

OSS Note 796998 contains more details on the parameter maintenance. We didn't create a new category and entered the standard SAP category *CCMS TEMPLATE* instead.

12. The copy process caused the release to be deactivated. Therefore, click on the **Release** tab and select the radio button **Auto-reaction method** in the group box **Execute method as**. Once you have saved your entry, the auto-reaction method is activated for the method execution.
13. Schedule Report `SXMSALERT_PROCESS_DATA_GET` on the work client (periodically every 30 minutes) so that you are informed about new alerts when they occur. To schedule the job, you must possess the SAP_XI_ADMINISTRATOR role.

Now you can store the copied and customized method `ZXI_CCMS_Send_Alert_to_ALM_V2` in any node in the CCMS (Transaction RZ20), for example, for the immediate dispatch of alerts and email. We did this in our XI system for the GRMG (Java monitoring). In the following section, *Configuring Java Monitoring (GRMG)*, we'll provide a brief example to describe how you can store the auto-reaction method.

For alert management, you must make additional settings in the work client. To do that, you can use Transaction ALRTCATDEF in the XI work client. In our XI system, this is client 100.

Note If the central alert server runs on the local system, you don't need to maintain an RFC connection. Simply enter NONE in Transaction SALRT1.

For authorizations, you can specify the following roles:

- SAP_BC_ALM_CUST for the entire application-specific customizing
- SAP_BC_ALM_ADMIN for the administrative activities to be performed and for the tools
- SAP_BC_ALM_ALERT_USER for the alert box or the external communication via RFC (email, SMS, fax)

Alert configuration is predominantly carried out via Transaction ALRTCATDEF, *Defining an Alert Category in the Work Client* (or web-based via *http://[hostname]:[portnumber]/rwb/index.jsp* Alert Configuration).

Once all the requirements have been met and you have entered a recipient for a specific category (e.g., *CCMS TEMPLATE*), all XI system alert messages will be stored in your alert inbox. The alert messages are triggered when an error occurs in the CCMS (caused by a job), by clicking on a link, when a function module is used, or by the post processing framework (PPF). What is most important is that the RFC destination has been maintained for the central alert server in Transaction SALRT1 (client 000). SAP provides a sample report called

RSALERTDEMO1 that you can use to trigger your own defined alert events (SALERT_LOCAL package). You can copy that program into the customer-specific namespace to define objects with the respective properties for events that can then be triggered through the function module. In Transaction SWE2, you can store the event triggering for the alert category, the recipient type, for function module SALRT_CREATE_VIA_EVENT, and for the receiver function model in the XI system.

In the alert configuration, you can define restrictive alerting rules via Transaction SXMSALRT, for example, regarding the alert categories that are supposed to notify you about errors. You can also perform this setting on the web via *http://[hostname]:[portnumber]/rwb/index.sp Alert Configuration*.

You can use Transaction ALRTCATDEF to make additional settings in the work client (see Figure 6.22).

For central monitoring (CEN), we have stored the category *CCMS TEMPLATE* when we entered the parameters for the auto-reaction method. The texts for the alerts are dynamically generated by the stored parameterization in the auto-reaction method. For this reason, you must activate the **Dynamic Text** checkbox (see Figure 6.22).

To activate the escalation, you must schedule Report RSALERTPROC as a job. For that job, you must create a report variant and activate the **Escalate** option. Only then can the required escalation to the specified person be performed at a predefined time in Transaction ALRTCATDEF. Moreover, you need this program for reorganization purposes and for the multiple dispatch of unconfirmed alerts. You should therefore create several variants of this report for the job scheduling.

Transaction SA38 provides the following additional tools (reports):

- RSALERTDISP (this report includes display and deletion tools)
- RSALERTTEST (using a test alert with or without addition)
- The alert category maintenance (see Figure 6.22) provides the following additional options:
- You can use the **Fixed Recipients** button to specify individual users for the alert messages.
- You can store authorization roles by using the **Recipients Via User Roles** button. This function enables you to implement a distributed dispatch of alerts to specific users. For example, you can specify that all

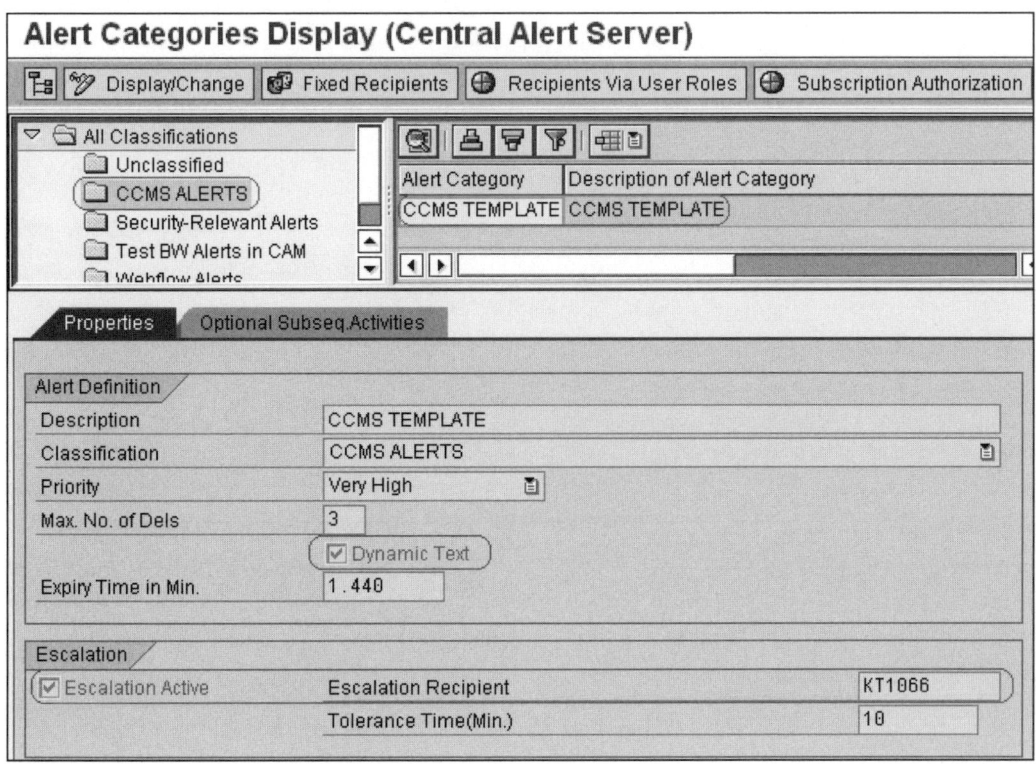

Figure 6.22 Maintaining Alert Categories

users with the role SAP_ALM_ADMINISTRATOR are to receive alerts and emails.

- You can use the **Subscription Authorization** button to determine who is allowed to subscribe to a specific category in the alert box. In this way, the user can access different alert categories via a subscription. That can be done in the alert inbox of the runtime workbench. When a user subscribes to a new alert category, the system automatically enters that user into the list of recipients. But that can only happen if the subscription role has been stored in the user master record of that user.

You can call the alert inbox either on the web via *http://[hostname]:[portnumber]/rwb/index.jsp* · *Alert Inbox* or via Transaction ALRTINBOX.

There you can view the content of the error messages and confirm the alert after checking or troubleshooting an error. Furthermore, the alert inbox contains the function to forward an alert message. The personalization function enables you to assign a substitute or restrict the period in which you can or want to process alerts (see Figure 6.23).

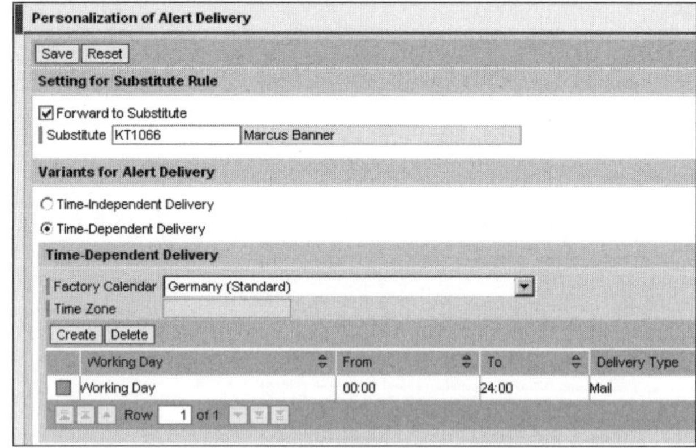

Figure 6.23 Alert Inbox: Personalization of Alert Delivery

Configuring Java Monitoring (GRMG)

Several configuration steps are necessary to use the Generic Request and Message Generator (GRMG) for monitoring the availability of your XI system's J2EE component. Call Transaction GRMG. The system now displays the dialog shown in Figure 6.24.

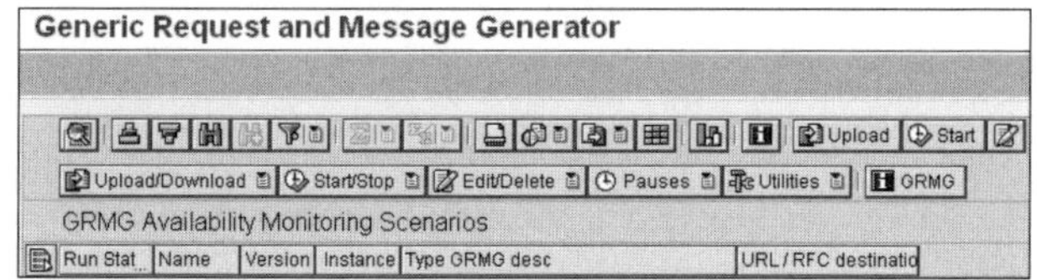

Figure 6.24 GRMG Availability Monitoring Scenarios for the J2EE Component

In the first step, you should read OSS Note 634771. Then download the customizing template mentioned in the OSS Note (*SAP_XI[XX]_GRMG_Cust_Template.txt*). You can find the XML file in the **Attachments** tab. For our configuration, we need the template for release status XI 3.0. Before you load the template into your XI system, you should examine it. You'll see that the relevant parts already contain a comment in the XML template. Customize the file in those parts for your system according to OSS Note 634771.

Then use the **Upload** function in Transaction GRMG to upload the file into your XI system (see Figure 6.25).

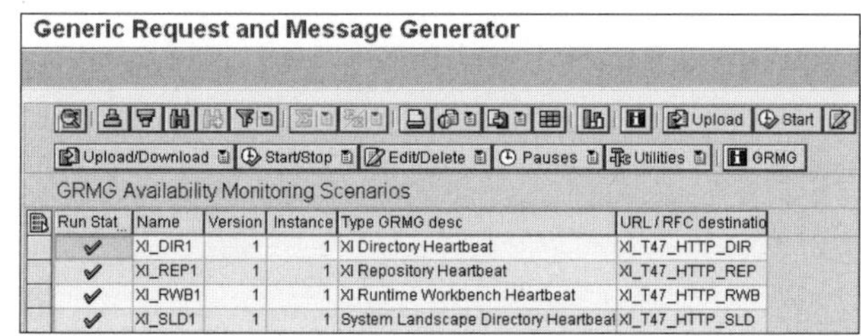

Figure 6.25 GRMG: Heartbeat Monitoring of the J2EE Part

In Figure 6.25, you can see that we monitor the availability of the following components only:

- Integration Directory
- Integration Repository
- XI Runtime
- SLD

Of course, you can also monitor your adapter engine here as well.

In the next step you must create the corresponding connections to your XI components by using Transaction SM59. We created them as illustrated in Figure 6.26.

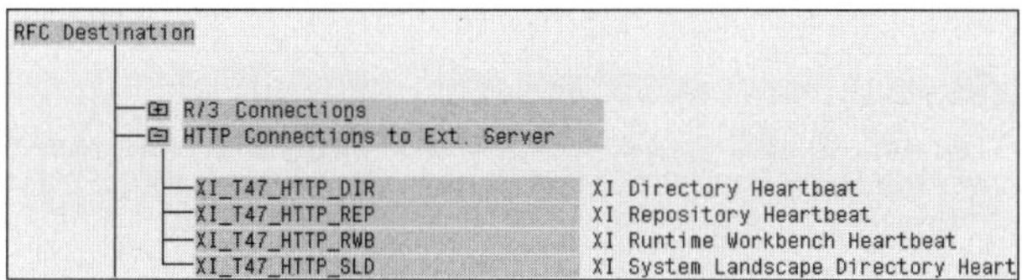

Figure 6.26 Creating HTTP Connections for GRMG

For the http connection, you must maintain the following two tabs: **Technical Settings** and **Logon/Security**. In our XI system, we have stored the following entries in the connection maintenance view **XI_T47_http_DIR** (directory heartbeat):

- Target machine: sapt47
- Service no.: 53500
- Path prefix: /dir/rtc

Please create the other RFC connections in accordance with the example.

Once you've created the http connections using Transaction SM59, go back to Transaction GRMG and assign the destinations to the respective components by highlighting the component to be edited and calling it using the **Edit/Delete** function. Then, activate GRMG monitoring using the **Start/Stop** function in the same transaction. You can now see the heartbeat of your XI components as shown in Figure 6.27 using Transaction RZ20, *CCMS Monitor Sets*. To do that, go to the **SAP CCMS Technical Expert Monitors** tree and open the node **SAP CCMS Technical Expert Monitors**.

Note Note that GRMG requires a configured and active Internet Communication Manager (ICM) on your ABAP instance.

In order for alerting to function properly, you must add the auto-reaction method `CCMS_Send_Alert_to_ALM_V2` that you copied earlier to the individual relevant nodes in the **GRMG Selfmonitoring** node (see Figure 6.28). We recommend the following configuration sequence:

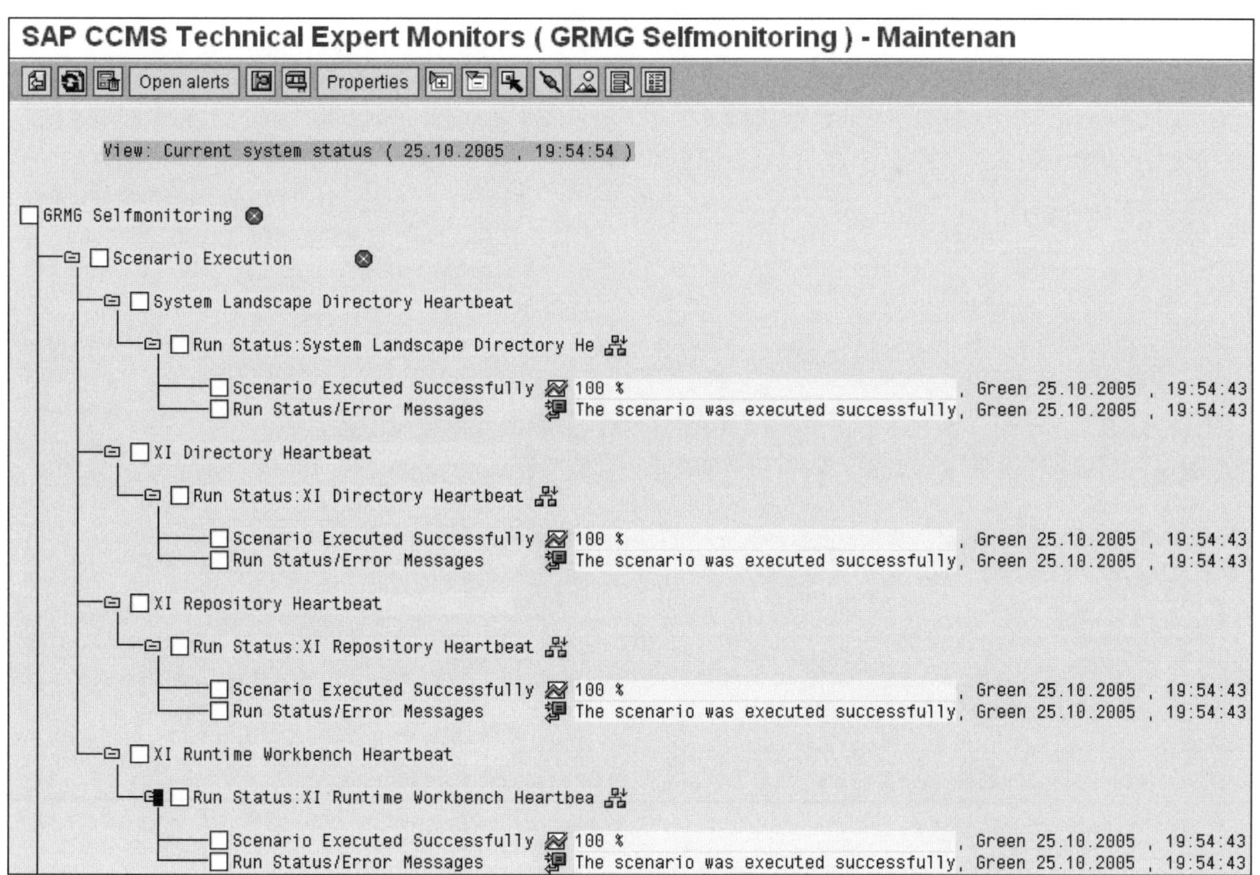

Figure 6.27 Overview of Monitored Components in Transaction RZ20

1. Call Transaction RZ20.
2. Expand the main node **SAP CCMS Technical Expert Monitors**.
3. Double-click on the subnode **GRMG Selfmonitoring**.
4. Expand the tree down to the lowest end node. You can add the method to any node. Caution: If you select a main node in the tree structure, the method will be added to all subnodes of this main node. We assigned the auto-reaction method only to the end nodes.
5. Switch on the maintenance function via the menu path **Activate maintenance function**.
6. Highlight an end node (where errors or problems are usually displayed).
7. Then click on the **Properties** button. This brings you to the **Monitoring: Properties and Methods** maintenance screen where you can assign your auto-reaction method via the **Methods** tab.
8. Click on the **Method assignment** button and select the **Auto-reaction** tab.
9. Switch on the change mode by clicking on the **Display <-> Change** button.
10. In the **Method assignment** group box, click on the **Method name** button and enter the copied auto-reaction method `CCMS_Send_Alert_to_ALM_V2`.
11. Save the method assignment for the node.

Then leave the maintenance screen and go to the CCMS (**GRMG Selfmonitoring**) via menu path **Views · Method allocation** to check whether the method has actually been assigned (see Figure 6.28).

Carry out the assignment for the other nodes as well.

6.8 Cache Monitoring

Figure 6.29 displays the web-based call of the cache monitoring.

Cache monitoring enables you to monitor the runtime cache in the integration engine or in the adapter engine and thus to display mapping programs that have been executed, for example.

You can monitor or select the following cache types:

- Value mapping groups
- Mapping programs
- Software components

Value mapping enables the mapping of different views of an object to each other. For instance, if a customer of company A is also an employee of company B. In SAP Exchange Infrastructure, the integration is defined via the view of an object through the assigning agency (organization, company, technical unit, system) and the corresponding identification schema (value schema). By combining the agency and the schema, an object is uniquely identified by an ID or value, for example, by the ID "customer number" (company A) and "personnel number" (company B). The representation of an object is complete if the agency, the identification schema, and the value are known. These relationships must be stored

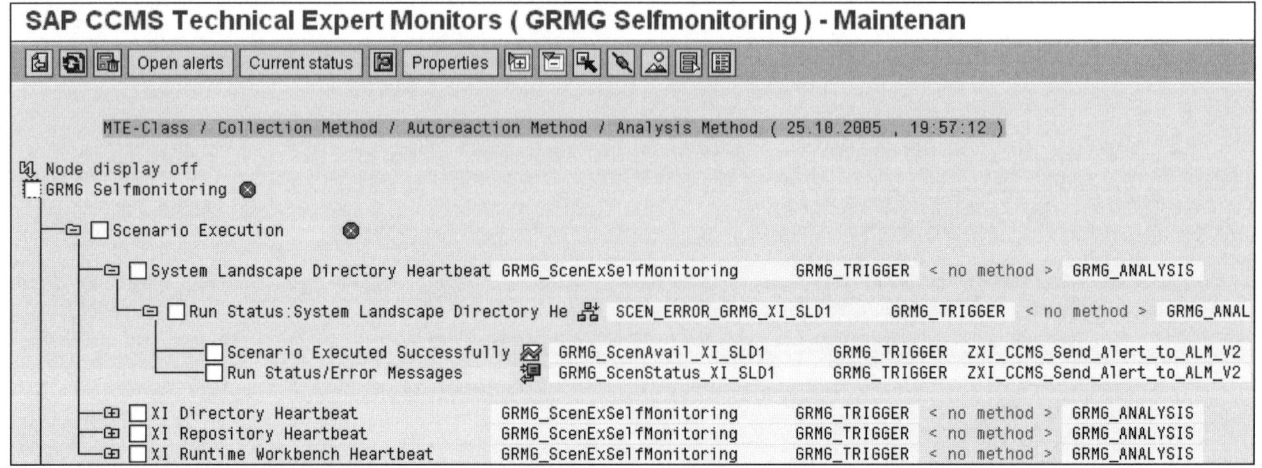

Figure 6.28 CCMS: Method Assignment

in specific tables in the Integration Builder configuration. In the main menu, you can access these tables via the following path: **Tools • Value Mapping**. A source and target ID is defined per value mapping group and agency (GUID).

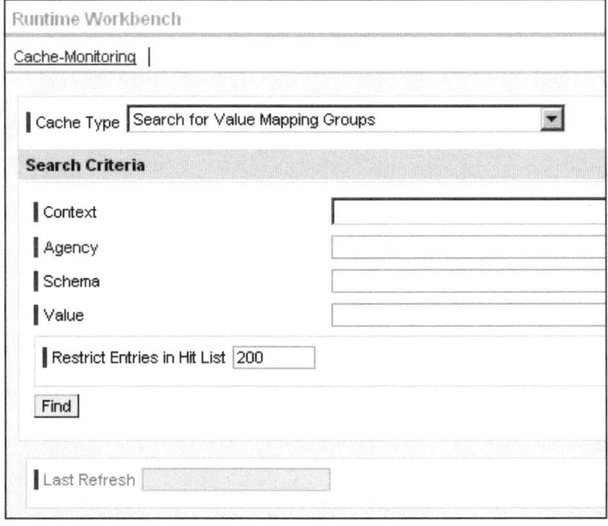

Figure 6.29 Cache Monitoring

Program mapping involves the search for runtime instances (programs) of message mappings in the Integration Repository. A graphical mapping editor (Integration Repository Design) enables you to design and edit message mappings (two XML structures). At the same time, this design represents the link to value mapping. Consequently, Java source code is generated from the graphical mapping description. That source code is translated and as a compressed JAR file it is executed at runtime by the integration engine. Chapter 2 contains further details on this topic.

The final analysis option for cache monitoring involves the search for software components. The creation and maintenance of the component versions takes place in the Integration Repository. Chapter 2 also contains information on how you can do that.

For instance, in order to start an analysis for mapping programs, go to the cache monitoring main menu and select the **Cache Type** dropdown box. As you can see in Figure 6.30, you can now choose between the analysis options described in the previous sections.

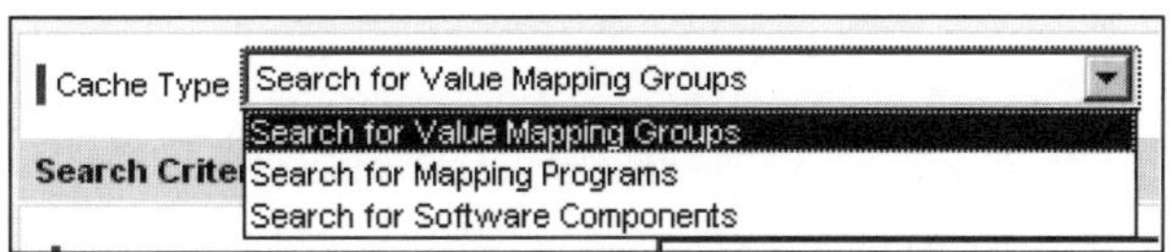

Figure 6.30 Cache Monitoring—Selecting the Cache Type

For our example, we'll select the **Search for Value Mapping Groups** function, which we can start by clicking on

Select Entries

Software Components Version	Namespace	Program	Date of change
41c17ae06dfe11d99f26d2e50ac8e68c	http://itellium.com/XI/KKM2RETAIL	com/sap/xi/tf/_ZST_MAP_CREMR_2_CREMAS04_.class	2005-06-28 15:33:51.0
33751b30438e11d98db9e8b80a114c15	http://sap.com/xi/ELSTER/VAT/2005	Elster2RFC2.xsl	2005-03-16 18:25:11.0
33751b30438e11d98db9e8b80a114c15	http://sap.com/xi/ELSTER/VAT/2005	Elster2RFC1.xsl	2005-03-16 18:25:11.0
33751b30438e11d98db9e8b80a114c15	http://sap.com/xi/ELSTER/VAT/2005	RFC2Elster.xsl	2005-03-16 18:25:11.0
3b787a8035c111d6bbe0efe50a1145a5	http://sap.com/xi/XI/Demo/Agency	com/sap/xi/tf/_BookingOrder_BPM2AirlineIDoc_.class	2005-04-18 09:27:09.0
3b787a8035c111d6bbe0efe50a1145a5	http://sap.com/xi/XI/Demo/Agency	com/sap/xi/tf/_FBOCancelation_BPM2AirlineIDoc_.class	2005-04-18 09:26:40.0
3b787a8035c111d6bbe0efe50a1145a5	http://sap.com/xi/XI/Demo/Agency	com/sap/xi/tf/_FSACheck_Agency2AirlineRFC_Fault_.class	2005-04-18 09:27:08.0
3b787a8035c111d6bbe0efe50a1145a5	http://sap.com/xi/XI/Demo/Agency	com/sap/xi/tf/_FSACheck_Agency2AirlineRFC_Resp_.class	2005-04-18 09:26:50.0
3b787a8035c111d6bbe0efe50a1145a5	http://sap.com/xi/XI/Demo/Agency	com/sap/xi/tf/_SplitMultipleBookingOrder_BPM_.class	2005-04-18 09:26:43.0
3b787a8035c111d6bbe0efe50a1145a5	http://sap.com/xi/XI/Demo/Agency	com/sap/xi/tf/_CreateBookingOrderCancelation_BPM_.class	2005-04-18 09:27:02.0
3b787a8035c111d6bbe0efe50a1145a5	http://sap.com/xi/XI/Demo/Agency	com/sap/xi/tf/_FBOConfirmation_Airline2Agency_.class	2005-04-18 09:26:55.0
3b787a8035c111d6bbe0efe50a1145a5	http://sap.com/xi/XI/Demo/Agency	com/sap/xi/tf/_BookingOrder_Agency2Airline_.class	2005-04-18 09:26:29.0
3b787a8035c111d6bbe0efe50a1145a5	http://sap.com/xi/XI/Demo/Agency	com/sap/xi/tf/_BookingOrderDataInfo_Agency2AgencyReporting_.class	2005-04-18 09:27:07.0
3b787a8035c111d6bbe0efe50a1145a5	http://sap.com/xi/XI/Demo/Agency	com/sap/xi/tf/_FBOConfirmation_AirlineIDoc2BPM_.class	2005-04-18 09:26:59.0
3b787a8035c111d6bbe0efe50a1145a5	http://sap.com/xi/XI/Demo/Agency	com/sap/xi/tf/_FSACheck_Agency2AirlineRFC_Req_.class	2005-04-18 09:27:01.0
3b787a8035c111d6bbe0efe50a1145a5	http://sap.com/xi/XI/Demo/Agency	com/sap/xi/tf/_MergeOrderConfirmations_BPM_.class	2005-04-18 09:27:00.0
3b787a8035c111d6bbe0efe50a1145a5	http://sap.com/xi/XI/Demo/Agency	com/sap/xi/tf/_BookingOrder_Agency2AirlineIDoc_.class	2005-04-18 09:27:02.0
3b787a8035c111d6bbe0efe50a1145a5	http://sap.com/xi/XI/Demo/Agency	com/sap/xi/tf/_CreateFailureNotification_BPM_.class	2005-04-18 09:27:05.0
3b787a8035c111d6bbe0efe50a1145a5	http://sap.com/xi/XI/Demo/Agency	com/sap/xi/tf/_FBOConfirmation_AirlineIDoc2Agency_.class	2005-04-18 09:26:53.0
3b787a8035c111d6bbe0efe50a1145a5	http://sap.com/xi/XI/Prototyping	com/sap/xi/tf/_ZMAP_CREMR_2_CREMAS_.class	2005-04-18 09:27:04.0

Page 1 / 2

Figure 6.31 Cache Monitoring—Result of a Search for Mapping Programs

the **Search** button. The system will now display an analysis similar to the one shown in Figure 6.31.

In that dialog you can determine the ID of the respective software component version depending on the relevant namespace and program name of the mapping program. The display of the date of the last change rounds off the output.

Similar to the search for mapping programs you can perform the **Search for Mapping Programs** and the **Search for Software Components**.

Appendix

1 Overview of Relevant XI System Parameters

Area	Parameter	Description
default	com.sap.aii.util.xml.schemaValidator	Class name of schema validator
default	com.sap.aii.util.sql.loglevel	This parameter is used for log SQL accesses that are executed by the software. 0 = no logging 1 = logging of SQL statements 2 = logging of value fields 3 = output of stack trace (back trace)
default	com.sap.aii.util.sql.stmtCacheOff	If *true*, the prepared statement won't be used by the SQL layer.
default	com.sap.aii.docu.url	Beginning with the root directory (start URL) in which the installed HTML files can be accessed by the web browser (use *zero*, if there's no documentation available)
default	com.sap.aii.docu.languages	Specifies whether a comma-separated language code list is installed for all documentation languages (set *zero* if there's no documentation available; otherwise, set the language keys of your installed documentation)
Connections	com.sap.aii.connect.integrationbuilder.startpage.url	Specifies a relative address of the XI tool start page (on the repository server)
Connections	com.sap.aii.connect.repository.name	Contains the host name of the repository server
Connections	com.sap.aii.connect.repository.httpport	Contains the HTTP port number of the repository server
Connections	com.sap.aii.connect.repository.rmiport	Contains the Java Remote Invocation (RMI) port number of the repository server
Connections	com.sap.aii.connect.repository.contextroot	Contains the context root of the repository
Connections	com.sap.aii.connect.directory.name	Contains the host name of the directory server
Connections	com.sap.aii.connect.directory.httpport	Contains the HTTP port number of the directory server
Connections	com.sap.aii.connect.directory.rmiport	Contains the RMI port number of the directory server
Connections	com.sap.aii.connect.directory.contextroot	Contains the context root for the HTTP services of the directory
Connections	com.sap.aii.connect.integrationserver.name	Contains the host name of the integration server
Connections	com.sap.aii.connect.integrationserver.httpport	HTTP port of the J2EE Engine on the integration server. This port is used by the XI integration directory to connect to the XI runtime environment.
Connections	com.sap.aii.connect.integrationserver.contextroot	Contains the context root of the integration server
Connections	com.sap.aii.connect.integrationserver.r3.httpport	HTTP port of the integration server. This port is used to connect to the Internet Communication Framework (ICF)(ABAP).
Connections	com.sap.aii.connect.integrationserver.r3.sysnr	SAP system number of the integration server (see JCo documentation of the *jco.client.sysnr* property)

Area	Parameter	Description
Connections	com.sap.aii.connect.integrationserver.r3.client	SAP client of the integration server (see JCo documentation of the *jco.client.sysnr* property)
Connections	com.sap.aii.connect.landscape.name	Contains the host name of the landscape directory server
Connections	com.sap.aii.connect.landscape.httpport	Contains the HTTP port number of the landscape directory server (listens to WBEM requests—communication standard in CIM)
Connections	com.sap.aii.connect.landscape.contextroot	Contains the context root of the landscape directory server
Connections	com.sap.aii.connect.cr.name	Contains the host name of the component repository server
Connections	com.sap.aii.connect.cr.httpport	Contains the HTTP port number of the component repository server
Connections	com.sap.aii.connect.cr.contextroot	Contains the context root of the component repository server
Connections	com.sap.aii.connect.rwb.name	Contains the host name of the Runtime Workbench (RWB)
Connections	com.sap.aii.connect.rwb.httpport	Contains the HTTP port number of the RWB
Connections	com.sap.aii.connect.rwb.contextroot	Contains the context root for the HTTP services of the RWB
Connections	com.sap.aii.connect.rwb.r3.sysnr	R3 system of the Web AS on which the RWB is running. Required for JCo connections from the RWB on J2EE to the ABAP component of Web AS.
Connections	com.sap.aii.connect.rwb.r3.client	Client of the XI system (Web AS 6.40) on which the Java components are monitored by GRMG. Also required for the JCo connections between the RWB and the ABAP component of Web AS 6.40.
IntegrationBuilder	com.sap.aii.repository.mapping.additionaltypes	In addition to the standard mapping types like *class* for Java mapping programs or xsi for XSLT programs, you can register other mapping types. These additional mapping types activate the call of mapping programs that aren't stored in the integration repository. Technically, the integration server calls the ABAP function CALL_PARTNER_MAPPING and the additional mapping type names as a destination. Therefore, the additional mapping type name must be registered as an RFC destination in the integration server. When you create an interface mapping, you can select the additional mapping type in the interface mapping editor of the integration builder. During interface mapping, you can click on a link to a mapping program of an SAP partner which the BAdI runs through when it is executed. For an additional mapping type, you must specify a key and a name. The key field is registered for 20 characters and should therefore contain no other characters than a, … , z and A, … , Z, the numbers 0, … , 9 and the underscore "_". The name shouldn't exceed a length of 25 characters. The name and the key are separated by a | character. Different additional mapping types are separated by a semicolon. Example: PA_TYPE|Partner Mapping; pa_trafo|Partner Transformation Note: Use the *none* value, if no additional mapping types are used.
IntegrationBuilder	com.sap.aii.repository.serviceuser.name	Service user. This user is required for the repository, if the user connects to other components.
IntegrationBuilder	com.sap.aii.repository.serviceuser.pwd	Service user password
IntegrationBuilder	com.sap.aii.repository.serviceuser.language	Service user language
IntegrationBuilder	com.sap.aii.ibrep.core.cms.activated	If this parameter is *true*, the CMS transport system has been activated.

Area	Parameter	Description
IntegrationBuilder	com.sap.aii.ibrep.core.cms.enableClTransport	Described in Chapter 3
IntegrationBuilder	com.sap.aii.ibrep.core.cms. enableTransportWizard	Described in Chapter 3
IntegrationBuilder	com.sap.aii.directory.serviceuser.name	Service user. This user is required for the directory, if the user connects to other components.
IntegrationBuilder	com.sap.aii.directory.serviceuser.pwd	Service user password
IntegrationBuilder	com.sap.aii.directory.serviceuser.language	Service user language
IntegrationBuilder	com.sap.aii.ibdir.core.cms.activated	If this parameter is *true*, the CMS transport system has been activated.
IntegrationBuilder	com.sap.aii.ibdir.core.cms. enableTransportWizard	Described in Chapter 3
IntegrationBuilder	com.sap.aii.ib.client.jnlp.j2se.initialheapsize	Minimum heap size of the Java Virtual Machine (JVM) client
IntegrationBuilder	com.sap.aii.ib.client.jnlp.j2se.maxheapsize	Maximum heap size of the JVM client
IntegrationBuilder	com.sap.aii.ib.client.applicationname. directory	Application name of the directory required for the Java Naming and Directory Interface (JNDI) search of the bean.
IntegrationBuilder	com.sap.aii.ib.client.applicationname. repository	Application name of the repository required for the JNDI search of the beans.
IntegrationBuilder	com.sap.aii.ib.server.localbeanjndiprefix. repository	Prefix that is needed for the JNDI search of the local beans in the integration repository.
IntegrationBuilder	com.sap.aii.ib.server.localbeanjndiprefix. directory	Prefix that is needed for the JNDI search of the local beans in the integration directory.
IntegrationBuilder	com.sap.aii.ib.client.login. InitialContextFactory	*Factory*; required for the initial context
IntegrationBuilder	com.sap.aii.ib.client.login.languages	Available login languages (format: comma-separated list)
IntegrationBuilder	com.sap.aii.ib.client.content.languages	Available content language (format: comma-separated list) The first language in the list is set as the default content language.
IntegrationBuilder	com.sap.aii.ib.client.properties	List of settings; needed for the client (format: comma-separated list)
IntegrationBuilder	com.sap.aii.ib.server.connect.webas. r3.usefastrfc	Connection between the Java and ABAP stacks of the Web AS: This flag defines whether FastRFC will be used for connecting to the R/3 component of the Web AS. Possible values: *true* and *false*.
IntegrationBuilder	com.sap.aii.ib.server.connect.webas.r3.client	Connection between the Java and ABAP stacks of the Web AS: JCo connection from the J2EE Engine to the ITS R3 instance: SAP client (see JCo documentation of the jco.client.client property)
IntegrationBuilder	com.sap.aii.ib.server.connect.webas.r3.ashost	Connection between the Java and ABAP stacks of the Web AS: JCo connection from the J2EE Engine to the R3 instance: SAP application server (see JCo documentation of the *jco.client.ashost* property)
IntegrationBuilder	com.sap.aii.ib.server.connect.webas.r3.sysnr	Connection between the Java and ABAP stacks of the Web AS: JCo connection from the J2EE Engine to the IST R3 instance: SAP system number (see JCo documentation of the *jco.client.sysnr* property)
IntegrationBuilder	com.sap.aii.ib.server.lockauth.activation	Activates the locking and authorization services. You should always set the value of this parameter to *true*. The *false* value deactivates the locking and authorization service.

Area	Parameter	Description
IntegrationBuilder	com.sap.aii.ib.server.concurrent_edit	This parameter controls the editing of the same object by several users. However, if several users have the same object in their change list, this can cause conflicts when the second change list is activated. Possible values are *true* and *false*.
IntegrationBuilder	com.sap.aii.ib.core.sso.enabled	Described in Chapter 4
IntegrationServer	com.sap.aii.ib.client.applicationname.runtime	Runtime application name required for the JNDI search of the beans.
IntegrationServer	com.sap.aii.ib.server.localbeanjndiprefix.runtime	Prefix that is required for the runtime JNDI search of the local beans.
IntegrationServer	com.sap.aii.integrationserver.serviceuser.name	Service user. This user is required by the integration server when it connects to other components (e.g., directory).
IntegrationServer	com.sap.aii.integrationserver.serviceuser.pwd	Service user password. This user is required by the integration server when it connects to other components (e.g., directory).
IntegrationServer	com.sap.aii.integrationserver.serviceuser.language	Service user language. This user is required by the integration server when it connects to other components (e.g., directory).
ApplicationSystem	com.sap.aii.applicationsystem.serviceuser.name	Service user. This user is required by the application when it connects to the integration server.
ApplicationSystem	com.sap.aii.applicationsystem.serviceuser.pwd	Service user password. This user is required by the application when it connects to the integration server.
ApplicationSystem	com.sap.aii.applicationsystem.serviceuser.language	Service user language. This user is required by the application when it connects to the integration server.
RuntimeWorkbench	com.sap.aii.rwb.serviceuser.name	Service user. This user is required by the RWB when a connection to another server is established.
RuntimeWorkbench	com.sap.aii.rwb.serviceuser.pwd	Service user password. This user is required by the RWB when a connection to another server is established.
RuntimeWorkbench	com.sap.aii.rwb.serviceuser.language	Service user language. This user is required by the runtime workbench when a connection to another server is established.
RuntimeWorkbench	com.sap.aii.rwb.server.centralmonitoring.r3.ashost	Host name of the application server of the Web AS on which the central Process Monitoring Infrastructure (PMI), the central
		Computing Center Management System (CCMS) and the central alert server are running. Please also refer to OSS Note 757373 (SSO problem).
RuntimeWorkbench	com.sap.aii.rwb.server.centralmonitoring.r3.client	Client on which the central PMI, the CCMS, and the alert server are running. Required for JCo connections.
RuntimeWorkbench	com.sap.aii.rwb.server.centralmonitoring.r3.sysnr	System number of the Web AS on which the central PMI, the CCMS, and the alert server are running. Required for JCo connections.
RuntimeWorkbench	com.sap.aii.rwb.server.centralmonitoring.httpport	HTTP port of the Web AS (ABAP component) on which the central PMI, the CCMS, and the alert server are running. Required for HTTP connections to the monitoring server.
AdapterFramework	com.sap.aii.adapterframework.serviceuser.name	Service user. This user is required by the adapter framework when a connection to another server is established.
AdapterFramework	com.sap.aii.adapterframework.serviceuser.pwd	Service user password. This user is required by the adapter framework when a connection to another server is established.
AdapterFramework	com.sap.aii.adapterframework.serviceuser.language	Service user language. This user is required by the adapter framework when a connection to another server is established.

2 Checklist—Interface Configuration

The following list can be used as a checklist to verify the completeness of the implementation activities to be performed for an interface configuration.

Step	Activity	Transaction or link
1	**Sending system**	
1.1	Create logical systems (system, XI, and receiver)	BD54
1.2	Create type 3 RFC connection to the XI system	SM59
1.3	Create IDoc port address	WE21
1.4	Create IDoc partner profile (specify outbound IDoc)	WE20
2	**Integration Server (XI)**	
2.1	Create logical systems for sending system, XI, and receiver	BD54
2.2	Create type 3 RFC connection to the XI system	SM59
2.3	Maintain port in IDoc adapter	IDX1
2.4	Load IDoc metadata into IDoc adapter	IDX2
3	**XI: System Landscape Directory**	
3.1	Enter technical system (technical landscape)	*http://[Hostname]:[Port]/sld/index.jsp*
3.2	Enter business systems (business landscape)	*http://[Hostname]:[Port]/sld/index.jsp*
3.3	Define software product	*http://[Hostname]:[Port]/sld/index.jsp*
3.4	Define catalog and assign product	*http://[Hostname]:[Port]/sld/index.jsp*
4	**XI: Integration Repository**	Activate objects after each step!
4.1	Import software component in integration repository (Integration Builder: design)	*http://[Hostname]:[Port]/rep/start/index.jsp*
4.2	Import SAP objects (IDoc and RFC interfaces)	*http://[Hostname]:[Port]/rep/start/index.jsp*
4.3	Create namespace in the repository	*http://[Hostname]:[Port]/rep/start/index.jsp*
4.4	Create message mapping objects	*http://[Hostname]:[Port]/rep/start/index.jsp*
4.5	Perform field assignments	*http://[Hostname]:[Port]/rep/start/index.jsp*
4.6	Development	*http://[Hostname]:[Port]/rep/start/index.jsp*
4.7	Create interface mapping object	*http://[Hostname]:[Port]/rep/start/index.jsp*
5	**XI: Integration Directory**	
5.1	Configure business system service via configuration wizard (communication channels, sender and receiver determination, receiver agreement, and interface determination)	*http://[Hostname]:[Port]/rep/start/index.jsp*
6	**Receiving system**	
6.1	Create logical system	BD54
6.2	Create IDoc port number	WE21
6.3	Maintain inbound receiver agreement and assign port number	WE20

Index

A

Administration of the SLD namespace 34
Alert categories 83
Alert configuration 82
Alert Inbox 80
Alert management 82
Alert monitoring 80
Architecture, CMS 42
Archiving 66
Archiving and deletion procedures in XI 3.0 66
Authorizations 51

B

Basic administration 29
Basic administration of the SLD 29
Business system 39
Business system groups 40

C

Cache contents 42
Cache monitor 86
CEN 81
Central information provider 7
Central monitoring (CEN) 71, 81
Change Management Service 41, 43
CIM dependencies 34
Component monitoring 74
Configuration of SLD profiles 31
Configuration within the repository and directory 12
Configuring the distribution 13
Configuring the IDoc adapter 16
Configuring the receiving system 27
Configuring the sending system for the distribution 13
Configuring the system landscape 29
Configuring the system parameters 10
Creating an interface mapping object 23
Creating an RFC connection 14
Creating a namespace in the repository 20
Customizing the system landscape directory 35

D

Data collection programs 33
Defining outbound and inbound interfaces 23
Deletion procedure 67
Distribution model 15

E

End-to-end monitoring 76
Exchange Infrastructure landscape topology 7
Exchange Infrastructure tools 16

G

Gateway service name 33
GRMG 82, 84

H

Heartbeat monitoring, J2EE 84

I

IDoc adapter 16
Implementing the architecture 10
Importing a software component version 19
Importing SAP objects 19
Integration Directory 24
Interface configuration 93

J

J2EE ApplicationThreadManager 69
Java monitoring (GRMG) 84
Java VM Tuning 69
JCo Service Provider on the J2EE Side 58
Job scheduling 34

L

Landscape Configurator 45
Locks on objects 42

M

Mapping editor 22
Mapping programs 23, 86
Message mapping objects
creation 20
Message monitoring 75
Minimum Configuration of the Transport System 49
Monitoring requirements 72

N

Namespace 20, 34

P

Parameter settings on the J2EE side 69
Parameter settings on the R/3 side 60
Partner profile 15
Performance monitoring 79
Performance optimization 57
Persistence 30
Port maintenance in the IDoc adapter 16
Product 18

R

Receiver determination 26
Registering a mapping program 23
Repository 20
RFC quota on the R/3 side 57
Role authorizations 55

S

SAP NetWeaver 5
SAP roles 53
Security role 53
Server Log 30
Service user 54
Set up data persistence 30
Set up SLD bridge 32
Single Sign-On 51
Sizing SAP Exchange Infrastructure 3.0 9
SLD bridge 32
SLD profiles 31
Software catalog 36
Software component versions 19, 36, 86
Support package 9
System data and sizing 9
System Information, display 30
System landscape 29
System landscape directory 7

T

Technical system 37
Transport groups 40
Transport system 42

U

UME 52
User group 53
User Management Environment 52

V

Value mapping groups 86

W

Web Administrator 55
Web AS 6.40, adapting for XI 3.0 57
Web AS 6.40—communication parameters 60
Web AS 6.40—gateway parameters 60

X

XI 3.0 Parameter Settings—Runtime Category 64
XI monitoring types 71
XI Role Concept 52
XI system parameters 89

ISBN 1-59229-074-4

SAP PRESS is an imprint of Galileo Press,
Fort Lee (NJ), USA
Bonn, Germany

Copy Editor Nancy Etscovitz, UCG, Inc., Boston, MA
Cover Design Vera Brauner
Printed in Germany